Economic History of the European Energy Industry

Global climate change and the war in Ukraine have put energy back on the agenda for Europe in a way that has not been seen since the oil crisis of the 1970s. But the economics and business of supplying energy to Europe has a long and rich history going back to the nineteenth century. This book explores changes in energy markets, strategies, firms and investments during the nineteenth and twentieth centuries. The primary focus is on manufactured gas—the gas that was initially produced from coal distillation until new ways of manufacturing gas emerged after the Second World War.

The expert contributors to this volume draw on their extensive research and utilise primary sources to explore a wide range of issues, including technological adaptation, market regulation, energy investments (particularly the role of foreign capital), gas consumption and supply issues. The case studies are particularly drawn from Spain, France and Italy, but the authors provide a comparative and global perspective to consider the wider context. The volume closes with an epilogue that brings the story into the present day to consider current issues affecting gas markets in the EU, including war, geostrategy and pipelines.

This book will be of interest to readers in economic history, business history, energy history, the history of public utilities and modern European history more broadly.

Alberte Martínez-López is Professor of Economic History at the University of A Coruña (Spain), where he coordinates the Business History Study Group.

Jesús Mirás-Araujo is Senior Lecturer of Economic History at the Department of Economics of the University of A Coruña (Spain).

Nuria Rodríguez-Martín is Lecturer in Contemporary History at the Complutense University of Madrid (Spain).

Routledge Explorations in Economic History
Edited by Lars Magnusson
Uppsala University, Sweden

Property, Power and the Growth of Towns
Enterprise and Urban Development, 1100–1500
Catherine Casson and Mark Casson

The Age of Global Economic Crises
(1929–2022)
Edited by Juan Manuel Matés-Barco and María Vázquez-Fariñas

The Sustainability and Development of Ancient Economies
Analysis and Examples
Clement A. Tisdell and Serge Svizzero

The Economy of Classical Athens
Organization, Institutions and Society
Emmanouil M. L. Economou

The Political Economy of Interwar Foreign Investment
Economic Nationalism and French Capital in Poland, 1918–1939
Jerzy Łazor

The Development of European Competition Policy
Social Democracy and Regulation
Edited by Brian Shaev and Sigfrido Ramírez Pérez

Economic History of the European Energy Industry
Lighting up Western Europe, 19th to 21st centuries
Alberte Martínez-López, Jesús Mirás-Araujo and Nuria Rodríguez-Martín

For more information about this series, please visit: www.routledge.com/Routledge-Explorations-in-Economic-History/book-series/SE0347

Economic History of the European Energy Industry

Lighting up Western Europe, 19th to 21st centuries

Edited by Alberte Martínez-López, Jesús Mirás-Araujo and Nuria Rodríguez-Martín

Routledge
Taylor & Francis Group
LONDON AND NEW YORK

First published 2025
by Routledge
4 Park Square, Milton Park, Abingdon, Oxon OX14 4RN

and by Routledge
605 Third Avenue, New York, NY 10158

Routledge is an imprint of the Taylor & Francis Group, an informa business

British Library Cataloguing-in-Publication Data
A catalogue record for this book is available from the British Library

ISBN: 978-1-032-55034-3 (hbk)
ISBN: 978-1-032-55035-0 (pbk)
ISBN: 978-1-003-42869-5 (ebk)

DOI: 10.4324/9781003428695

Typeset in Times New Roman
by SPi Technologies India Pvt Ltd (Straive)

Contents

Figures

Tables

Contributors

Joan Carles Alayo-Manubens. PhD in Industrial Engineering from the Universitat Politècnica de Catalunya (UPC) (Spain). Expert in Electrical Engineering. He has worked from 1971 to 2001 in different utilities in Spain, in the areas of Planning and Projects (Hidroeléctrica de Cataluña S.A.) and Technical Audit (ENDESA). He began to develop his historical research on electricity and electrification in 1987 at the chair of UPC electrical engineering. His doctoral thesis obtained, in 1996, the Bonaplata award, granted by the Associació del Museu de la Ciència i de la Tècnica i d'Arqueologia Industrial de Catalunya. He is the author or co-author in many books. His research has focused on the history of the electricity in Catalonia and Spain, and also the gas technology, focused in Spain.

Carlos Alvarado-García. PhD in Economics and Law from the University of Deusto, Bilbao (Spain). Former Lecturer of Business Strategy and Economics at the Deusto Business School. Former Board Member and Former Director of energy and gas companies (Cadem, Ente Vasco de la Energía, Naturcorp, Bilbogas and Sedigas). He is the author of several articles and books, among others: J.M. Valdaliso (dir.), C. Alvarado and P. Suárez (eds.), *Nortegas (1845-2021). Historia de la industria del gas en el Norte de España* (Marcial Pons, 2022); C. Alvarado, *Petronor. Un estudio histórico sociológico de la refinería en los municipios de su entorno* (Universidad de Deusto, 2014, with Jon J. Leonardo, Angel M. Ormaechea and Javier Torres Ripa); C. Alvarado (dir.) et al., *Arteche. Historia de los hechos empresariales, 1946-2006* (Universidad de Deusto, 2008).

Francesc Xavier Barca-Salom. PhD in Industrial Engineering from the Universitat Politècnica de Catalunya (UPC) (Spain). He obtained the Diplôme d'Études Approfondies of Energy Economics at the Université de Sciences Sociales de Grenoble (1977) and the Master of History of Science at the Universitat Autònoma de Barcelona (1995). He has been associate professor of History of Science and Technology at the UPC from 1991 to 2011 and professor at the Escola del Treball de Barcelona, where he taught organisation and energy projects until 2014. He is a founding partner and was the first secretary of the Catalan Society of History and Technology (SCHCT), branch of the Institut d'Estudis Catalans since its establishment in 1990 until 1998. He was designated as "International Scholar" for the biennium 1999–2000 by the Society for the History of Technology (SHOT). Among his publications, we must highlight the contributions to several journals such as *Minerva*, *Icon*, *History of Technology*, *Dynamis* and *Asclepio*. He is the author of biographical studies of scientists and technicians; his research has focused on the history of astronomy, mathematics and technical education. In this field he has focused his interest on the history of nuclear energy, gas technology and water.

Mariano Castro-Valdivia. BS. Economics (University of Valencia, 1991), PhD in Economics (2012), is Associate Professor of Economic History and Business History at the Department of Economics of the University of Jaén (Spain). He has carried out research stays of more than three months at the Università degli Studi di Roma "La Sapienza", University of Salamanca and the University Michel de Montaigne Bordeaux III. He is coordinator of several research projects, member of the Research Group Historical Studies on Business, and secretary of the journal *Agua y Territorio / Water and Landscape* (AYT / WAL). His main research lines are the teaching of Economics at the Spanish University, the diffusion of classical economic thought in Spain and the evolution of foreign investment in Spanish utilities (water, electricity and gas). Some recent publications are: *Companies and Entrepreneurs in the History of Spain. Centuries Long Evolution in Business since the 15th century* (Palgrave, 2021, with María Vázquez-Fariñas and Pedro Pablo Ortúñez-Goicolea); *Derecho ex cathedra. 1847-1936: diccionario de catedráticos españoles* (Dykinson, 2019, with several authors); *Cambio y crecimiento económico* (Universidad Rey Juan Carlos, 2015, with Leonardo Caruana).

Pere-A. Fàbregas. Graduated in Business Administration and holds a master's degree from ESADE Business School and a PDG from IESE. He was senior executive at Catalana de Gas and Gas Natural Fenosa for 47 years, in the areas of strategy, finance, information systems and corporate social responsibility. His concern for the preservation of the gas industry's historical heritage led him to create the company's Historical Archive (1987), the *Cuadernos de Historia* journal (1989–1991), the Gas History book collection (2006), and to direct the project of the Gas Museum (2012). He has specialised in the history and strategy of energy and the gas sector in Spain with research activities starting since 1974. He has published eight books, amongst which are the biographies of José Roura, the introducer of gas-lighting (1993), and that of the introducer of natural gas, Pere Duran (2014). Moreover, in 2003, he wrote a book about the international relations in the beginning of the gas sector in Spain, which won the history prize at the Ateneo de Sevilla 2001. He has also published two books about the most important gas company in Spain: *Gas Natural Fenosa, de Barcelona al* *mundo. Los primeros 170 años de historia* (2014), and *Naturgy, 175 años de compromiso con la energía y la sociedad (1843-2018)* (2018). He has also collaborated on more than 70 collective works published in Spain, Argentina and Mexico, and has given more than a hundred conferences and lectures on energy, the environment, history and other related subjects. He is currently honorary president of Coordinadora Catalana de Fundacions, and ESADE Alumni. He is also a member of the Board of Directors of the Association of the Museum of Science, Technology and Industrial Archaeology of Catalonia.

Antonio Rafael Fernández-Paradas. Lecturer in Social Science Didactics at the Department of Social Science Didactics at the University of Granada (Spain). He holds a PhD in Art History and a PhD in Educational Sciences. He is a specialist in Sculpture, Furniture and Decorative Arts. His lines of research deal with religious iconography, Art History, gender and homosexuality, Baroque sculpture, Didactics of Social Sciences, and so on. Currently, he is a member of the research project "Gas in Latin Europe: A Comparative and Global Perspective (1818–1945)". His research has appeared in journals such as *International Visual Culture Review*, *Historia y Comunicación Social* and *International Journal of New Education*.

Mercedes Fernández-Paradas. Head Professor of Contemporary History at the University of Malaga (Spain). She is head of some research projects about gas and other utilities, and head researcher of the research project "Gas in Latin Europe: A Comparative and Global Perspective (1818–1945)" (with A. Martínez-López). She has been visiting fellow in several European and American universities. Her research fields are utilities (gas, electricity) and business history, on which she is the author of several articles and books, such as, recently, *Bajo la cálida luz del gas: los mercados regionales de la industria gasista en España (siglos XIX y XX)* (Sílex, 2022, with I. Bartolomé Rodríguez and J. Mirás); *Business History in Spain (19th and 20th centuries)* (Peter Lang, 2021, with C. Larrinaga); *Cercanas pero distintas: la desigual trayectoria de la industria del gas en las regiones del sur de Europa (siglos XIX-XX)* (Marcial Pons, 2020, with I. Bartolomé Rodríguez and J. Mirás); *Globalización, nacionalización y liberalización de la industria del gas en la Europa latina (siglos XIX-XXI)* (Marcial Pons, 2017, with I. Bartolomé Rodríguez and J. Mirás).

Andrea Giuntini. Associate Professor of Economic History, at the Department of Economics of the University of Modena and Reggio Emilia (Italy). M.A. in Economic History, University of Florence (1980). PhD in Economic History, Istituto Universitario Navale of Naples (1988). He has been Director of the Istituto di Studi Storici Postali in Prato (2002–2019), and member of the Centro di Documentazione Storica ed Economica dell'Impresa in Rome (1985–2008), and of the Management Committee COST 340 European Project on Transports (1999–2005). Member of the Editorial Boards of several journals and of several European academic associations.

His research deals with contemporary economic history and his main fields of research are history of networks, energy, transport and communications, public infrastructure and urban history. Some recent publications are: *L'Italia e il canale di Suez (1856-1869)* (Pacini, 2021); Editor of *The Gas Industry in Latin Europe. Economic Development during the 19th and 20th Centuries* (Palgrave Macmillan, 2023, with J. Mirás).

Carlos Larrinaga Rodríguez. Associate Professor of Economic History at the University of Granada (Spain). His research deals with the history of tourism, railways in the nineteenth century, and the service sector (gas, electricity and water). He has undertaken research in several stays, among others, at Bordeaux-Montaigne University (France) and at Aberystwyth University (United Kingdom). He has participated in several research projects. He is a member of the editorial board of *Historia Contemporánea*, and has edited several books: *El impacto de la Guerra Civil española en el sector terciario* (Comares, 2019, with M. Fernández-Paradas); *Italia e Spagna nel turismo del secondo dopoguerra* (FrancoAngeli, 2021, with A. Berrino); *Business History in Spain (XIXth and XXth centuries)* (Peter Lang, 2021, with M. Fernández-Paradas); *Luis Bolín y el turismo en España entre 1928 y 1952*, Marcial Pons, 2021; and *Coastal Tourism in Southern Europe in the XXth Century: New Economy and Material Culture*, Peter Lang, 2021 (with P. Battilani).

José Joaquín Luque García. Pre-doctoral researcher with an FPI contract at the University of Malaga (Spain). He specialises in economic history. His main line of research deals with the gas industry in Latin Europe. He analyses, through specialised gas periodicals and the documentation generated by the main gas associations, how knowledge and techniques in this industry circulated between France, Spain, Italy and Portugal, without losing sight of the advances and expansion of the British gas industry. In this way, his main contribution to the history of energy is the cataloguing, systematisation and analysis of the written press specialising in this field and the main companies operating in the sector.

Nuno Madureira. Professor at Lisbon University Institute (Portugal), he works currently in the areas of economic history, contemporary history of energy and environmental history. Visiting scholar at University of Harvard and visiting scholar at University of Berkeley, USA; member of the permanent pool of referees of the European Science Foundation (2006–2013) and of the College of Reviewers of the European Science Foundation (2016–2023). Consultant of the NWO—Netherlands Organization for Scientific Research and of the Bucharest University. Member of ISCTE's General Board. Coordinator of several collective research projects. Author of 12 books as single author, the last of which, *Key Concepts in Energy: Technology, Economy and History,* Springer, was published in 2014. Author of academic articles published in the following journals: *Energy Policy*, *Environment and*

History, Technology & Culture, *Business History*, *Business History Review*, *Journal of the Philosophy of History*, *Journal of Global History*, *Contemporary European History*, *European Review of History-Revue Européenne d'Histoire*, and *Journal of Contemporary History*. Short articles can also be found in several international encyclopaedias.

Alberte Martínez-López. Professor of Economic History at the University of A Coruña (Spain), where he coordinates the Business History Study Group. He has been head of some research projects about gas and other utilities, and head researcher of the research project "Gas in Latin Europe: A Comparative and Global Perspective (1818–1945)" (with M. Fernández-Paradas). Visiting fellow in several European and American universities. His main recent research fields are utilities (gas, electricity, transport, water) and foreign investment in utilities. Author of several articles, chapters and books about these topics in *Business History*, *Continuity and Change*, *Journal of Urban Technology*, *Journal of Urban History*, and so on.

Juan Manuel Matés-Barco. BSc Geography and History (University of Saragossa), PhD in History (University of Granada), is Full Professor of Economic History and Business History at the University of Jaén (Spain). He has made research stays at the Università degli Studi di Firenze, at the European University Institute (Italy), at the Université Michel de Montaigne Bordeaux 3 (France) and at the University of Évora (Portugal). He has carried out studies on the Public Drinking Water Supply Service and is Director of the journal *Agua y Territorio / Water and Landscape (AYT/WAL)*, and has published studies on the economic evolution of contemporary Spain. Researcher at the Permanent Seminar on Water, Territory and the Environment: Public Policies and Citizen Participation. Coordinator of several research projects. Head Researcher of the Group of Historical Studies on the Company (GEHESE-UJA).

Jesús Mirás-Araujo. Senior Lecturer of Economic History at the Department of Economics of the University of A Coruña (Spain). He is an associate editor of the *International Journal of Economics and Business Modelling*, and previously a member of the editorial board of *Transportes, Servicios y Telecomunicaciones*. He has participated in several research projects, and in contracts with companies, most of them related to energy history. His main research interests are on public utilities, particularly gas and electricity, as well as urban history, business history and transport history. He is the author of several books about these topics, chapters in Peter Lang, Routledge or Presses de l'Université Paris-Sorbonne, and articles in *Business History*, *Continuity and Change*, *Urban History* or *Journal of Urban History*.

Antonio Jesús Pinto Tortosa. Full-time Lecturer in History of Thinking and Social Movements at the Universidad Europea, Madrid (Spain). Though he got his PhD in Contemporary Spanish History, focusing on the impact of the Haitian Revolution on Spanish Santo Domingo, he has published several works on the history of gas industry and the Spanish industrial take off. Among other journals in which he has published his results, it is necessary to underline *Llull* and *Asclepio*. In addition to that, he has published his contributions in editorial firms such as Marcial Pons, Catarata, and Tirant lo Blanch. He is currently enrolled in the research project "Gas in Latin Europe: A Comparative and Global Perspective (1818–1945)".

Nuria Rodríguez-Martín. Lecturer in Contemporary History at the Complutense University of Madrid (Spain). She holds a degree in Journalism, and she earned her PhD in History from the UCM in 2013, with a dissertation on the social changes in Madrid during the 1920s and 1930s, which received the Distinguished Doctoral Dissertation Award from the Spanish Association of Contemporary History. Before joined the UCM's Faculty of Geography and History she was a Lectrice d'espagnol at Université Paris-Sorbonne (Paris IV) and a Juan de la Cierva Postdoctoral Fellow at University of the Basque Country. In 2006 she joined the research group Espacio, Sociedad y Cultura en la Edad Contemporánea, where she explores the social and cultural transformations in Madrid during the first third of the twentieth century. Her research is concerned with the history of urban infrastructures and public utilities, particularly gas and electricity. She is the author of *La capital de un sueño. Madrid en el primer tercio del siglo XX* (2015), awarded as best book in Art and Humanities at the XIX Spanish University Presses Prizes, and of several articles and book chapters in Routledge, Peter Lang, and so on.

Patricia Suárez Cano. PhD in Economics from the University of Oviedo, Spain (2011) and Extraordinary Doctorate Award. Associate Professor (2020) in the Department of Economics (History and Economic Institutions). She has carried out different research stays in Switzerland (Università della Svizzera Italiana), Spain (University of Alcalá), Washington DC (Inter American Development Bank) and Italy (Bologna University). She has published more than 20 publications (Scopus), in journals such as *Papers in Regional Science*, *Small Business Economics*, *Transportation Research Part A: Policy and Practice*, *Business History*, *Labor History*, and *The Annals of Regional Science*. She has also published five book chapters in prestigious publishers such as Springer and Physica-Verlag and five books on different business histories. In the last year she has focused her work on the preparation of a book for Nortegas on the positioning of this company in the natural gas industry in Spain.

Russell Thomas. BSc (Hons) Microbiology and Biotechnology (University of Sunderland). PhD (University of Birmingham), CBIOL FRSB MIENVSc CEnv MSCI FIGEM EngTech. He is a Technical Director at the international engineering professional services firm WSP. He has spent much of his career researching different aspects of the gas industry, pioneering technologies to investigate and remediate gas manufacturing sites. In recent years his focus has turned to preserving the history and the heritage of the gas industry. He is chair of the Institution of Gas Engineers and Managers (IGEM), History Panel and co-editor of its publication, *The Historic Gas Times*. The author of several books, plus countless reports and academic papers, Russell is invited to speak at conferences around the globe. He is a Visiting Professor at the Department of Civil and Environmental Engineering at the University of Strathclyde and a Visiting Lecturer at the University of Manchester's School of Earth, Atmospheric and Environmental Science. He is a charted fellow of the Royal Society of Biology, Chartered Environmentalist and a Fellow of IGEM.

Jesús María Valdaliso Gago. Professor of Economic History at the School of Economics and Business of the University of the Basque Country (Bilbao, Spain). Visiting Research Fellow at the London School of Economics (1995), Visiting Scholar at the Universidad de Barcelona (1997), Universidad de Los Andes (2009) and the Institute for Strategy and Competitiveness of the Harvard Business School (2010/2011). He has served as Head of the Department of Economic History and Institutions of the University of the Basque Country (2013–2020), and President of the International Maritime Economic History Association (2008–2012) and of the Spanish Association of Economic History (2015). Principal Investigator of several research projects funded by public and private organisations. He currently leads the Research Group Cliobasque, funded by the Basque Government, and a Research Project of the Spanish Ministry of Science and Innovation, both focused on the processes of path dependence and change in the institutions and organisations of old industrial regions and on the economic resilience of sectors and regions. He has recently directed and published a commissioned history of Nortegas, the second gas distributor of Spain: *Nortegas (1845-2021). Historia de la industria del gas en el norte de España* (Marcial Pons, 2022).

María Vázquez-Fariñas. Lecturer in Economic History (Department of Economic Theory and History) at the University of Malaga (Spain). PhD in Social and Legal Sciences and Degree in Business Administration and Management from the University of Cadiz. Actively involved as a component of the Research Group of Historical Studies on the Enterprise (GEHESE-UJA). Research stays in Spanish and prestige foreign centres, such as the School of Hispanic American Studies (CSIC, Seville), the University Michel de Montaigne Bordeaux 3 and the University of Cadiz. General lines of research are focused on the economic and business history of nineteenth-century Cadiz (Spain), and the development of gas and public utilities in contemporary Spain. Author of several works on these topics that have been published in national and international journals and publishing houses, such as Routledge, Peter Lang and Palgrave, in which she has coordinated the book *Companies and Entrepreneurs in the History of Spain. Centuries Long Evolution in Business since the 15th Century* (2021). She has also participated in several research and teaching innovation projects, and is part of the Editorial Board of the journal *Agua y Territorio / Water and Landscape* (AYT/WAL), from 2018 to the present.

Jean-Pierre Williot. Professor of Contemporary History at the Faculty of Letters of the Sorbonne University, Paris. PhD in History, Sorbonne University Paris IV (1995). Visiting fellow in several European universities. He was formerly director of the research team LéA (Équipe Alimentation), and head of the Master "Histoire et Culture de l'Alimentation", both at the University François Rabelais of Tours. Member of the Scientific Board of the journal *Actes d'Història de la Ciència i de la Tècnica (SCHCT)* and *Histoire, Economies, Sociétés*, he has also been member of several scientific committees, and has participated in several national and international research projects, as well as scientific research mission with companies. His fields of specialisation are economic and social history (nineteenth and twentieth centuries), energy history (gas companies and networks), railway history and the history of food innovation. His research focuses on the actors and methods of innovation, which he studies in three fields: gas energy, railways and the food chain. In the field of gas history, he is the author or co-author of several books on the history of gas in Paris, France, and Europe. Some recent publications related to gas include: *Les routes du gaz* (Le Cherche Midi, 2012, with Alain Beltran); *Gaz. Deux siècles de culture gazière* (Le Cherche Midi, 2009, with Alain Beltran).

Acknowledgements

This book forms part of the results of the research project “Gas in Latin Europe: A Comparative and Global Perspective (1818–1945)”, PID2020-112844GB-I00. It has been supported and financed by the Ministry of Science and Innovation of the Spanish Government and European Regional Development Funds.

1 Introduction

Alberte Martínez-López, Jesús Mirás-Araujo and Nuria Rodríguez-Martín

Energy is an essential factor for societies and economic activities. In fact, the major economic transformations (emergence of agriculture, different phases of industrialisation, modern transport systems, public services, etc.) were only possible thanks to the profound changes in the energy paradigm: from human to animal, firewood and hydraulic energy, from these to coal and, subsequently oil, natural gas and nuclear energy and, more recently, the transition towards renewable energies, such as wind, solar, tidal and geothermal energies.

The transcendence and complexity of these processes of change in energy sources has meant that the energy transitions have attracted much interest, not only among historians but also among professionals from other disciplines, such as economics or ecology, and they have become prominent in the political agenda. The initial interest of historians was focused on the energy transformations that accompanied the industrialisation processes, that is, from a predominance of human and animal power, biomass and hydraulic energy to a model based, mainly, on fossil fuels such as coal.

Subsequently, the growing importance of the profound and relevant transformations that accompanied the second technological revolution (among others, electrification, the shift from coal to oil, the consolidation of the network systems) renewed the academic interest in energy, reinforced by the strong impact of the oil crisis of the 1970s.

In recent years, the general public and leaders (politicians and entrepreneurs) have gradually assimilated and accepted the warnings from the academic world about the risks and environmental impact (pollution, climate change) of the production and consumption model of the west and emerging countries. Particularly, these warnings refer to the strong growth in the use of fossil fuels (coal, oil, natural gas) and the resulting and imperative need for their progressive and rapid replacement with clean and renewable energies. This has reinforced, once again, the attention of social and environmental scientists on the energy transition processes, their conditioning factors and implications (Gales et al., 2007; Fouquet, 2016; Lamard and Stoskopf, 2019; Bartoletto, 2020).

DOI: 10.4324/9781003428695-1

From different perspectives, this tension and the dynamic interplay between different energy alternatives are present in many of the studies in this book, particularly Chapters 1, 2, 3 and 5.

Currently, the war in Ukraine has crudely highlighted the essential importance of energy in the functioning of the economy and the daily lives of people, its strategic nature (with the resulting reluctance of the entry of foreign capital in this sector) and the vulnerability and the risk derived from depending on its external supply concentrated in a few countries, particularly in situations of conflict. These types of problems are reflected in one way or another in Chapters 4, 6, 7, 8 and 10.

The literature on energy from a historical perspective includes works of reference that analyse the issue from an overall point of view and from a long-term perspective. Particularly noteworthy are those of Fouquet (2008), Madureira (2014), Kander, Malanima and Warde (2015) and Smil (2017). For Southern Europe, the studies by Madureira (2005), Malanima (2006), Teives (2009) and Sudrià (2010) are of note.

The hot topic within energy has, undoubtedly, been electricity. One of the seminal works in this field is that of Hughes (1993). More recently, we can refer to the study by Lagendijk (2008) on a European scale. Within the framework of Latin Europe, the reference studies are those by Caron et al. (1991–1996) for France and Bartolomé Rodríguez (2007) for Spain.

In the case of gas, the essential work on a European scale is the one conducted by Paquier and Williot (2005). However, other important studies had been previously published on the gas industry in different countries of Southern Europe, such as Spain (Sudrià, 1983), France (Beltran and Williot, 1992) or Italy (Bigatti et al., 1997). An overall vision of the oil and gas industry in Europe from a historical perspective, but with a geological approach, can be found in Craig et al. (2018).

In the case of natural gas, studies have been conducted for the European scale, such as Victor, Jaffe, and Hayes (2006) and for individual countries, such as Ballestero (2017) for Spain or Beltran and Williot (2012) on natural gas transportation in France.

In the last decade, a research group led by Mercedes Fernández Paradas has consolidated, made up of researchers from different disciplines (economic history, social history, cultural history, technological history) and from different countries (Spain, France, Italy and Portugal), who have developed different research projects based on the gas industry in these territories within the framework of Latin Europe. This collective work, together with the collaboration of other professionals, has given rise to the publication of several monographs in journals and books. These studies represent the most complete and updated sample of the historiographical production on gas in Southern Europe. In some cases, several of the members have also published documented studies, for example, on the evolution of gas technology (Alayo and Barca, 2011), the full history of the leading gas company in Spain (Fàbregas, 2018), or a long-term perspective of the entrepreneurial evolution of the sector, also in Spain

(Fernández-Paradas, Martínez-López, and Mirás-Araujo, 2022), together with detailed monographs on different Spanish cities and regions, some written by authors who do not form part of this research group.

Many of the studies conducted by this group use the comparative method between different countries or even the whole of Latin Europe as a frame of reference. Owing to a lack of space, we will cite the collective works in monograph format in journals or books. The initial publications represented a first approach to the topic (Bartolomé Rodríguez, Fernández-Paradas, and Mirás Araujo, 2017). Later, the studies began to specialise in different geographical perspectives, such as cities (Fernandez and Martínez-López, 2021) or different regions (Bartolomé Rodríguez, Fernández-Paradas, and Mirás Araujo, 2020, 2022). The most recent works show the maturity of the group and its international projection (Mirás and Giuntini, 2023; Cardoso, Fernandez and Pinto, 2023).

This volume also forms part of another important thematic line, namely urban network infrastructures or technical public services, which have aroused the interest of historians, economists, geographers, urban planners and engineers. In fact, technological history and urban history have perhaps been the predominant approaches to studying the relationships between networks and urban spaces. To a great extent, although not exclusively, energy networks, particularly in their early stages of development, were related to the urban context, given their high cost and the need for agglomeration economies.

The networked city (Tarr and Dupuy, 1988) took shape in advanced countries in the period 1880–1920, coinciding with the onset of the second technological revolution, although in certain countries, some networks, such as gas and water, began to be formed in the mid-nineteenth century (Cardesín and Mirás, 2008). The intense urban growth derived from the industrial revolution placed intense pressure on the network structures in cities, namely water (in volume and quality), sanitation, mobility and energy. During the second half of the nineteenth century, they almost reached breaking point, particularly the water and sanitation networks, but also those of mobility and energy. This obliged the local governments to urgently search for reliable and long-lasting solutions.

The dominant doctrinal liberalism and the lack of economic resources, technological knowledge and management capacity led the local authorities to enlist the help of the private initiative, frequently of foreign origin, for the construction and management of these new infrastructures through administrative concessions. The chronology, exploitation regime and relative weight of private and foreign capital varied in accordance with the degree of economic development and institutional systems of the different countries. The laying and implementation of the corresponding public utilities, associated with the idea of modernity, significantly contributed to the profound sociological changes that took place in the advanced societies in the period 1880–1930 (Otero, 2020; Gunn et al., 2022).

Initially, these network systems were confined to urban environments and even more specifically to the town centres, where the population with the highest purchasing power was concentrated (initial target market of the concessionaire companies) and where the agglomeration economies made the laying of distribution networks more feasible and profitable. At first, even the transport networks of the different fluids (water, gas, electricity) had an eminently local radius of action, as the provision or production systems (based on coal for gas and electricity) at that time required a proximity between producing centres and consumption areas, given the high cost (and leaks) of transporting it across long distances.

Over time (after the First World War for electricity and the Second for LPG and natural gas), the technological advances such as hydroelectricity and the transport of high voltage electricity or the obtaining of gas through the refining of petroleum and the extraction of natural gas facilitated the territorial expansion of the energy transport networks from an initially local scale to the regional, national and finally international level. This international dimension reached by the networks in their final phase and the strategic nature of what they distributed (water in the case of the shared basins, energy, information) gave rise to new challenges related to the interconnection of systems, the notion of sovereignty, national security and the guarantee of supply, depending ultimately on delicate and unstable geopolitical balances, such as the oil crisis of the 1970s or the current conflict in Ukraine have highlighted. These types of problems are analysed in Chapters 7, 8 and 10.

The historiography on the networks of urban technical services is too vast and mature to summarise in a few paragraphs. Apart from the aforementioned seminal work of Tarr and Dupuy (1988), the work of reference in this field is, undoubtedly, Millward (2005). This author began by researching the water and gas companies, the first network suppliers, in the United Kingdom throughout the nineteenth century. As Millward's research matured, he broadened the sectoral, geographic and chronological scale of the analysis of the networks, also examining the complex relationships between private and public actors in infrastructure industries, particularly electricity, within the most developed countries during the nineteenth and twentieth centuries. In the aforementioned work, Millward has conducted an encyclopaedic level of analysis of the network services companies over the long term, including not only energy but also telecommunications and transport.

In the specific case of Latin Europe, we can refer to the monograph publication coordinated by Giuntini and Martínez-López (2011) or the collective book by Matés and Torres (2019) on Spain. Given the high cost of the infrastructures, their finance has also attracted the attention of economic historians. In this respect, particularly noteworthy is the collective study by Cassis, De Luca and Florio (2016).

Herein, we will refer to the principal studies on different energy network services mentioned previously. The urban water supply as an essential and critical provision has generated a vast amount of academic studies. Here, we will indicate some of those that we consider as being the broadest and most relevant. These include those by Melosi (2008) and Matés Barco (2013).

The studies on urban transport and mobility have aroused the interest of many researchers from different disciplines, given the relevance and implications of the subject. Among the most global contributions, we can refer to the studies by McKay (1976), Oyón (1999), Capuzzo (2000), Divall and Bond (2003) or Giuntini and Núñez (2007) for Mediterranean Europe. The telecommunications networks and their relationships with geopolitical interests have been studied by, among others, Headrick (1991) and Hugill (1999).

The flows of knowledge on an international level and, more specifically, of technological knowledge have played a fundamental role in the implementation of the urban infrastructures and the management of public network services. These research lines include the recent studies by Pretel and Camprubí (2018), Roca et al. (2019), or Le Bot and Michel (2021). The technological transfer in the Mediterranean region, which is the object of this book, has been addressed by Merger (2006) and Medina-Ruiz et al. (2022), with several chapters on the role of the engineers and the gas industry in this process.

Generally speaking, these international technological transfers have been conducted with foreign investment. In this regard, the companies from the "nucleus" of capitalism (initially the United Kingdom and France and then also the United States and Germany; Belgium in the tram sector) played a crucial role in enabling the construction of the networks and their management, due to their investment capabilities, technical knowledge and know-how. There has been some level of specialisation in certain public services by the investing countries in accordance with their comparative advantages, particularly derived from their experience and technological superiority, but also from their historical connection with certain geographical areas, such as the case of France in Mediterranean Europe. In this way, the British were leaders in railways (also in animal pulled trams) and telegraphy, the French in water and gas, while the Germans, together with the Americans, dominated the electricity markets, with the Belgians as leaders in electrical trams, although frequently acting as an instrument of the powerful German electrical consortia, which also used Switzerland to this end.

The historiographical production on foreign investment is already copious and has reached a high level of maturity. Focusing on the urban public services sector and from an international perspective, we can highlight the studies by Broder (1982b), Hertner (1990), Martínez-López (2003) and Hausman, Hertner and Wilkins (2008). In the geographical area of Latin Europe, significant contributions have been made, although many elements have yet to be studied. An overall view of the Spanish case can be found in Castro-Valdivia, Matés-Barco and Vázquez-Fariñas (2020). The water supply in Spain has been studied mainly by Matés (2002). In terms of electricity, the reference works are those of Broder (1982a), Lanthier (1991), Segreto (1994) and Bartolomé Rodríguez (2014). In the case of gas, we can cite the recent studies by Martínez-López and Mirás-Araujo (2021) and Vázquez-Fariñas, Castro-Valdivia and Matés-Barco (2023).

The natural monopoly nature of network systems has historically justified their need for regulation, although in recent decades this trend has been reversed (Clifton, Lanthier and Schröter, 2014).

The private/public tension in the management of urban public services is a reflection of the intense theoretical debates on the advantages and drawbacks of the two models in relation to notions such as equity or efficiency (Hausman and Neufeld, 1994). In the case of network infrastructures, the research has been focused on the types of management, of which there are two principal models. On the one hand, one in which there is a predominance of the private company, following the French concessional model (Barjot, 2011), which was implemented in the majority of Latin Europe, although less so in the Italian case due to the weight of the municipalisation of services developed in the light of the law of 1903 (Berselli, Della Peruta and Varni, 1988), and other European countries. The second model is the shift towards the municipalisation of certain services, as in the case of the United Kingdom at the end of the nineteenth century and in other states of Central Europe such as Germany or Austria, among others (Kühl, 2014). The privatisation process initiated in the 1990s, which particularly affected network public service companies, has also attracted the interest of economic historians, such as Clifton, Comín and Díaz Fuentes (2006).

From the urban economics field, recent and interesting contributions have been made on the influence of the political institutions on infrastructures, expressly using the historical perspective as an instrument of analysis (Bogart, 2022).

The term "Latin Europe" generally refers to the European territories, not necessarily complete states (as in the case of Belgium or Switzerland, for example), in which a language derived from Latin is spoken and which have inherited the Roman culture and Catholic tradition (Friedman and Pérez-Perdomo, 2003). In our case, we refer to a more economic, institutional and historical notion. Therefore, we limit Latin Europe to those states of South-western Europe (Spain, Italy, Portugal), which, sharing cultural, geographical and climate similarities, enjoyed golden ages in the Late Middle Ages and/or beginning of the Modern Age, but had serious difficulties to adapt to modernity, particularly the industrialisation process. We also include France, which, sharing a Latin cultural and institutional heritage and Catholic religion, was attractive to the other three countries and greatly influenced them, particularly from the eighteenth century, from a cultural, political, institutional, economic and technological point of view.

These similarities and the relatively unitary nature can also be observed in their energy systems. In all of them, with the partial exception of France, coal was practically non-existent, scarce and/or of a low quality and sometimes was difficult to access and exploit and was not located close to the industrial and more urbanised regions. This obliged these countries to import it from Great Britain or, to a lesser extent and, for the case of France, Belgium and to continue the mass use of hydraulic energy, which conditioned an industrial structure dominated by light industry, more suited to this energy mix. This energy restriction strongly conditioned the performance of these countries during the industrial revolution. However, their position improved with hydroelectricity as they were better equipped with this resource.

In the case of gas, the peculiarities of this European region have been analysed in depth by Cardoso, Fernandez and Pinto (2023). These authors highlight the supply problems (scarcity of coal, small number of gas factories, networks that were not very dense) and demand problems (limited industrialisation and urbanisation, low per capita income). All of this led to a late beginning and a low level of implementation of the gas industry on both territorial and social levels, with the exception of France. This country became the principal issuer of the regulatory model (concession), investments, technology, entrepreneurs and technicians to the other Latin countries.

The book aims to contribute an in-depth analysis of several topics related to the changes in energy in Western Europe in the long term, from the nineteenth to the twenty-first century. It focuses mostly on manufactured gas, that is, the gas that was produced from coal distillation, but also the new ways of manufacturing gas that emerged after the Second World War. A multidisciplinary approach is adopted as the authors come from different fields: economic history, business history, social history, cultural history and history of technology.

The book opens with a chapter written by Nuno Madureira, which defines, from a long-term perspective, the reference theoretical framework for the rest of the chapters: the energy transitions in Europe and the adaptation strategies that were adopted by the different energies. Madureira analyses two large energy transitions: from animal, firewood and hydraulic to coal and from coal to oil and natural gas, highlighting the differences between the two processes.

The rest of the chapters analyse different aspects of these dynamics, focusing on the case of gas and on a chronological and evolutionary line from manufactured gas to natural gas.

José Luque and Alberte Martínez analyse how electricity was perceived and received by the gas sector during the last third of the nineteenth century and their adaptation strategies in response to the new competitor. To do this, they conduct a detailed study of the contents of one of the references of the European gas press.

Antonio Fernández and Nuria Rodríguez use a new approach from social and cultural history to analyse the competition between gas and electricity. With this objective, they analyse the communication and marketing strategies of the companies of these sectors in Spain and France during the period 1890–1936.

Meanwhile, the study by María Vázquez, Mariano Castro and Juan M. Matés analyses the relevant weight of foreign gas companies in Spain and their withdrawal process from the Spanish markets from the time of the First World War. Several of these companies formed energy conglomerates engaged in both gas and electrical activities, which constituted a strategy to overcome the traditional rivalry between the two sectors.

Continuing this comparison between the two competing energies, the chapter by Mercedes Fernández, Carlos Larrinaga and Antonio Pinto makes a comparative study on two levels: between the energies (gas and electricity) and between countries (Spain and France) during the depression of the 1930s.

The chapter by Mercedes Fernández, Alberte Martínez and Jesús Mirás analyses the impact of the Second World War on the gas industry in Western Europe, its adaptation strategies and, particularly, how the different types of demand were affected.

The study by Jesús M. Valdaliso, Patricia Suárez and Carlos Alvarado opens the series referring to natural gas. It analyses the different gas connection projects between Spain and France presented from 1959 and the complexity of the factors in play in the decision-making process regarding their construction and implementation.

Jean-Pierre Williot and Andrea Giuntini continue the line of comparative studies, in this case focusing on the provision of gas in two relevant European countries: France and Italy. Their respective energy mixes, resource endowment, gas infrastructures and geopolitical conditions explain the differences in the volume and origin of the supplies.

Russell Thomas takes a different approach. From an industrial archaeology perspective, this author analyses the major challenges involved in the recovery and reuse of the old, manufactured gas producing factories due to, among other factors, the toxicity of their waste and the complexity of the urban planning processes.

By way of an epilogue, the book ends with a very topical chapter. Pere Fàbregas analyses the external supply of gas to Europe over the last half-century, its conditioning factors and risks. As a case study, the chapter compares the different options chosen by Germany and Spain.

References

Alayo, Joan Carles, and Barca, Francesc X. 2011. *La tecnología del gas a través de su historia*. Barcelona: Fundación Gas Natural Fenosa.

Ballestero, Alfonso. 2017. *El gas natural en España*. Barcelona: Lid Editorial.

Barjot, Dominique. 2011. Public utilities and private initiative: The French concession model in historical perspective. *Business History* 53 (5): 782–800.

Bartoletto, Silvana. 2020. *Energy Transitions in Mediterranean Countries. Consumption, Emissions and Security of Supplies*. Cheltenham: Edward Elgar.

Bartolomé Rodríguez, Isabel. 2007. *La industria eléctrica en España (1890-1936)*. Madrid: Banco de España.

Bartolomé Rodríguez, Isabel. 2014. La inserción internacional de la primera electrificación española y los antecedentes del mercado ibérico (1890-1940). *Revista de la historia de la economía y de la empresa* 8: 97–122.

Bartolomé Rodríguez, Isabel, Fernández-Paradas, Mercedes, and Mirás Araujo, Jesús eds. 2017. *Globalización, nacionalización y liberalización de la industria del gas en la Europa Latina (siglos XIX-XXI)*. Madrid: Marcial Pons.

Bartolomé Rodríguez, Isabel, Fernández-Paradas, Mercedes, and Mirás Araujo, Jesús eds. 2020. *Cercanas pero distintas. La desigual trayectoria de la industria del gas en las regiones del sur de Europa (siglos XIX-XX)*. Madrid: Marcial Pons.

Bartolomé Rodríguez, Isabel, Fernández-Paradas, Mercedes, and Mirás Araujo, Jesús eds. 2022. *Bajo la cálida luz del gas. los mercados regionales de la industria gasista en España (siglos XIX y XX)*. Madrid: Sílex.

Beltran, Alain, and Williot, Jean-Pierre. 1992. *Le noir et le bleu: 40 ans d'histoire de Gaz de France*. Paris: P. Belfond.

Beltran, Alain, and Williot, Jean-Pierre. 2012. *Les Routes du gaz: Histoire du transport de gaz naturel en France*. Le Cherche Midi.

Berselli, Aldo, Della Peruta, Franco, and Varni, Angelo. 1988. *La Municipalizzazione nell'area padana: storia ed esperienze a confronto*. Milano: Franco Angeli.

Bigatti, Giorgio, Giuntini, Andrea, Mantegazza, Amilcare, and Rotondi, Claudio. 1997. *L'acqua e il gas in Italia*. Milano: Francoangeli.

Bogart, Dan. 2022. Infrastructure and institutions: Lessons from history. *Regional Science and Urban Economics* 94, 103626.

Broder, Albert. 1982a. Le financement et le contrôle de l'industrie électrique dans les pays de la façade nord de la Méditerranée: 1890-1929. In *Banque et investissements en Mediterranée a l'époque contemporaine*, Marseille: Chambre de commerce et d'industrie de Marseille: 85–102.

Broder, Albert. 1982b. L'expansion internationale de l'industrie allemande dans le dernier tiers du XIXe siècle: Le cas de l'industrie électrique: 1880-1913. *Relations Internationales* 29: 65–87.

Capuzzo, Paolo. 2000. La conquista della mobilità. Contributo ad una storia sociale dei transporti urbani in Europa (1870–1940). *Richerche Storiche* 30 (3): 621–639.

Cardesín Díaz, José María, and Mirás Araujo, Jesús. 2008. La modernizzazione delle città spagnole tra il tramonto della restaurazione e la guerra civile. *Storia Urbana* 119: 9–20.

Cardoso, Ana, Fernandez, Alexandre, Pinto, Antonio J. 2023. *The Gas Sector in Latin Europe's Industrial History: Lighting and Heating the World*. Cham: Springer Nature.

Caron, François, Cardot, Fabienne, Lévy-Leboyer, Maurice, and Morsel, Henri. 1991–1996. *Histoire de l'électricité en France*. 3 tomes. Sévres: Fayard.

Cassis, Youssef, De Luca, Giuseppe, and Florio, Massimo. 2016. *Infrastructure Finance in Europe: Insights into the History of Water, Transport, and Telecommunications*. Oxford: Oxford University Press.

Castro-Valdivia, Mariano, Matés-Barco, Juan Manuel, and Vázquez-Fariñas, María. 2020. Capital extranjero y desarrollo urbano en España: la inversión en los servicios públicos durante el primer tercio del siglo XX. In *Las infraestructuras en la construcción de la ciudad moderna. España y México, 1850-1936* edited by Luis Enrique Otero-Carvajal, 177–193. Madrid: La Catarata.

Clifton, Judith, Comín, Francisco, and Díaz Fuentes, Daniel. 2006. Privatizing public enterprises in the European Union 1960–2002: Ideological, pragmatic, inevitable? *Journal of European Public Policy* 13 (5): 736–756.

Clifton, Judith, Lanthier, P., and Schröter, H. eds. 2014. *The Economic and Social Regulation of Public Utilities: An International History*. New York: Routledge.

Craig, John J., Gerali, Francesco, MacAulauy, Fiona, and Sorkhabi, Rasoul. eds. 2018. *History of the European Oil and Gas Industry*. London: Geological Society of London.

Divall, Colin, and Bond, Winstan. 2003. *Suburbanizing the Masses: Public Transport and Urban Development in Historical Perspective*. Aldershot: Ashgate.

Fàbregas, Pere A. 2018. *Naturgy. 175 años de compromiso con la energía y la sociedad*. Barcelona: Naturgy – Planeta.

Fernandez, Alexandre, and Martínez-López, Alberte. eds. 2021. *La energía en las ciudades de la Europa latina*. Madrid: *Ayer. Revista de Historia Contemporánea* 122 (2).

Fernández-Paradas, Mercedes, Martínez-López, Alberte, and Mirás-Araujo, Jesús. 2022. The gas companies in Spain, a long-run approach (1842-2018). *Business History* 64 (1): 75–97.

Fouquet, Roger. 2008. *Heat, Power and Light: Revolutions in Energy Services*. Cheltenham, UK: Edward Elgar Publications.

Fouquet, Roger. 2016. Historical energy transitions: Speed, prices and system transformation. *Energy Research & Social Science* 22: 7–12.

Friedman, Lawrence M., and Pérez-Perdomo, Rogelio. eds. 2003. *Legal Culture in the Age of Globalization: Latin America and Latin Europe*. Stanford: Stanford University Press.

Gales, Ben, Kander, Astrid, Malanima, Paolo and Rubio, María del Mar. 2007. North versus South. Energy transition and energy intensity in Europe over 200 years. *European Review of Economic History* 2: 219–253.

Giuntini, Andrea, and Núñez, Gregorio. 2007. Reti di trasporti urbani nell'Europa meridionale. *Richerche Storiche* 2: 273–433.

Giuntini, Andrea, and Martínez-López, Alberte. eds. 2011. Utilities del mondo latino. Economia, finanza e tecnologia dei servizi tecnici a rete (secc. XIX-XX). *Memoria e ricerca* 36.

Gunn, Simon, Butler, Richard, De Block, Greet, Høghøj, Mikkel, and Thelle, Mikkel. 2022. Cities, infrastructure and the making of modern citizenship: The view from north-west Europe since c. 1870. *Urban History* 50 (3): 1–19.

Hausman, William J., Hertner, Peter, and Wilkins, Mira. 2008. *Global Electrification: Multinational Enterprise and International Finance in the History of Light and Power, 1878–2007*. Cambridge: Cambridge University Press.

Hausman, William J., and Neufeld, John L. 1994. Public versus private electric utilities in the United States: A century of debate over comparative economic efficiency. *Annals of Public and Cooperative Economics* 65 (4): 599–623.

Headrick, Daniel R. 1991. *The Invisible Weapon: Telecommunications and International Politics, 1851-1945*. New York: Oxford University Press.

Hertner, Peter. 1990. Estrategias financieras y adaptación a los mercados exteriores: la industria electrotécnica alemana y sus actividades multinacionales de 1890 a 1939. In *Empresas multinacionales, finanzas, mercados y gobiernos en el siglo XX*, edited by Maurice Lévy-Leboyer, Alice Teichova, and Helga Nussbaum, 197–214. Madrid: Ministerio de Trabajo y Seguridad Social.

Hughes, Thomas P. 1993. *Networks of Power. Electrification in Western Society, 1880-1930*. Baltimore: Johns Hopkins University Press.

Hugill, Peter. 1999. *Global Communications since 1844: Geopolitics and Technology*. Baltimore: Johns Hopkins University Press.

Kander, Astrid, Malanima, Paolo and Warde, Paul. 2015. *Power to the People. Energy in Europe over the Last Five Centuries*. Princeton and Oxford: Princeton University Press.

Kühl, Uwe. ed. 2014. *Der Munizipalsozialismus in Europa/Le socialisme municipal en Europe* (Vol. 57). Walter de Gruyter GmbH & Co KG.

Lagendijk, Vincent C. 2008. *Electrifying Europe: the power of Europe in the construction of electricity networks*. Eindhoven: Technische Universiteit Eindhoven.

Lamard, Pierre, and Stoskopf, Nicolas. 2019. *La transition énergétique: Un concept historique?* Villeneuve d'Ascq: Presses Universitaires du Septentrion.

Lanthier, Pierre. 1991. *Las multinacionales y la industria eléctrica francesa 1889-1940*. Madrid: Ministerio de Trabajo y Seguridad Social.

Le Bot, Florent, and Michel, Alain P. 2021. Le travail des ingénieurs en entreprises. formation, socialisation et activités des ingénieurs en perspective européenne de longue durée. *Artefact. Techniques, Histoire et Sciences Humaines* 13: 9–46.

Madureira, Nuno Luis. 2005. *A história da energia: Portugal 1890-1980*. Lisboa: Livros Horizonte.

Madureira, Nuno Luis. 2014. *Key Concepts in Energy*. Cham: Springer.

Malanima, Paolo. 2006. *Energy Consumption in Italy in the 19th and 20th centuries. A Statistical Outline*. Naples: CNR Edizioni.
Martínez-López, Alberte. 2003. Belgian investment in tramways and light railways: an international approach, 1892–1935. *The Journal of Transport History* 24 (1): 59–77.
Martínez-López, Alberte, and Mirás-Araujo, Jesús. 2021. British investments in the gas industry in Spain: the role of the free-standing companies. In *Business History in Spain: 19th and 20th centuries*, edited by Mercedes Fernández-Paradas and Carlos Larrinaga Rodriguez, 113–129. Berlin: Peter Lang.
Matés Barco, Juan Manuel. 2002. Strategies of foreign firms in the sector of water supply in Spain. In *Transnational Companies, 19th-20th Centuries*, edited by Hubert Bonin et al., 301–316. París: P.l.a.g.e.
Matés Barco, Juan Manuel. 2013. La conquista del agua en Europa: los modelos de gestión (siglos XIX y XX). *Agua y Territorio/Water and Landscape* 1: 21–29.
Matés Barco, Juan Manuel, and Torres-Rodríguez, Alicia. eds. 2019. *Los servicios públicos en España y México (siglos XIX-XXI)*. Madrid: Sílex.
McKay, John P. 1976. *Tramways and Trolleys: the Rise of Urban Mass Transport in Europe*. Princeton: University Press.
Medina-Ruiz, Israel-David, Pinto Tortosa, Antonio Jesús, Ravina Ripoll, Rafael, and Rodríguez-Martín, Nuria. eds. 2022. *Los ingenieros en la Europa del sur (siglos XVIII-XX)*. Valencia: Tirant lo Blanch.
Melosi, Martin V. 2008. *The Sanitary City: Environmental Services in Urban America from Colonial Times to the Present*. Pittsburgh: University of Pittsburgh Press.
Merger, Michèle. 2006. *Transferts de technologies en Méditerranée* (Vol. 25). Paris: Presses Paris Sorbonne.
Millward, Robert. 2005. *Private and Public Enterprise in Europe. Energy, Telecommunications and Transport, 1830–1990*. Cambridge: Cambridge University Press.
Mirás-Araujo, Jesús, and Giuntini, Andrea. eds. 2023. *The Gas Industry in Latin Europe: Economic Development during the 19th and 20th Centuries*. Cham: Springer Nature.
Otero Carvajal, Luis Enrique. 2020. *Las infraestructuras en la construcción de la ciudad moderna. España y México, 1850–1936*. Madrid: Los Libros de la Catarata.
Oyón, José Luis. 1999. Transporte público y estructura urbana (de mediados s. XIX a mediados s. XX): Gran Bretaña, España, Francia y Países germánicos. *Ecología Política* 17: 17–35.
Paquier, Serge, and Williot, Jean-Pierre. dirs. 2005. *L'industrie du gaz en Europe aux XIXe et XXe siècles. L'innovation entre marchés privés et collectivités publiques*. Bruxelles: Peter Lang.
Pretel, David, and Camprubí, Lino. 2018. *Technology and Globalisation: Networks of Experts in World History*. Cham: Springer.
Roca, Antoni M., Cardoso de Matos, Ana, Martykánová, Darina, Gouzévitch, Irina, and Grelon, André. 2019. La gran expansión de la ingeniería: Una perspectiva internacional. In *Técnica e Ingeniería en España. VIII. Del noventayochismo al desarrollismo*, edited by Manuel Silva Suárez, 163–244. Zaragoza: Real Academia de Ingeniería Institución «Fernando El Católico», Prensas de la Universidad de Zaragoza.
Segreto, Luciano. 1994. Le rôle du capital etranger dans l'industrie électrique. In *Histoire générale de l'électricité en France, tome deuxième, L'interconnexion et le marché 1919-1946*, edited by Maurice Lévy-Leboyer and Henri Morsel, 982–1019. Paris: Fayard.
Smil, Vaclav. 2017. *Energy and Civilization: A History*. Cambridge, MA: MIT Press.
Sudrià, Carles. 1983. Notas sobre la implantación y el desarrollo de la industria del gas en España 1840-1901. *Revista de Historia Económica* I (2): 97–119.

Sudrià, Carles. 2010. A historical outline of energy in the industrialization of Spain. In *Energy regulation in Spain: From monopoly to market*, edited by José Luis García Delgado and Juan Carlos Jiménez, 39–63. Pamplona: Civitas.

Tarr, Joel A., and Dupuy, Gabriel. eds. 1988. *Technology and the Rise of the Networked City in Europe and America*. Philadelphia: Temple University Press.

Teives, Sofia. 2009. *Energy Consumption in Portugal 1856-2006*. Naples: Consiglio Nazionale delle Ricerche.

Vázquez-Fariñas, María, Castro-Valdivia, Mariano, and Matés-Barco, Juan Manuel. 2023. The Internationalisation of the British Gas Industry in Latin Europe in the Nineteenth Century. In *The Gas Sector in Latin Europe's Industrial History: Lighting and Heating the World*, edited by Ana Cardoso, Alexandre Fernandez, and Antonio J. Pinto, 13–24. Cham: Springer Nature Switzerland.

Victor, David G., Jaffe, Amy M., and Hayes, Mark H. eds. 2006. *Natural Gas and Geopolitics: From 1970 to 2040*. Cambridge: Cambridge University Press.

2 Energy transitions in Europe

Nuno Madureira

2.1 Introduction

Most fundamentally, the transition concept covers the shifts in dominant energy sources and technologies that have occurred throughout history, such as the transition from biomass to coal or that from coal to oil and natural gas (Lu and Nemet, 2020). However, from the perspective of historical actors, the touchstone of changes are the modifications occurring in heating, lighting, mechanical power and cooling. While the realm of structural and civilisational energy transitions revolves around the replacement of existing energy systems with new energy sources and technologies, historical consciousness places a considerably greater emphasis on the delivery of energy services. Hence, any major energy transition may be broken down as the sum of the many small changes in energy services.

Peter O'Connor (2010, p. 10) captures this duality between structure and action with the ensuing definition:

> If the hallmark of an energy transition is a significant impact on society, quality of life, and the economy, then changes in resources, carriers, services, or converters can constitute an energy transition. We then have "energy resource transitions", "energy carrier transitions", "energy service transitions" and "energy converter transitions". These transitions are connected.

In this chapter, we explore the diverse patterns of energy transitions that have unfolded in Europe, highlighting one significant aspect throughout this process: the pivotal role played by shifts in energy resources, carriers, services or converters in driving substantial growth in total energy demand. Indeed, the global amount of raw materials directly consumed (domestic material consumption—DMC) per capita and per year has grown from an average of 3.4–4 tonnes per capita in 1850 to 10 tonnes in 2010. These advances resulted in an increased need for commodities and equipment which has, in turn, driven the growing demand for minerals and fossil fuels. In fact, fossil fuels ushered in a frenzied period of metals production. Additionally, there has been a stabilising

DOI: 10.4324/9781003428695-2

effect on the per capita demand for biomass (Haberl et al., 2016, p. 204). From this viewpoint, energy transitions are intimately linked to hungry economy contexts characterised by emerging needs, novel products and advanced technologies. The availability of energy at reduced prices has also stimulated enhanced consumption, while energy has itself replaced land, labour and capital in various domains.

2.2 Biomass: European contrasts

The shift from the epoch-long solar energy regime to the fossil fuel regime in its multifarious forms stands out as a pivotal energy transition from the perspective of the planet's metabolism. With the beginning of fossil fuel usage through coal, this in effect marked a shift both in the process of energy conversion and in global energy flows. These changes have consequently exerted a notable influence on the intricate biogeochemical cycles of our planet.

Up to the nineteenth century, the solar energy regime prevailed across Europe. This deployed the capacity to produce work both through the muscular force of men and animals and by means of firewood. As such it was dependent on the effects of solar energy upon the growth of plants, trees, cyanobacteria and algae. Food and firewood, the mainstay of agrarian societies, hinge on the provision of solar energy through photosynthesis. The dominant form of energy conversion is therefore the transformation of heat into mass: plant growth is regulated by the chemical transformations of a light-absorbing pigment called chlorophyll, which absorbs energy from solar blue and red-light to produce oxygen (O_2) and chemical energy stored in glucose (a sugar). In the next stage, men, oxen and horses draw their muscular force from this foodstuff. Ultimately, up to the nineteenth century, all the energy of European societies came from the sun.

The resources available nonetheless began shrinking due to population growth: Europe entered the eighteenth century with 125 million inhabitants, attained 195 million by 1800 and 288 million by 1850 (Livi-Bacci, 1990, p. 2). The intensification of agricultural production along with new crop rotations ensured more food for the people. However, this trend was achieved largely at the expense of deforestation. Considering only domestic consumption, Europeans needed 1–2.5 m^3 of solid wood per person per year in the Mediterranean and with rising to a peak of 5 m^3 in the coldest climates of Scandinavia. Accordingly, each eighteenth-century newborn accrued the demand for at least one more hectare of coppiced forest for timber production (Warde, 2006). In large inland concentrations of people, fuel shortages led to drastic measures. Such was the case of Berlin and Madrid, for example, where for large stretches of time the public authorities held responsibility for ensuring the urban firewood supply. In Madrid, small amounts of firewood came from the city's immediate surroundings, within a 20-kilometre radius, whilst the bulk of demand was satisfied by charcoal (less volume for transportation with enhanced calorific power) produced within a 39-kilometre radius.

The depletion of the innermost zones led to the expansion of the charcoal supply, out to a radius of 111.5 kilometres, later reshuffled to 167 kilometres. To ensure that domestic consumers received their fuel, a complex transportation network was extended ever further to reach all the nearby forests (Ortego and Madrazo, 2017). In rural areas, peasants had to cope with a broad range of less efficient fuels. These included cattle dung, furze, heather, broom and sticks from hedgerows and copses and would account for at least a third of the overall consumption (Davidson, 1983, p. 73; Warde, 2007, p. 38).

The eighteenth century was an epoch of enclave fuelwood shortages rather than an epoch of energy crises. Owing to high transportation costs, certain regions would get completely stripped of all timber, such as Madrid's surroundings despite being near copiously forested mountains and hills. With wood prices doubling every 4–7 kilometres on roads in good condition, and with charcoal carriage carrying the risk of breakage, the boundary for fuel supply transportation ended up at 15 kilometres (Warde, 2006, p. 39; Sieferle, 2010, p. 59). Larger distances, such as the exceptional supply area of Madrid, had to be enforced with investments in road maintenance plus an organised transport system based on the remarkable deployment of 30,000 to 35,000 oxen-driven carts.

Charcoal burning consequently became an itinerant occupation with workers travelling from place to place to find new timber stocks. Likewise, industries had to maintain their own workforce of charcoal burners engaged across supply belts of coppiced forests. This created ceilings for the installation of factories beyond which supply became much trickier. All over Europe, the clash between the installation of energy intensive industries and the peasant economy left a track record of protests, claims and official ordinances. Ironworks, salt making from sources of brine, glass making, porcelain and creamware were the sectors that drove the consumption of massive quantities of firewood between the sixteenth and eighteenth centuries. These industries often required temperatures between 800° and 1300° Celsius. As a result, they triggered social conflicts with the peasant economy and, in fact, most of these factories only thrived due to state protection, be this through crown licences, exclusive rights to crown lands or mandatory fixed timber prices. Ultimately, the predatory effects upon forests became so large that some factories had to foreclose their activities: the case of iron smelting in south Denmark, glassworks in central Portugal or saltworks in eastern France. These, above all, produced the affluent commodities of an expanding energy consumer society: tiles and brick houses with porcelain, creamware or white salt-glazed stoneware teapots, cups, plates and sets of matching dishes; iron stoves, cast iron chimney plates, cooking pots, frying pans, kettles, pipes, agricultural hardware, cannon, mortars and ammunition; drinking glasses, window glass and mirrors; improved protein intake with salted pork and salted fish. Hence, comfort and refinement imbued in growing incomes exerted additional pressure upon timber and forests.

Over time, wood became an increasingly valuable asset in local and regional economies. Historically, institutions adapted themselves to the mounting valuation of assets through the creation of new property rights. The weakest links in the property rights over forests and meadows were the commons: land which everyone belonging to a village could use to collect wood or graze animals. This common property offered peasants the opportunity to exploit the economies of scale of resource pools granting additional means of subsistence. Since non-members of the village were generally excluded from access, forests became a sort of club goods (Kasper and Streit, 1998, pp. 180–185). Little by little, timber valuations drove the exclusion of increasing numbers of people from the common usage rights. This trend culminated with the expropriation of any rights held by local populations and the takeover of this essential resource by the crown. By the middle of the nineteenth century, the commons had all but disappeared from most of Europe with just some residual manifestations in Southern regions. In the ongoing energy transition, this reflects how the major outcome of wood shortages was the decoupling of forests from the peasant economy (Moor, 2009; Matteson, 2015). Forests were turned into scientifically managed spaces, entailing the protection of shoots from pasturing and thereby enabling a more robust regeneration of coppices and, furthermore, the adoption of fast-growing trees with the predominance of deciduous forests, particularly in Central Europe (Sieferle, 2010; McGrath et al., 2015).

Nevertheless, from a national perspective, three contrasting regions surfaced in Europe: First, there stands out the Europe rich in wood with at least one quarter of the national surface area forest covered: Austria-Hungary, Germany, Poland, the Balkans, Russia, Finland and Sweden (Endres, 1922, p. 6; Kjaergaard, 1994, p. 112; Kander et al., 2013, p. 56). Moreover, Central and Eastern Europe also display the highest availability of woods per capita. The woodlands heart was particularly located in two nations in this geography: Russia and Sweden. Russia because it was the largest exporter of timber to Europe owing to the widely available wood resources in the forest-steppe regions of European Russia and Ukraine; Sweden, because it was also an exporter of lumber and wood energy intensive products and the only country with a moving logging frontier still able to exploit new commercial forest regions, namely northern Sweden, that is, Norrland (Fries, 1996).

Moving in a westerly direction, we encounter the middle term nations: those who held between 10% and 25% of forested surfaced area at the dawn of the eighteenth century: Belgium, France, Italy and Switzerland. Although not entirely devoid of resources, these nations experienced mounting social conflicts around forests and common lands. Heading a little further west one finally arrives in the woodland depleted regions of Great Britain, the Netherlands, Denmark, Spain and Portugal. Altogether, these were the main ocean-going colonial empires of the modern epoch. However, the explanation that forests were continuously felled mainly due to national maritime expansion and the associated shipbuilding only partially accounts for the environmental scarcity. In any case, it was in these wood scarce landscapes that the energy transition took off. The Netherlands and Great Britain were the first nations to spearhead the adoption of alternatives to biomass: peat, wind power and coal.

The Netherlands enjoyed a unique geological condition owing to the closure of an area of mud flats and salt marshes from the sea's incursions that resulted in accelerated peat growth. Peat is an unconsolidated deposit of semi-carbonised plant remains that displays a persistent high water content, therefore being inferior to coal in terms of calorific power. Mostly treeless, the Dutch had first begun exploiting these energy deposits in the Middle Ages. Population growth boosted a new cycle of large-scale peat digging after 1750. Resorting to low-cost transportation costs through waterways and canals, peat fuelled the energy needs of domestic life, industry and trade, chiefly within a polygon that comprised Naarden, Utrecht, Gouda, Rotterdam, Delft, Leiden, Haarlem, Alkmaar and Amsterdam, one of the wealthiest European regions. There is some casuistic evidence that this low price peat economy precluded the adoption of coal in Dutch cities (Allen, 2009, p. 104; Ryckbosch and Saelens, 2023). Simultaneously, the need to remove water from peat bogs after their cutting and from lakes led to the development of drainage windmills, whose technology was much more efficient in harnessing wind power and converting it into mechanical force. Exhibiting a distinct octagonal smock, this mill came to be known as the Dutch mill (holloender, holländare or Holländermüh) and was furthermore adapted for grinding gain (Davids, 1998). Because of such unique conditions, the Dutch experienced a singular energy transition with fuelwood consumption replaced by peat and wind power. Suffice to say that while wind power (windmills plus sailing ships) represented only 1% or 2% of the total primary energy consumption in other European nations by 1850, wind power fulfilled 12% of Dutch primary consumption needs (Gales et al., 2007, p. 224; Teives, 2009, p. 96).

Likewise, recent research has shown that the transition towards a fossil fuel economy in England and Wales occurred not during the industrial revolution but rather from 1540 onwards. The first signs of a dynamic economy powered by coal appeared in the mining districts of the northeast coast (Northumberland and Durham) spurred by the demand for fuel from the salt and glass industries, with regionally sourced metallic ores, and by domestic consumption. The rise in alternative charcoal prices during the seventeenth century and the demand from urban growth in London developed a bustling market for coal consumption within the imperial capital. The urban domestic consumption was fed by shipments from the mining district of Newcastle transported down the coast. Meanwhile, the advance of domestic consumption was consolidated by the development of a new style of house with its central room equipped with a narrow chimney that induced a draft through the burning of coal. Even though the increase in coal consumed was the product of regional economies pivoted around mining zones with cheap energy and the more expensive cost of energy in London (transport costs raised coal prices there by eight times), fossil fuel demand already accounted for 50% of overall primary energy consumption by 1700, that is, as much as all the human and animal muscular force, firewood, wind power and water power put together. At the close of the eighteenth century, the coal share had surged to 77% in England and Wales (Warde, 2007; Allen, 2009).

Strikingly, the energy transition loomed in modern Britain amid the agrarian society solar regime rather than in an era shifting to mechanical work. Steam technology took a long time to perfect (Crafts, 2004). This well-established fact set off debate about what steered the course of change in the agrarian society. According to Robert Allen, coal was adopted because England was a high wage economy with very low energy prices near the coalfields. This peculiar wage/energy cost ratio was the historical outcome of the boom in British foreign trade. High wage economies are particularly important when, for each unit of income growth, there is more than a unit of demand for certain commodities or services (income elasticity). When this is the case, transitions are speeded up through large increases both in the consumption of energy resources and in energy embedded goods (Allen, 2009; Fouquet, 2016).

2.3 The second coal transition

Continental Europe experienced a quite different type of energy transition. In effect, two patterns of historical energy transition are herein at stake: the first, the energy resource transition driven by the substitution of fuelwood sources in England, Wales and Scotland; the second, the converters energy transition driven by the adoption of new technologies that transformed the chemical energy of coal into heat and motion, which took hold in continental Europe and emulated the second British transition to coal (Malanima, 2016). This reflects how coal consumption on the continent was the consequence of the diffusion of steam engines in coal mines, mills for puddling and rolling pig-iron, blast furnaces for iron ore smelting, railway locomotives fuelled by coke and coal briquettes, steam engines applied in conjunction to weave and new ovens for brick production. To sum up, these new energy converters brought coal into the markets.

Throughout this process, the key triggering factor was not the availability of coal in Belgium, France and Germany. As Sydney Pollard (1988, p. 121) remarks: "On the Continent, coal rarely came first, and it was the apparently favourable cost ratios of non-coal methods, such as using water-power for spinning-mills and bellows, and charcoal for metallurgy, which frequently held back some of the major continental centers". Coal converters found favourable ground to thrive in the well-developed fuelwood and water-power centres of continental Europe. The paradox of this incorporation of new technologies into the old industrial landscape is vividly illustrated by the hybridisation phenomenon of the iron industry during the transition to the fossil fuel age. Rather than fully adopting the entire range of the new converters for iron production, German and French ironmasters concentrated just on the final stages of production devoted to refining the pig-iron, that is, the transformation of the brittle and hard iron that came out of the furnaces into a malleable, wrought iron for shaping into bars and rails. The process entailed reducing the carbon content of pig-iron and carried out via using coal in the new puddling and rolling mills that increased both output and productivity. Often these refineries obtained their semi-finished pig-iron material from local charcoal furnaces, thus resulting in a hybrid technological process, partly coal-based, partly wood-based. In the short run, the new coal developments drove change in the wood fuel technologies of blast furnaces. This helps explain the survival of traditional charcoal furnaces and new spurts of investment and modernisation in old technologies (Madureira, 2012). Regarding coke fired blast furnaces, the new methods for ore smelting sprang up from a pioneering hub around Liège (Belgium) active in the 1820 and 1830s. With some time lag, these coke furnaces then arrived in the regions of the Saar, Rhineland and Westphalia in Germany, and Saône et Loire, Moselle and Champagne in central and north eastern France. Despite the lack of quantitative information available, there is evidence of further hybridisation in the ore smelting stage with the recurrent usage of mixtures of charcoal and coke in several coke blast furnaces (Schainberg, 2004; Banken, 2005). In any case, metallurgical research has proven that the coke furnace effectively represents a different type of energy converter with new equilibria between the flame temperature at the tuyeres and the solids heating up with the gas in a counter current, consequently providing a new process for reducing iron oxides (Nicolle, 2023). On the heels of metals, the dissemination of coal was further spurred by the steam engine in two sectors: the scattered mechanised textile industry with its main centres were the Belgium Borinage; northern France; the German regions of Rhine Valley, Saxony, Silesia, Bavaria; St. Galen and Zurich (Switzerland). The second and decisive sector was the railways. In truth, despite the excessive fuel requirements of early locomotives, railway consumption made only a marginal contribution to the overall demand for coal. Its effects on the energy transition were rather indirect: on the one hand, railways deepened the demand for iron; on the other hand, they provided a cheap alternative for transporting coal beyond the local markets of mining regions and paved the way for the exploration and development of coalfields, specifically the Ruhr and Upper Silesia (O'Brien, 1983; Fouquet, 2008, pp. 162–169). Overall, energy fulfilled a relevant role in an economic cycle of positive feedback: cheaper resource inputs enabled tangible goods and intangible services to be produced and delivered at ever lower cost (Ayres and Warr, 2005, p. 182).

Whilst by 1860 and 1870s, the core nations of continental Europe had accomplished the transition towards the fossil fuel age, peripheral countries such as Italy, Portugal, Spain, Greece, Sweden and Russia remained locked in the solar-agrarian regime making recourse to biomass energy. They consumed less and more expensive coal largely because they were unable to implement the backward linkages that were changing industrial production. Energy converters were adopted singly rather than in mutually reinforcing networks. Likewise, these regions were left out of the coal market price convergence that took place in Europe at the turn of the nineteenth century (Grubler, 2012; Murray and Silvestre, 2020).

2.4 Fossil fuel's cold war

As the transition to coal gathered pace, a new fuel arrived in Europe from the United States, spreading widely across both the East and the West. In fact, lamp oil obtained by distilling petroleum achieved outstanding popularity because it provided a cheaper and smell-free luminous flux. Petroleum made its inroads lighting Europe. However, it would nonetheless take a while for oil demand to start changing European societies: the transition to oil only occurred after 1950 in a trend that might best be described as the Americanisation of European energy systems. This expression conveys two dimensions: the emulation of the American life style, with greater mobility based on the high-energy consumption of individual automobile travel; on the other hand, an oil glut financed by the American Marshall Plan to fuel Europe while simultaneously "maintaining markets for U.S. oil companies" (Painter, 1984, p. 362). Additionally, the European Reconstruction Plan also sponsored a few oil refineries.

Swift, overwhelming and shattering, the oil and natural gas transition was quite distinct from the slow, regional and hybrid coal transition. Briefly, several transitions became immersed into a single Schumpeterian change. First and foremost, oil brought about a transition in energy services. Gasoline, diesel and jet-fuel, for which coal was no substitute in combustion engines, enabled individual mobility over short and long distances and new practices of work, shopping, travel, sport, leisure and holidays. Second, oil was furthermore a resource transition that could displace coal particularly in lighter industries where boiler fuels did not require great changes in production equipment. Price advantages over coal per unit of heat produced also enabled the replacement of coal in domestic heating with the adoption of automated central heating systems and in electricity generation through the usage of fuel oil and natural gas. Between 1950 and 1973 oil demand forced down coal consumption. The image of coal miners marching silently through the streets and waving black flags become the social hallmark of resource substitution. Third and finally, petroleum also represented a transition in energy converters with the revolution in petrochemicals, particularly from the 1960s onwards. Petroleum refineries, applying catalytic cracking technologies, were the bedrock of the new energy conversion technologies: thanks to cumulative scientific discoveries, chemical companies were henceforth able to produce feedstocks from natural gas or from the by-products obtained from crude oil refining, such as naphtha. This then enabled the production of a wide variety of petrochemicals products through resorting to these feedstocks, including artificial rubber, artificial fibres, plastics, celluloids and synthetic fertilisers. From this point of view, the oil age opened a revolution in material culture thereby driving enhanced levels of demand for food, commodities and equipment. The oil transition pressed mass culture forwards and underpinned habits of mass consumption. To mention just the most important: appliances, luggage and cases, industrial machinery, photographic material, magnetic tape and metallised film, pipes and fittings, consumer electronics, furniture, stationery and drafting material, clothes and garments, ropes, and packages (Caines and Shen, 1980; Melsted and Pallua, 2018; Gross, 2023).

Given the prevailing scenario of an almost simultaneous energy transition in services, resources and converters, it is little wonder that the pace of events quickened significantly. On top of that, two decades of income growth after the Second World War—the so-called European "miracle"—further eased the changeover towards petroleum. Sweden ranks at the top of nations for the swiftest and most intense transitions. Italy, Switzerland, Spain and Portugal followed suit despite being the laggard countries in the coal age. At the beginning of the twentieth century, they experienced some diversification away from coal when beginning to exploit the exceptional natural conditions of their watercourses for generating hydroelectricity. After the most productive spots for dam construction had already been brought on stream and with hydroelectricity generated no longer meeting the prolific growth in national demand, the switch towards the modern energy carrier—oil—came rapidly and intensely. To a certain extent, Sweden, Italy, Switzerland, Spain and Portugal became offspring of the Marshall Plan. The case of Switzerland deserves particular attention because the country was an energy-saving nation with one of highest levels of per capita Gross Domestic Product. This partly results from Switzerland efficiently harnessing its proficient natural resources, capable of incorporating the environmental inputs of sun, rain, rivers and geology into its productive structure. Consequently, the dependence on imported fossil fuels was largely counterbalanced by exports of goods and services that took advantage of natural energy flows. Globally, the water tower of Europe developed a low intensive energy economy based on the balanced contribution of services, light industry, agriculture and tourism. After the Second World War, oil became overwhelming because these sectorial activities jointly contributed to raising the demand for petroleum. In just two decades, oil ended up accounting for about 75% of Swiss commercial primary energy consumption. A sign of the times, the Swiss even attempted to strike oil in their own country (Pillet and Odum 1984; MBES, 1987; Walter et al., 2015).

Longer established coal strongholds, such as Britain and Germany nonetheless lagged in the transition to oil. This peculiar situation led Grubler (2012) to pinpoint a sort of "first-in last-out" feature to historical energy transitions. Pioneering advantages were turned into goldbricking disadvantages. The continuity of coal in industrial nations set higher factor cost prices for resource usages, with oil beating the costs of bituminous coal particularly in the economics of energy conversions for industrial power, domestic heating and electricity generation. In this respect, a far worse situation occurred in Eastern Europe. Basically, the oil transition seems to skip the regions of the Black Sea coast and the Balkan Mountains. Under the Soviet curtain, oil came only later, slower and weaker. Part of the explanation lies in the comparatively low number of cars per inhabitants, the obsolete road networks and rare motorways. With scarce personal vehicles, the demand for gasoline and diesel never rose

(Berendt, 2009, p. 135). Aside from this factor, the stark reality curtailing the oil transition was geopolitics. Throughout Eastern Europe, the Soviet system of central planning then under operation introduced urgency into investments in defence and heavy industry. Priority was granted to iron, steel, aluminium, coal, power stations and heavy engineering, the largest gluttons of energy. On all these fronts, the Eastern Bloc avoided dependence on Western supplies, instead advancing with national energy carriers, particularly coal mining in Poland, Czechoslovakia, Hungary and Bulgaria plus uranium from Czechoslovakia.

As it turned out, Europe experienced a *fossil fuel cold war*: the Americans fostering oil usage in the western world by means of the Marshall Plan, the Soviet Bloc stipulating the growth of coal in its satellite states. Keen to boost energy resources, the Socialist self-sufficiency policy began to tap coal pits with less calorific power and minor commercial value: lignite from the Urals and Moscow basin (USSR); lignite from the Lubin and Silesian basin (Poland); lignite from the Western region of Tatabánya (Hungary); and, most of all, brown coal from the basins of Northern Bohemia (Czechoslovakia). In this manner, a sort of energy specialisation took place with the worst coals applied for thermal electricity generation and domestic consumption while saving bituminous and sub-bituminous coal for coke production, the fuelling of iron and steel furnaces and heavy machinery production.

In the 1960s, the wheel was again turning towards oil and natural gas imports in Eastern Europe. Hungary, the most heavy-industry-concentrated Soviet satellite nation, took the lead. The transition was a centrally managed process, triggered by the decisions of the Hungarian Socialist Workers' Party in 1960 and 1961. There was the decision to moderate the development of unproductive domestic coal mining and introduce petrochemical processes into the chemical industry previously based on coal. This implied a trade-off between Hungarian coal and petroleum and natural gas imports from the Soviet Union. The conversion of the coal-based Borsod Chemical Combine (BVK–BCC) to natural gas marked a milestone in this new era (Hopkins et al., 1973; Kuskovaa et al., 2008; Germuska, 2013). Even so, on the eve of the first oil shock, coal still accounted for nearly 50% of the Hungarian primary commercial energy consumption.

Between 1969 and 1973, global oil demand skyrocketed, pushed by consumption in the United States, Japan and Europe. The result was a tight market with a lack of spare capacity. The market imbalance was kept hidden owing to the institutional system of posted prices settled between Middle East governments and oil multinationals. Then, in October 1973, the Yom Kippur war between Egypt/Syria and Israel opened Pandora's Box. The time was ripe for Arab states to take advantage of Western dependence and deploy a new weapon: oil. In just one quarter, oil prices picked up momentum with a fourfold increase. All this came about as an absolute surprise, a shock. It was, accordingly, dubbed the first oil shock with only a handful of oil analysts having foreseen the event.

Everything subsequently changed. Inasmuch as the noticed event coincided with a new business cycle characterised by double digit inflation, collapses in investment and soaring unemployment, indignation rose a notch higher in Europe. However, the fourfold increase in oil prices only explained a small proportion of the inflationary cycle. The main mechanism of propagating this crisis stemmed from the downsizing of energy-using goods, especially automobiles. Cars, travel and gasoline consumption in effect emerged as the most impacted areas. Per capita energy consumption declined in Europe. However, it also took six or seven years for this adjustment to actually take place reflecting on how people changed their habits in reaction to the oil price hikes even while tending not to do so immediately (this technically corresponds to the difference between the short-run and long-run elasticity in oil demand) (Barsky and Kilian, 2004; Salvador, 2005).

In the end, people feelings were right: something had changed forever. The era of cheap energy had come to an end.

2.5 What next?

The fossil fuel age came at a price. The combustion of coal, oil and natural gas emits carbon dioxide (CO_2) and the concentration of this and other gases in the atmosphere (principally methane—CH_4 and nitrous oxide—N_2O) causes a greenhouse effect that inhibits the exit of solar long-wave energy from earth. The result is an increase in global temperature with devastating consequences upon the environment. Global warming set in motion the urgency of a new energy transition away from fossil fuels. However, this entails a different type of transition. Unlike historical transformations, the green transition is driven by scientific knowledge, public opinion and international politics. As such, it is, to a large extent, a purposeful process made by design. Moreover, the pace of the green energy transition is measured in real time given the long-term goals for CO_2 concentration in the atmosphere: under scenarios of international cooperation, everyone knows where they stand regarding the abatement of fossil fuel emissions.

Globally, the European Union (EU) has endeavoured to be a world leader. With a groundbreaking initiative, the EU set national objectives for member states regarding the substitution of fossil fuels by renewable energy under the Renewable Energy Directive (2009/28/EC). This furthermore detailed a clear route for this transition. Later, 173 countries followed suit. Revised in 2014 and 2018, the EU directives established the target year of 2030 to fulfil three main objectives: a decrease of at least 40% in greenhouse gas emissions in comparison with 1990 levels; a 32% share of renewable energy in the gross final energy consumption (updated in 2023 to 45%); and a 32.5% improvement in energy efficiency.

The current leading countries in the adoption of renewable energy are Sweden, Denmark, Portugal, Germany and Finland. Some of the countries that apparently fared well in the historical transition to coal but worse in the transition to oil are also lagging in the transition towards renewable energy (the United Kingdom and Belgium). On a per capita basis, Sweden and Denmark lead the way in wind energy production, Germany and Netherlands in solar energy production, Luxembourg and Austria in hydroelectricity and Finland in biofuels. Aside from the European Union, it is worth mentioning the United Kingdom's progress in wind energy with enhanced results in offshore exploration and Norway´s success in the transport revolution with 82% of all vehicles registered in the electric and plug-in hybrid class of vehicles (Elliott, 2019; Muneer et al., 2022; Stec and Grzebyk, 2022).

Europe seems on track towards a decarbonised economy but the pace and direction of this transition is likely to fluctuate after 2030. Firstly, because the last few steps are always the hardest, meaning that the costs and the efficiency of solar, wind and biofuel energy decrease beyond a certain threshold of installed capacity. Secondly, because at advanced stages, supply solutions are no longer enough. Energy systems will require more capacity but, above all, more flexibility. The development of "smart grid" systems, with "demand side management", will prove crucial to shifting consumer power demand to times when supply from renewable supplies is available. This creating "smartness" accounts for the means of keeping energy costs affordable by saving on recourse to storage and long distance transmission. Lastly and finally, the historical energy transitions herein examined went along with growing demand for materials, equipment, commodities and services. The great challenge in the green transition ahead is to continue to assure reasonable supplies of health, mobility, food and comfort but with lower levels of energy and consumption (Moriarty and Honnery, 2012; Mills and Wiser, 2012; Ueckerdt et al., 2013).

In summary, the lesson from the aforementioned historical energy transitions is that they reinforced European asymmetries, since some nations changed in the medium term their resources, converters and services, while others found themselves entrenched in protracted and incomplete processes of change. It is essential to underscore that, under similar circumstances, those nations that acted as early adopters in the realm of energy transitions enjoyed a distinct comparative advantage. This advantage was derived from their ability to redirect their economies towards more cost-effective and efficient energy inputs, subsequently fostering a ripple effect of innovations across leading productive sectors. The downside is that rapid energy transitions often entailed environmental debacles.

References

Allen, Robert C. 2009. *The British Industrial Revolution in Global Perspective*. Cambridge: Cambridge University Press.

Ayres, Robert U., and Warr, Benjamin. 2005. Accounting for growth: The role of physical work. *Structural Change and Economic Dynamics* 16 (2): 181–209.

Banken, Ralf. 2005. The diffusion of coke smelting and puddling in Germany 1796–1860. In *The Industrial Revolution in Iron* edited by Chris Evans and Goran Rydén, 55–74. Aldershot: Ashgate.

Barsky, Robert B., and Kilian, Lutz. 2004. Oil and the macroeconomy since the 1970s. *The Journal of Economic Perspectives* 18 (4): 115–134.
Berendt, Ivan T. 2009. *From the Soviet Bloc to the European Union: The Economic and Social Transformation of Central and Eastern Europe since 1973*. Cambridge: Cambridge University Press.
Caines, L. L. and Shen, S. Y. 1980. *Energy and Materials Flows in the Production of Olefins and Their Derivatives*, S. Y. Springfield VA: Argonne National Laboratory.
Crafts, Nicholas. 2004. Steam as a general purpose technology: A growth accounting perspective. *Economic Journal*, 114: 338–351.
Davids, Karel. 1998. Successful and failed transitions. A comparison of innovations in windmill-technology in Britain and the Netherlands in the early modern period. *History and Technology* 14 (3): 225–247.
Davidson, Caroline. 1983 *A Woman's Work Is Never Done. A History of Housework in the British Isles 1650–1950*. London: Chatto & Windus, 2nd edition.
Elliott, David. 2019. *Renewable Energy in the UK. Past, Present and Future*. London: Palgrave Macmillan.
Endres, Max. 1922. *Handbuch der Forstpolitik mit besonderer Berücksichtigung der Gesetzgebung und Statistik*. Berlin: Verlag von Julius Springer.
Fouquet, Roger. 2008. *Heat, Power and Light: Revolutions in Energy Services*. Cheltenham, UK: Edward Elgar Publications.
Fouquet, Roger. 2016. Historical energy transitions: Speed, prices and system transformation. *Energy Research & Social Science* 22: 7–12.
Fries, Clas. 1996. *Human Transformation of the Swedish Boreal Forest*. International Institute for Applied Systems Analysis. Working paper 96–86 (1996-July), https://pure.iiasa.ac.at/id/eprint/4941/1/WP-96-086.pdf (accessed July 20, 2023).
Gales, Ben, Kander, Astrid, Malanima, Paolo and Rubio, Mar. 2007. North versus South: Energy transition and energy intensity in Europe over 200 years. *European Review of Economic History* 11: 219–253.
Germuska, Pál. 2013. Socialist Miracle? Hungarian industrial development policy and economic growth, 1950–1975. *Journal of European Economic History* 42 (1): 87–136.
Gross, Stephen G. 2023. The Politics of Creative Destruction: West German Hard Coal and the Postwar Oil Transition. In *New Energies. A History of Energy Transitions in Europe and North America* edited by Stephen G. Gross and Andrew Needham, 48–61. Pittsburgh: University of Pittsburgh Press.
Grubler, Arnulf. 2012. Energy transitions research: Insights and cautionary tales. *Energy Policy* 50: 8–16.
Haberl, Helmut, Fischer-Kowalski, Marina, Krausmann, Fridolin and Winiwarter, Verena. 2016. *Social Ecology. Society-Nature Relations across Time and Space*. Basel: Springer.
Hopkins, George, Korens, Nick, Schmidt, Richard and Trexel, Carl, 1973. *Analysis of Energy Resources and Programs of the Soviet Union and Eastern Europe*. Stanford: Stanford Institute Menlo Park.
Kander, Astrid, Malanima, Paolo and Warde, Paul. 2013. *Power to the People. Energy in Europe over the Last Five Centuries*. Princeton: Princeton University Press
Kasper, Wolfang, and Streit, Manfred. 1998. *Institutional Economics. Public Order and Public Policy*. Cheltenham: Edward Elgar.
Kjaergaard, Thorkild. 1994. *The Danish Revolution,1500–1800. An Eco-Historical Interpretation*. Cambridge: Cambridge University Press.
Kuskovaa, Petra, Gingrichb, Simone and Krausmann Fridolin. 2008. Long term changes in social metabolism and land use in Czechoslovakia, 1830–2000: An energy transition under changing political regimes. *Ecological Economics* 68 (1–2): 394–407.
Livi-Bacci, Massimo, 1990. *Population and Nutrition. An Essay on European Demographic History*. Cambridge: Cambridge University Press.

Lu, Jiaq and Nemet, Gregory F. 2020. Evidence map: Topics, trends, and policy in the energy transitions literature. *Environmental Research Letters* 15 123003: 1–18.

Madureira, Nuno Luis. 2012. The iron industry energy transition. *Energy Policy*, Special Issue: Past and Prospective Energy Transitions, Roger Fouquet and Peter Pearson (eds.) 50: 24–34.

Malanima, Paolo. 2016. Energy consumption in England and Italy, 1560–1913. Two pathways toward energy transition. *Economic History Review* 69 (1): 78–103.

Matteson, Kieko. 2015. *Forests in Revolutionary France. Conservation, Community, and Conflict, 1669–1848*. Cambridge: Cambridge University Press.

MBES- Mitgeit yom Bundersamt fur Energiewitschaft vom Schweiz. 1987. *Energiestatistik der Schweiz 1910–1985*. Bern and Lausanne: Schweizerischer Elektrotechnischer Verein.

McGrath, M. J., Luyssaert, S., Meyfroidt, P., Kaplan, J. O., Bürgi, M., Chen, Y., Erb, K., Gimmi, U., McInerney, D., Naudts, K., Otto, J., Pasztor, F., Ryder, J., Schelhaas, M.-J. and Valade, A., 2015. Reconstructing European forest management from 1600 to 2010. *Biogeosciences* 12: 4291–4316.

Melsted, Odinn and Pallua, Irene. 2018. The historical transition from coal to hydrocarbons: Previous explanations and the need for an integrative perspective. *Journal of History* 53 (3): 395–422.

Mills, Andrew and Wiser, Ryan. 2012 *Changes in the Economic Value of Variable Generation at High Penetration Levels: A Pilot Case Study of California*. Berkeley: Berkeley National Laboratory

Moor, Tine de. 2009. Avoiding tragedies: a Flemish common and its commoners under the pressure of social and economic change during the eighteenth century. *Economic History Review*, 62 (1): 1–22.

Moriarty, Patrick and Honnery, Damon. 2012. Preparing for a low-energy future. *Futures* 44 (10): 883–892.

Muneer, Tariq, Jadraque Gago, Eulalia, and Berrizbeitia, Saioa Etxebarria. 2022. *The Coming of Age of Solar and Wind Power*. Cham, Switzerland: Springer.

Murray, John and Silvestre, Javier. 2020. Integration in European coal markets. *Economic History Review* 73 (3): 668–702

Nicolle, Rémy. 2023. History of the iron furnace using the physical-chemical blast furnace model. *Metallurgical Research & Technology* 120 (1): 1–9.

O'Connor, Peter A. 2010. *Energy Transitions*, THE PARDEE PAPERS, 12.

O'Brien, Patrick (ed.). 1983. *Railways and the Economic Development of Western Europe, 1830–1914*. London: Macmillan.

Ortego, Javier Hernando and Madrazo García de Lomana, Gonzalo. 2017. Firewood and Charcoal Consumption in Madrid during Eighteenth Century and Its Effects on Forest Landscape. In *Environmental History in the Making. Volume I: Explaining*, edited by Estelita Vaz, Cristina Joanaz de Melo, and Lígia M. Costa Pinto, 321–340. Heilderberg: Springer.

Painter, David S. 1984. Oil and the Marshall Plan. *The Business History Review* 58 (3): 359–383.

Pillet, Gonzague and Odum, Howard T. 1984. Energy externality and the economy of Switzerland. *Swiss Journal of Economics and Statistics (SJES)* 120 (3): 409–435.

Pollard, Sydney, 1988 [1981]. *Peaceful Conquest. The Industrialization of Europe 1760–1970*. Oxford: Oxford University Press.

Ryckbosch, Wouter and Saelens, Wout. 2023. Fuelling the urban economy: A comparative study of energy in the Low Countries, 1600–1850. *The Economic History Review* 76: 221–256.

Salvador, Amos. 2005. *Energy: A Historical Perspective and 21st Century Forecast*. Tulsa: AAPG Studies in Geology.

Schainberg, Hartmut. 2004. *Die belgische Beeinflussung der Frühindustrialisierung im Aachener Raum, ca. 1820–1860.* Trier: Universität Trier. https://d-nb.info/971663068/34 (accessed 25 July 2023).
Sieferle, Rolf Peter. 2010. *The Subterranean Forest: Energy Systems and the Industrial Revolution.* Cambridge: White Horse Press.
Stec, Malgorzata, and Grzebyk, Mariola. 2022. Statistical analysis of the level of development of renewable energy sources in the countries of the European Union. *Energies* 15: 8278.
Teives, Sofia. 2009. *Energy Consumption in Portugal 1856–2006.* Naples: Consiglio Nazionale delle Ricerche.
Ueckerdt, Falko, Hirth, Lion, Luderer, Gunnar and Edenhofer, Ottmar. 2013. System LCOE: What are the costs of variable renewables? *Energy* 63: 61–75.
Walter, François, Steinauer, Jean and Planzi, Lorenzo. 2015. *Paysages sous tension. Électricité et politique en suisse occidentale.* Fribourg: Alphil.
Warde, Paul. 2006. Fear of wood shortage and the reality of the Woodland in Europe, c.1450–1850. *History Workshop Journal* 62 (1): 29–57.
Warde, Paul. 2007. *Energy Consumption in England & Wales 1560–2000.* Naples: Consiglio Nazionale delle Ricerche.

3 The emergence of a competitor

The impact of the development of electricity on the gas sector through *Le Gaz Journal* in the last third of the nineteenth century*

José Joaquín Luque García and Alberte Martínez-López

3.1 Introduction

The current controversial and uncertain process of replacing fossil fuels with renewable energies has placed the spotlight on the importance of the energy transition processes and their open and complex nature. Within this context, the study of how these transitions occurred in the past has become more relevant: the real and changing situation of the different technological alternatives in play, their strengths and weaknesses, the factors that favoured or delayed their use, the variety of market niches available, how they were perceived by those of their time (scientists, entrepreneurs, politicians, users) and so on.

The historiographical debate initially focused on the shift of traditional energies in the pre-industrial era (human, animal, hydraulic, wind, etc.) to coal within the framework of the industrial revolution. However, an increasingly prominent field of study in recent decades is concerned with the different alternatives arising during the Second Technological Revolution such as gas, electricity or oil and their respective adaptations (Madureira, 2014; Craig et al., 2018; Fernández-Paradas and Sudrià, 2018) or the analysis of the different energy transitions in the long term (Madureira, 2005). This study forms part of this line of research.

Gas began to be used to light the cities from the beginning of the nineteenth century (Falkus, 1982). The invention of the gasometer enabled the large-scale production of gas using coal. Despite its advantages, such as constant light or the ease of use, it had some drawbacks. For example, its production and transport were relatively expensive, it had problems related to safety and produced an unpleasant smell. It gradually replaced the traditional lighting systems such as oil or petroleum lamps (Peebles, 1980). In this way, gas enjoyed its golden age during the third quarter of the century (Paquier and Williot, 2005).

* This research forms part of the results of the R+D+I Research Project "Gas in Latin Europe: a comparative and global perspective (1818–1945)", PID2020-112844GB-I00, financed by the Ministry of Science and Innovation of the Government of Spain and ERDF Funds.

DOI: 10.4324/9781003428695-3

Electricity, on the other hand, had been discovered at the beginning of the nineteenth century, but, in general, it had been simply experimental, until the invention of the incandescent light bulb in 1879 by Edison and the alternating current electric motor by Tesla and Westinghouse in the 1880s.

Electricity had several advantages over gas. It was cleaner and easier to transport through electric cables and was more versatile. As electricity became more available and affordable, it began to compete with gas as a source of energy. The first applications of electricity included the lighting of streets and public buildings, but soon this extended to homes and factories.

The attitude of the gas sector towards the competition from electricity evolved over time. Initially, it sought to discredit it, using scientific publications and the press as a platform, insisting on its limitations and dangers. Simultaneously, it attempted to prohibit its introduction into urban markets, reinforcing the legal protection of its concessions. Later, and in light of the failure of the previous measures, particularly in the lighting sector, it sought to improve its efficiency (mechanisation, Auer lamp, etc.) (Matthews, 1987) and find new market niches (cooking, heating, motors, etc.) (Smil, 2010), using modern marketing and advertising methods, largely targeting female audiences, who were its main users in the domestic domain (Fernández-Paradas and Rodríguez-Martín, 2022; Fernández-Paradas et al., 2022). In this way, contradicting the "technological determinism", gas exhibited considerable resilience, as other "old" technologies had historically done, such as sail boats with the arrival of steamboats, which can be explained, at least partially, in terms of "path dependence" (Kander, Malanima and Warde, 2014; Smil, 2017).

Until the end of the nineteenth century, electrical technology was not sufficiently mature and suffered from a series of defects. The alternating/direct current dilemma was not fully resolved. Nor was the flow security. The costs were relatively high as it was obtained through burning coal. It had to be consumed locally, as the losses were very large when it was distributed across long distances (Shiman, 1993).

It was not until the full triumph of alternating current, the advent of hydroelectrical generation and of the transmission of high voltage electricity that the balance leaned clearly in its favour, definitively displacing gas lighting from the beginning of the twentieth century and, particularly, after the First World War (Rose, 1988). This transition in lighting was especially relevant as it was the energy sub-sector that was able to bring about a major reduction in real costs by a long way and in the long term (Smil, 2017).

This chapter focuses on the first phase of the competition between gas and electricity, the last third of the nineteenth century, that is, before the major electrical innovations at the beginning of the twentieth century. In a Schumpeterian sense, this period occurred between two expansive phases of the business cycle and energy innovations: 1843–1869, with the application of the steam engine to land and sea transport and 1898–1924, with the triumph of electricity in industrial motorisation and domestic uses (Smil, 2017). This study focuses on analysing the emergence and development of the electricity industry in the second half of the nineteenth century based on the articles published by the Parisian journal *Le Gaz* and how it was perceived by the gas sector.

3.2 *Le Gaz* within the context of scientific publications

Scientific and technical periodical publications undoubtedly contributed to the expansion of knowledge on the new forms of production of the industrial model. These publications began to emerge in the mid-eighteenth century, with generalist approaches and a distinct Enlightened nature (Alayo and Barca, 2021). The development of the different scientific disciplines and their practical applications in the nineteenth century demanded the creation of specialised spaces for communication and debate. This is how *Gaz Gazette* emerged, the first specific gas journal, founded in 1846, or the *Journal of Gas Lighting*, in 1848 (Williot, 2004).

These first initiatives were soon followed by similar publications in Europe and the United States. In this way, in 1852, *Le Journal de l'Éclairage au Gaz* began to be published in Paris. The following year *Gas and Water Times* appeared in London. In 1857, again in Paris, *Le Gaz* began to be published and one year later, in Germany, the *Journal für Gasbeleuchtung* was born. A final pioneer of the technical gas journals that should be mentioned is the *American Gas-Light Journal*, founded in the United States in 1859.

Due to the enormous volume of information contained in the journals, they have constituted a valuable source for the historical study of the gas industry since the mid-nineteenth century. However, the study of them as the focus of analysis is scarce and has received little attention by the historiography (Alayo and Barca, 2021). Meanwhile, the mentions of electricity in the written press have been studied by French historiography (Kant, 1986), although journals specialised in electricity have received little attention to date (Chapuis, 1983; Bouvier, 2008).

The journal *Le Gaz* began its trajectory in Paris in 1857 and was published until 1939. Its founder and alma mater, Émile Durand, had worked since his youth on the management of lighting contracts with different city councils. In 1853, he began his career in the specialised press, collaborating with the *Journal de l'Éclairage au Gaz*. Subsequently, he began to publish *Le Gaz*.[1]

The journal was born with the aspiration of defending the users from the irregularities committed by the *Compagnie Parisienne d'Éclairage et de Chauffage par le Gaz*. However, the line followed by *Le Gaz* gradually transformed, which is revealed in its subtitle which changed from "journal des consommateurs des gaz" in 1857 to "Organe spécial des intérêts de l'industrie d'éclairage et de chauffage par le gaz" in 1862. Its relevance is evident in the many references made to it in the principal periodical scientific publications of Europe and the United States. On the other hand, Émile Durand was a partner of the Society for the Development of National Industry of France and a member of honour of the *British Association of Gas Managers* and of the

Table 3.1 References to electricity in *Le Gaz*

Decade	*Total number of references*	*Issues consulted*	*Average references per issue consulted*
1850s	15	117	0,13
1860s	17	98	0,17
1870s	26	77	0,34
1880s	41	66	0,62
1890s	43	24	1,79

Source: Own elaboration.

American Gas-Light Association (British Association of Gas Managers, 1866; Fourth Annual Meeting of the American Gas-Light Association, 1876).

After the death of Émile Durand in 1886, his son Paul Durand took over the management of the journals, while Gustave Jouanne became responsible for the technical editing. They were both engineers with professional experience in the gas sector.

Since its foundation, the journal contributed to the expansion of the gas industry through the diffusion and discussion of the principal technical advances in gas. Furthermore, it carried out an intense education and dissemination work aimed principally at consumers and, subsequently, at entrepreneurs and gas factory directors. All in all, the emergence of electricity represented a new challenge for the journal. Having been born and expanding during the "belle époque" of the gas monopoly, the development of electricity would be identified from an early date as a threat to the gas interests that could not be ignored. Each advancement in electricity was addressed and often questioned by *Le Gaz*. In this way, mentions of its competitor became more frequent with the passage of time, particularly from the industrial revolution in the 1880s, as we can observe in Table 3.1.

It goes without saying that in the study of the contents of the journal, the information collected has to be critically analysed (Chapuis, 1983). Specialised journals formed scientific and pressure communities, committed to defending the interests of their sectors. Therefore, Émile Durand, Paul Durand or Gustave Jouanne, renowned gas professionals, through the platform provided by *Le Gaz*, defended their industry, indicating the deficiencies of its competitors. Furthermore, the geographical bias is noteworthy, as the French and particularly Parisian affairs have a much greater weight with respect to foreign affairs.

3.3 *Le Gaz* and electricity

3.3.1 The origins of electricity and laboratory breakthroughs

At the beginning of the nineteenth century, the first inventions related to electricity were made, with Volta's battery and Davy's arc lamp (Jamin, 1878). The limitations of these two inventions were partially remedied by the

German-born Bunsen and the Frenchman Foucault (Figuier, 1884). However, in the mid-nineteenth century, electricity had not made it out of the laboratory, suffering from deficiencies that prevented its industrial use. The batteries designed until then were insufficient for any industrial application. Their large-scale production required the transformation of mechanical energy produced by a steam engine. The first magnetoelectric machines were developed by Clarke in around 1850.

The first reference made by *Le Gaz* to electricity was on 20 February 1858. It described the electric lamp developed by the Lyon-born J. B. Pascal, which was based on the principals of the voltaic arc. However, the interest did not reside in the information about the new invention, but in the reflection made by the editor. Durand considered that the technological issues could be divided into two highly differentiated domains. On the one hand, the academic or scientific world was conducting laboratory experiments, seeking to understand the nature of the new advances that were being made. On the other hand, the industrial world, although connected with the former, only adopted those scientific breakthroughs that had a commercial application and that were potentially profitable.

Despite the embryonic phase of electricity, Émile Durand, being prudent and to some extent visionary, gathered news referring to the possible competitor. Although the day when this would become a threat was still distant, it would come and the gas industry had to be prepared to face it. In the words of this Bordeaux-born editor, "*l'indifférence tue comme la crainte*". The large investments that had been made in the gas industry with long amortisation periods could be threatened if electricity reached an industrial level of application.

3.3.2 The 1860s: The Serrin regulator, lighthouses and the beginning of the public debate

As previously mentioned, the generation of electricity with a certain level of power, without depending on batteries, had been resolved with the creation of the magnetoelectric machine. Its patent was acquired in 1853 by the company Alliance, which would be fundamental in the first practical uses of electricity outside of the laboratory (*Le Gaz* 15/03/1861; Berlioz, 1869).

However, the lamps still had a serious drawback. The carbon rods burned away when the electricity passed through them, increasing the distance between them and leading to the extinction of the arc and, therefore, the brightness. In order to overcome this situation, regulators were developed that automatically brought the rods together depending on their wear. The most perfected regulator was the one developed by Serrin, enabling the self-regulation of the distance between the rods depending on their wear, ensuring the continuity of the light and eliminating, or reducing, the risk of extinction (*Le Gaz* 10/05/1859).

Of course, electric light was far from being perfect. In addition to its high cost of production and difficult distribution there was also a constant flickering due to the combustion of impurities contained in the carbon rods.[2] This made it unsuitable for indoor environments or as a widespread alternative to gas. Despite this, the improvements that the magnetoelectric machine and Serrin regulator made enabled electricity to be applied for certain very specific uses, in which the light power provided outweighed the disadvantages.

In this way, the first use of electricity, in terms of lighting, was made in a field where gas had not eliminated the traditional systems, namely in lighthouses. In the United Kingdom, the experiments had begun in 1857 in South Foreland. However, it was in France where, from 1863, the use of electricity in lighthouses progressed with force (*Le Gaz* 31/05/1868; Fichou, 1998).

The information referring to the lighthouses in the specialised gas press did not strictly respond to the fear of a threat or possible competition as gas was not used in these places. However, the demonstration of the feasibility of voltaic arc electric lamps for these uses gave rise to the first attempts to apply it to the cities. Due to its nature, the voltaic arc could be useful for lighting large spaces such as crossroads or squares. In fact, the first urban conquests of electricity were in these places. The enthusiasm shown by supporters of the new energy source was widespread. According to them, electric lighting would eliminate the insalubrity caused by gas and its filtrations and the fire risk. It would also be more comfortable, safer and cheaper (*Le Gaz* 15/03/1861). In response to this acclamation, *Le Gaz* (31/01/1862) plainly pointed out all of its weaknesses, namely, the flickering, extinctions, the cost of installation, the production cost and its excessive and unpleasant brightness.

In any event, the debate surrounding gas and electricity was a reality in the 1860s. In the preceding years, electricity had been used in lighting large port and urban spaces and for non-permanent illumination, such as that used for festivals or construction works. It was becoming a real alternative in large spaces. On the other hand, for widespread public street lighting and domestic lighting, the triumph of electricity over gas was still chimerical. In fact, its strong power was a disadvantage in these uses. The intensity of the light emanating from a single point in all directions created large shadows. Gas, on the other hand, was easily divisible and, although the lamps had a lower intensity, they could be distributed across the space, creating pleasant and homogeneous lighting (*Le Gaz* 30/09/1864; 31/05/1868).

Once the uses of the two lighting methods had been defined, the trend of opinion divided between those who considered that electricity would quickly dethrone gas and those who assigned it a complementary value. The emergence of electricity need not be detrimental to gas. On the contrary, the appearance of the new energy source would increase the demand for lighting, in the same way as the consumption of oil for lighting increased with the emergence of gas (*Le Gaz* 31/03/1864).

Despite the optimism of the electricity supporters, the attempts to light large urban spaces had been unsuccessful. The flickering and blinding light was not received well by the population and electricity demonstrations were abandoned (*Le Gaz* 15/07/1874). Nevertheless, despite its deficiencies and limitations, electricity had become part of the public, scientific and technical debates. General journals, such as *Le Temps* or *Revue des Deux Mondes*, similarly to *Le Gaz*, reported on the progress and demonstrations (Banal et al., 1996).

3.3.3 The 1870s: The Gramme Dynamo and Yablochkov candles. The beginning of the technical competition

The 1870s began with an enormous step forward. Zenobe Gramme designed a new electric generator that was much more efficient than previous generators and enjoyed immediate commercial success (Figuier, 1884, p. 198; Tomsin, 2005).

In 1876, Paul Yablochkov invented the electric candle, which did not need a regulator as it used alternating current produced by the Gramme dynamo. Although the electric candle did not resolve the characteristic flickering of the arc, it mitigated it. The symbiosis between the Gramme dynamo and the Yablochkov candle went beyond the technical environment and was formalised with the creation between the two of the Société Générale d'Électricité, with its head office in Paris, a little before the opening of the Universal Exhibition of 1878 (*Le Gaz* 15/09/1883).

We can pinpoint this date as when the technical competition between gas and electricity began. News began to arrive from the United States about experiments conducted by Thomas Edison with electric incandescence, although they were received with a certain level of scepticism (*Le Gaz* 15/11/1878). The imminent danger, now seen as such by the gas industry, came principally from the Société Générale d'Electricité. The discourse of *Le Gaz*, which, until then had been limited to reporting the electrical advances without judging them, became harder and more thorough. The comparative analyses between the economy and use of gas and electricity multiplied as did the indication of the deficiencies of the latter.

The actions taken by the gas companies were shaken by the demonstrations of the Yablochkov candle and the public opinion was divided between those who hailed the new light and those who considered its brightness to be unpleasant (Figure 3.1).

The high power of the electric lights revealed the light insufficiency of gas lamps. The burners had undergone few modifications with respect to the gas consumed. However, the urban development promoted by Napoleon III in Paris had expanded the public spaces, meaning that this consumption was no longer efficient for lighting the large squares and boulevards. The threat from electricity pushed the research efforts in the gas sector (*Le Gaz* 15/02/1879). The immediate result was the development of intensive burners. They proved that gas could compete in terms of light power with the new electric candles (*Le Gaz* 15/05/1880).

Prior to the emergence of electricity, the city councils had ensured the economy of gas. However, when electric lighting was introduced, the demand for a greater intensity was immediate. This alerted scientists and gas companies to

AVEUGLEMENT DE LA PLACE DE L'OPÉRA.

Éclairage électrique fondé par une société d'oculistes sans ouvrage.

Figure 3.1 Une ombrelle le soir pour traverser la place de l'Opéra. In *Les folies parisiennes: quinze années comiques 1864–1879*, par Cham. Paris: Calmann-Lévy, 1883, p. 43.

reinvent themselves, revealing the advantage of a dynamic industry as opposed to one that was sleeping in its comfort zone. The result of this initial conflict was favourable to gas. The comparative experiments of Paris showed that electricity could not compete in terms of price (*La lumière électrique*, 15/04/1879). Furthermore, the principal advantage of electricity, that is, its light intensity, was counteracted with the development of the intensive burners. Of course, the lighting of indoor spaces continued to be the untouchable domain of gas. With respect to the economic results, these were even more significant for the old source of energy (*Le Gaz* 15/09/1883).

3.3.4 The 1880s: The International Exhibition of Electricity of Paris and the incandescent lamp

The liberal, entrepreneurial and technological context in which electricity emerged was much more mature and advanced than that in which gas was born at the end of the eighteenth century. The construction of the scientific and technical community of electricity took place much before the consolidation of the sector, unlike the gas industry. In this respect, the first journal specialised in electricity was created in 1876, with the launch of *L'Électricité*, which was followed by *La Lumière Électrique* two years later (Bouvier, 2008, pp. 73-74).

Meanwhile, in the United States, in 1878, Edison was making significant progress with incandescent electricity (Figuier, 1884). He frequently used the press, through advertising, interviews and direct communication with the journalists of all types of publications (Bouvier, 2008). Edison referred to the beginning of electricity as a network system, like gas, which rang alarm bells in the gas press (*Le Gaz* 15/11/1878). Durand counter attacked, underlying the abandonment of investors and the lack of confidence in Edison's company in the United States (*Le Gaz* 15/02/1879). He also included articles from other gas journals that opposed Edison, such as *Gas and Water Engineering*.

The International Exhibition of Electricity in Paris in 1881 marked a tipping point and one of acceleration in the development of electricity, due to the media repercussions that it had and its investment attraction capacity (Carré et al., 1983). The specialised and general press reported on it with opposing views. *Le Gaz* continued with its sceptical discourse along with disqualifying elements (*Le Gaz* 15/10/1881).

The opening of the Exhibition was the ideal occasion for Edison to demonstrate the value of his invention. Electricity challenged gas in a place where its jurisdiction had been untouchable until then, that is, indoor spaces. After the event, Edison took advantage of the situation to create an incandescent lamp factory in Paris (Figuier, 1884).

Despite the turbulence caused by the inventor, electricity prices were not competitive until several decades later (Wilson, 1993). Electricity, similar to gas in its beginnings, was a luxury. In response to the mass persuasion campaign of the gas industry with respect to the advancement of electricity, the electricity supporters implemented a fragmentary persuasion strategy targeting the wealthy sectors of society, who saw the new source of energy as a way to flaunt their standard of living and as a status symbol (Nye, 1993).[3] In this way, before its use in street lighting, electricity was gaining ground in private spaces such as cafés and hotels. The accidents also multiplied, which were skilfully magnified in the gas press (*Le Gaz* 15/03/1887).

The proliferation of serious and deadly fires in gas-lit theatres throughout the world intensified the controversy regarding the safety of the different energies. The specialised electricity press claimed that the technology of electricity was safer while in *Le Gaz*, G. Jouanne wrote an article defending this energy source. In his opinion, these types of incident were not due to the nature of gas, but to the lack of regulation and the negligence of those responsible for its installation and maintenance (*Le Gaz* 15/06/1887). His arguments did not seem to convince the Parisian authorities, as shortly afterwards, electricity was being used to light all of the theatres in the French capital. Contrary to the economy of gas, electricity was seen as the materialisation of modernity and progress. As a result, the year 1889 marked the beginning of electricity as a network system in the French capital (Beltran, 1985).

3.3.5 The 1890s: The legal battle

With the proliferation of power stations, the panorama of public and private lighting exploitation transformed. Until then, electricity was produced in the same establishments where it was installed. Therefore, the companies engaged in its promotion only targeted the consumers. However, with the development of power stations, a new competing agent emerged that had been consolidating since the 1870s: the municipalities. In fact, the need to establish a distribution network along the public thoroughfares to reach the supply points required the complicity of the town councils. In their negotiations with the cities, the gas companies had obtained the monopoly of public lighting and often also that of private lighting. Throughout the whole of France, certain local governments ignored or only partially interpreted the concession contracts in order to allow electric power lines in the public streets. Meanwhile, the gas companies regarded these actions as a violation of the agreements signed and brought their claims before the judiciary, demanding compensation from their competitors and the local governments. The technical, commercial and propaganda battles of the 1870s and 1880s were taken to the courts in the 1890s.

From the outset, *Le Gaz* exhibited a preference for the legal and contractual issues of the gas industry over the technical details. The journal gave a detailed account of the jurisprudence resulting from the many conflicts between the gas companies and municipalities and congratulated those gas companies that committed to supplying electricity themselves, avoiding any possible conflicts with emerging companies (*Le Gaz* 15/12/1891).

In general, the lawsuits that were filed were structured around the more or less strict interpretation of the terms of contracts that were signed at a time when any alternative to gas lighting was unimaginable (*Le Gaz* 15/10/1891; 15/01/1892). The 1891 sentences of the French Council of State, favourable for the gas companies, marked the jurisprudence to follow in future lawsuits (*Le Gaz* 15/01/1892).

Of course, the journal celebrated this decision and reported on the immediate repercussions that it had in the cities, which had to cancel agreements with emerging electricity companies (*Le Gaz* 15/12/1891). Despite the optimism, the warning was clear. The gas companies had to use their privileged position and undertake the introduction of electricity according to their own terms. Meanwhile, the principal electricity companies, shaken by the hard decision taken by the Council of State, began to form a syndicate to protest against the decisions of the courts (*Le Gaz* 03/15/1892).

3.4 Conclusions

The scientific advances and the development in the electricity sector were closely followed from the outset by specialised gas publications, such as by *Le Gaz*. Initially, the new technology was merely a series of laboratory tests and the perspective of the journal was simply one of curiosity, informing its readers of the technological novelties within a sociocultural context of enthusiasm for science and progress. However, the insight and future vision of its creator, Émile Durand, led it to explore the potential of electricity and the threat that it could represent to gas when it matured.

During the 1860s and 1870s, scientific advances were made in electricity that enabled the elimination or, at least the reduction, of the previous drawbacks and limitations. This enabled it to start becoming a serious competitor to gas, at least in certain specific uses, for example in lighting large spaces such as squares or wide avenues. This new position of electricity generated greater interest in *Le Gaz*, which adopted a more critical stance, seeking to scientifically discredit the new competitor, highlighting its technical limitations and safety problems.

Electricity technologically matured during the last two decades of the century, and it openly competed for spaces that were formerly reserved for gas, such as public and domestic lighting. Within this new context, the battlefield shifted first to costs and then to the courts. The gas press emphasised the fact that the use of gas was more economical. On the other hand, it insisted on the need for the gas industry to improve its efficiency, particularly in terms of the brightness of the light. Finally, it turned to the use of the courts to defend its energy monopoly, and, in parallel, it took the initiative in the new electricity industry to prevent the entrance of competitors.

Notes

1 As well as being the author of an extensive bibliography, Émile Durand was the promoter of *Le Constructeur d'usines à Gaz* in 1863 and of *Annuaire général de l'industrie de l'éclairage et du chauffage* in 1875.

2 The search for a stable light that did not flicker in the electric arc continued throughout the century with little success. The unpleasant flickering caused by the electric arc was one of the arguments made by the gas professionals to defend the superiority of gas. The Jacquelain patent sought to resolve this problem. However, its inventor was ordered to compensate the company Alliance which had bought it, due to its inefficiency. This information provided by *Le Gaz*, formed part of the attempts of the journal to dampen the enthusiasm of possible investors in light of the theoretical advances made, as, according to the journal, scientific success was not a guarantee of commercial and industrial success (*Le Gaz* 20/05/1859; 15/03/1861).

3 From this date, the gas companies reinforced the market penetration campaigns, facilitating access to the supply of gas to poorer families with prepaid meters or developing new uses of gas, particularly in heating, cooking and driving force. These campaigns, together with the development of more efficient burners, such as the Auer burners, laid the foundations for continuity and expansion of the industry in the twentieth century.

References

Alayo, Joan C. and Barca, Francesc X. 2021. Gas y electricidad. La evolución de su tecnología a partir de los artículos y noticias aparecidas en publicaciones periódicas de carácter técnico en España y Francia entre 1855 y 1910. *Asclepio 73*(2): 565.

Banal, Michel, et al. 1996. *Histoire Générale de l'électricité en France*. Association pour l'histoire de l'électricité en France.

Beltran, Alain. 1985. La difficile conquête d'une capitale: L'énergie électrique à Paris entre 1878 et 1907. *Histoire, économie et société 4*(3): 369–395. https://doi.org/10.3406/hes.1985.1402

Berlioz, Auguste. 1869. *La Compagnie l'Alliance et la lumière électrique*. Paris: Chez Jules Bonaventure. https://gallica.bnf.fr/ark:/12148/bpt6k854590k

Bouvier, Yves. 2008. Les revues d'électricité et la construction d'une communauté internationale de pratique technologique à la fin du XIXe siècle. *Le Temps des médias 11*(2): 72–81. https://doi.org/10.3917/tdm.011.0072

British Association of Gas Managers. 1866. *Journal of Gas Lighting, Water Supply and Sanitary Improvement*.

Carré, Patrice et al. 1983. L'exposition internationale d'électricité de 1881 à travers quelques textes. *Bulletin d'histoire de l'électricité 2*(1): 63–84. https://doi.org/10.3406/helec.1983.892

Chapuis, Christine. 1983. L'électricité dans les périodiques. *Bulletin d'histoire de l'électricité 1*(1): 66–69.

Craig, Jonathan, et al. 2018. The history of the European oil and gas industry (1600s–2000s). *Geological Society, London, Special Publications 465*(1): 1–24.

Falkus, Malcolm E. 1982. The early development of the British gas industry 1790–1815. *Economic History Review XXXV* (2): 217–235.

Fernández-Paradas, Antonio R., Fernández-Paradas, Mercedes and Rodríguez-Martín, Nuria. 2022. Happiness and well-being. Economic, social and artistic analysis of the promotional strategies of gas companies in Madrid and Paris at the beginning of the 20th century. In *A thousand ways to understand happiness in the economy of the European Union's Next generation funds: A comprehensive vision under the lens of social marketing, history and happiness management*, edited by José Marchena Domínguez et al., 83–96. Granada: Comares.

Fernández-Paradas, Mercedes and Rodríguez-Martín, Nuria. 2022. Abrazar la felicidad a través del confort. Un estudio socioeconómico y comparado de la promoción del uso del gas en la cocina en España, Francia y Portugal hasta los años 1930. In *El Happiness Management. Un cisne amarillo que vuela hacia el marketing social, la felicidad y el bienestar*, edited by Rafael Ravina Ripoll et al., 281–302. Valencia: Tirant Lo Blanch.

Fernández-Paradas, Mercedes, and Sudrià, Carles. 2018. La transición de la industria del gas de carbón al gas natural: dos modelos, España y Cataluña. *Revista de Historia Industrial 27*(71): 121–149.

Fichou, Jean-Christophe. 1998. La lumière électrique sur les côtes de France. *Bulletin d'histoire de l'électricité 32*(1): 23–42. https://doi.org/10.3406/helec.1998.1406

Figuier, Louis. 1884. *Les nouvelles conquêtes de la science. L'électricité*. Librairie Illustrée. https://gallica.bnf.fr/ark:/12148/bpt6k105447t

Fourth Annual Meeting of the American Gas-Light Association. 1876. *American Gas-Light Journal and Chemical Repertory*.

Jamin, Jules. 1878. L'éclairage électrique. *Revue Des Deux Mondes 26*(2): 281–303.

Kander, Astrid, Malanima, Paolo and Warde, Paul. 2014. *Power to the People. Energy in Europe over the Last Five Centuries*. Princeton: Princeton University Press.

Kant, Simone. 1986. La presse et l'électricité dans les dernières années du XIXe siècle. In *La France des électriciens, 1880–1980*, edited by Fabienne Cardot, 389–398. PUF.

Madureira, Nuno. 2005. *A historia da energia: Portugal 1890–1980*. Lisboa: Livros Horizonte.
Madureira, Nuno. 2014. *Key concepts in energy*. Cham: Springer.
Matthews, Derek. 1987. The technical transformation of the late nineteenth-century gas industry. *Journal of Economic History* XLVII(4): 967–980.
Nye, David E. 1993. La commercialisation de l'énergie électrique aux Etats-Unis, 1880-1930. *Bulletin d'histoire de l'électricité 22*(1): 131–142. https://doi.org/10.3406/helec.1993.1224
Paquier, Serge, and Williot, Jean-Pierre. 2005. *L'industrie du gaz en Europe aux XIXe et XXe siècles*. Bruxelles: Peter Lang.
Peebles, Malcolm WH. 1980. *Evolution of the Gas Industry*. Macmillan.
Rose, Mark H. 1988. Urban gas and electric systems and social change, 1900–1940. In *Technology and the Rise of the Networked City in Europe and America*, edited by Joel Tarr, and Gabriel Dupuy, 229–245. Temple University Press.
Shiman, Daniel R. 1993. Explaining the collapse of the British electrical supply industry in the 1880s: Gas versus electric lighting prices. *Business and Economic History* 1(22): 318–327.
Smil, Vaclav. 2010. *Two prime movers of globalization: The history and impact of diesel engines and gas turbine*. MIT Press.
Smil, Vaclav. 2017. *Energy and civilization: A history*. MIT Press.
Tomsin, Philippe. 2005. Zénobe Gramme et l'éclairage électrique. *Annales historiques de l'électricité 3*(1): 97–112. https://doi.org/10.3917/ahe.003.0097
Williot, Jean-Pierre. 2004. Sprit associatif, vulgarisation scientifique et diffusion technologique: La Société technique du gaz de 1874–1937. In *Artisans, industrie: Nouvelles révolutions du Moyen âge à nos jours*, edited by Natacha Coquery et al., 433–440. Lyon: ENS – Editions Société française d'histoire des sciences et techniques.
Wilson, John F. 1993. La concurrence entre l'énergie électricité et le gaz en Grande-Bretagne (1880–1980): Cycles et tendances. *Bulletin d'histoire de l'électricité 22*(1): 55–66. https://doi.org/10.3406/helec.1993.1219

4 Electricity and gas in Spain, between competition and complementarity*

Joan Carles Alayo-Manubens and Francesc Xavier Barca-Salom

4.1 Electricity and gas in Spain at the end of the nineteenth century: An overall view

Almost 150 years ago, in Spain, the *Sociedad Española de Electricidad* began producing and selling electricity in the city of Barcelona and paved the way for electrification.

Before 1881, all Spanish cities were lit by coal gas, petroleum or with oil lamps. Years before, lighting experiments had sporadically been made with electricity. They were almost all ephemeral, but a more permanent electricity venture began in 1875 with the installation in Barcelona of the first electrical machines imported by the company Francisco Dalmau e hijo, which was based in this city.

The project of Dalmau began with private electrical installations in many Spanish towns. It even installed facilities in the island of Cuba, which was a Spanish colony at the time. On 30 April 1881 it became the Sociedad Española de Electricidad, engaged in the development and promotion of the application of electric light (Almanaque del Diario de Barcelona para 1882, 1881, p. 58).

With this creation, the Dalmau project extended its scope, hence its name "española" and its area of activity immediately expanded to the cities of Madrid and Valencia. La Sociedad Matritense de Electricidad was established on 4 December 1882 and the Sociedad Valenciana de Electricidad on 26 January 1883. The interest in supplying electric lighting was the principal reason for creating these companies so as to place the materials that they manufactured in Barcelona and imported from France (the Gramme machines) and England (the Swan lamps).

Science and technology had advanced significantly in Spain during the nineteenth century. With the new liberal regime, a change took place in Spain, beginning in 1851 in industrial teaching and, as a result, the industrial schools

* This research forms part of the results of the R+D+I Research Project "Gas in Latin Europe: A comparative and global perspective (1818-1945)", PID2020-112844GB-I00, financed by the Ministry of Science and Innovation of the Government of Spain and ERDF Funds.

DOI: 10.4324/9781003428695-4

of Madrid, Barcelona, Seville and Vergara were created. Industrial studies had been offered in Barcelona since 1769 by the city's Board of Trade and had helped the industrialisation of the country (Barca et al., 2009).

On the other hand, the enormous task undertaken by Ildefonso Cerdá from the year 1859 had a significant impact on the urban planning of Barcelona, which, together with the transformation of the industrial space, gradually became an economic hub, contributing to the growth of the city. Therefore, it is not surprising that the electricity revolution took place in Barcelona, where many years before there had also been a gas revolution. These two industries were sometimes complementary and other times competed with each other.

In this city, the scientists eagerly continued the electricity experiments developed in other countries, such as the comparative test between electric lighting through the Yablochkov ignition and arc system and that obtained with gas, which took place in Paris in 1879. Francisco de Paula Rojas, a professor at the Industrial Engineering School of Barcelona found two problems with it: the lack of safety in the continuity of the lighting and the divisibility of the electric lighting. Partially prophetic, he indicated that:

> After resolving the first drawback [...], electricity will fight against gas in the field of public street lighting and will then gain an advantage; with time, it will almost surely be the winner, limiting gas to homes, shops and modest establishments. After resolving the second drawback, this will be the last bastion for gas, which will not be able to retreat to the rural areas due to the obstacles involved in its transportation and because its father, coal, will not want to accompany it.
>
> (Rojas, 1879, p. 27)

When electric lighting was introduced in Spain between 1880 and 1889, the materials and equipment were initially imported. However, as the needs of the new equipment required for the incipient electrification became evident, they began to be manufactured in Spain, which was also an advantage for the development of electrification. The first companies engaged in the manufacture of electrical material to emerge were: Sociedad Española de Electricidad (Barcelona), which, with Gramme's patent from Paris, manufactured the electrical material used in the installations; Planas, Flaquer y Compañía (Girona), which adopted the technology of Ganz et Cie, of Budapest; La Electricidad (Sabadell), which, in 1896, manufactured and marketed electrical material with foreign patents.

However, the Spanish electricity market also attracted other European companies. such as: Anglo-Española de Electricidad (Barcelona); Julius G. Neville & Co. (Barcelona); Ahlemeyer Compañía Anónima de Construcciones e Instalaciones Electromecánicas (Bilbao); Siemens & Halske A.G (Madrid); Allgemeine Elektrizitäts Gesselschaft (Madrid).

All of these companies attempted to gain a share of the emerging electricity market, which they promoted themselves, in order to place their products and manufactured equipment and to develop the distribution networks.

Thus, after Barcelona, Madrid or Valencia, other initiatives emerged. One such initiative was in Irún, where electric lighting was installed in 1882 in some streets using the Brush system, created by Hammond Electrical Engineering. This was the fourth Spanish town to have electricity, but it was eventually eliminated in September 1883 due to its poor functioning.

At the end of 1890, Spain had 35 towns with electricity, of which 12 had a gas factory distributing to private customers and for public lighting. All of these were provincial capitals. The remaining 23 were towns without a gas factory, of which 10 were provincial capitals and they had no obstacles for introducing electricity (Table 4.1).

The gas companies of the above-mentioned towns acted in different ways, as shown in Table 4.2.

Table 4.1 Towns with electricity at the end of 1890

Town	*Electricity company*	*Start year*	*Gas company*	*Start year*
Barcelona	Sociedad Española de Electricidad	1881	Sociedad Catalana para el Alumbrado por gas	1842
Madrid	Sociedad Matritense de Electricidad	1882	Sociedad Madrileña para el Alumbrado por gas	1847
Valencia	Sociedad Valenciana de Electricidad	1882	Jules Pierre Lecocq y Charles Louis André Lebon	1844
Irún	Hammond Electrical Engineering	1882	-	
Bilbao	Ayuntamiento de Bilbao	1883	Société pour l'éclairage de la ville de Bilbao	1849
Portugalete	Alumbrado público del puerto de Abra y la Ría	1883	-	
Girona	Ayuntamiento - Planas, Flaquer y Cía.	1886	Barrau y Cia	1861
Andújar	José Fontagut y Aguilero	1886	-	
Malaga	Compañía Andaluza de Alumbrado Eléctrico	1886	Louis Gosse	1853
Burgos	Juan Gómez Medina	1887	Compañía General de Crédito en España	1863

(Continued)

Table 4.1 (Continued)

Town	*Electricity company*	*Start year*	*Gas company*	*Start year*
Écija	Custodio Díaz	1887	-	
Valencia	Fábrica de gas del Marqués de Campo	1887	Fábrica de gas del Marqués de Campo	1844
Albacete	Sociedad Albacetense de Electricidad	1888	-	
Calatayud	Sociedad de alumbrado Alonso y Compañía	1888	-	
Cazalla	Vela y Durán	1888	-	
Pamplona	Electra Municipal de Pamplona	1888	Compañía General de Crédito en España	1861
Pamplona	Ortigosa, Andreu, Carballo y Cía	1888	-	
Pontevedra	Sociedad de Alumbrado Eléctrico de Pontevedra	1888	-	
Talavera de la Reina	Sociedad Española de Electricidad	1888-89	-	
León	Sociedad Electricista de León	1889	-	
Salamanca	La Electricista Salmantina	1889	-	
San Sebastián	Empresa del alumbrado por gas	1889	Empresa de Alumbrado por gas	1869
Teruel	Fernández y Eced - Eléctrica Turolense	1889	-	
Cadiz	Francisco de la Viesca y de la Sierra	1889	Charles L.A. Lebon, and the British Grafton and Goldsmith	1846
Seville	Ramón Piñal, Empresa Sevillana de Alumbrado Eléctrico	1889	Juan Pedro Lacave (in the name of York & Co. - London)	1850
Algeciras	S.A. de Alumbrado Eléctrico	1890	-	
Azpeitia	Anastasio Beloqui	1890	-	
Benavides de Órbigo	Ángel García	1890	-	
Cuenca	Vicente Mogorrón	1890	-	
Elizondo	Francisco Corbea	1890	-	
Huesca	Francisco Casaús y Leopoldo Navarro	1890	-	
Jerez	Sociedad Jerezana de electricidad	1890	-	

(Continued)

Table 4.1 (Continued)

Town	*Electricity company*	*Start year*	*Gas company*	*Start year*
A Coruña	S.A. de Alumbrado, Calefacción y Fuerza Motriz	1890	Sociedad civil particular del alumbrado por gas de la Coruña	1855
Palencia	Sociedad Eléctrica Palentina	1890	-	
Segovia	La Eléctrica Segoviana	1890	-	
Toledo	La Electricista Toledana	1890	-	
Villafranca del Bierzo	Sociedad Electricista	1890	-	

Source: Own elaboration.

Table 4.2 Actions of the gas companies in response to the introduction of electricity

Town	*Electricity*	*Action of the gas company*
Barcelona	1881	The two competing gas companies joined together to create a new electricity plant in 1894
Madrid	1882	It became the shareholder of the principal electricity company of Madrid in 1889–1890
Valencia	1882	The gas factory also became an electricity factory from 1886
Bilbao	1883	The gas company was municipalised in 1886 and also introduced the distribution of electricity
Girona	1886	When public street-lighting became powered by electricity in 1886, it occasionally distributed gas for public lighting until 1891, but continued with private lighting and thermal uses
Malaga	1886	No action. It continued to supply gas-powered public street lighting according to its contract until 1940
Burgos	1887	With no concern about the advance of electricity, gas continued to light the city until 1925
Pamplona	1888	At this time it had no gas factory
San Sebastián	1889	The gas factory also supplied electricity
Cadiz	1889	Two gas companies in competition with each other: In 1896, one acquired the electricity plant which was supplying part of the public street-lighting with electricity. The other installed an electricity station in its gas factory in 1898
Seville	1889	In 1912, the gas company constructed a new gas and electricity factory in order to compete with the electricity company which had taken over the supply of public street lighting from gas in 1905
A Coruña	1890	The gas factory also supplied electricity

Source: Own elaboration.

4.2 Case studies

4.2.1 Barcelona

The emergence of electricity in Barcelona in 1881 did not pose a problem for the gas company. The gas network was well consolidated compared to the precarious situation with which the electricity sector began, with few networks and scarce consumption.

However, a few years later, the company Lebon lowered the price:

> The company Eugenio Lebon y compañía is honoured to announce to the people of Barcelona that from 1 January, the price of gas will be twenty cents of a peseta per cubic metre.
>
> (*La Vanguardia*, 29-11-1885)

> Last night the new street lighting on the Rambla del Centro and the Rambla de las Flores was lit for the first time by Schulke system gas lamps in the former and by large electric bulbs in the latter. The testing of these lights should last for six months, during which it will be determined which of the two offers more advantages both economically and in terms of better lighting.
>
> (*La Vanguardia*, 2-10-1885)

The electricity company attempted to modify the perception of the better performance of electrical lighting as opposed to gas with this test between October 1885 and March 1886, and it was determined that electrical lighting was the better of the two.

With the city council involved in the gas lighting contract, the tests were influential for the introduction of electric lighting but the preparation of the International Exhibition to be held in 1888 had an even greater influence. Therefore, Las Ramblas and other streets that connected with the Exhibition site were lit by electricity, but more electric lighting was installed by the construction companies inside the site than in the city itself. Two aspects should be taken into account: the gas company that provided public street lighting was controlled by the city council, and, therefore, it was not very interested in developing electric lighting; on the other hand, the price of gas in 1892 was 0.19 pesetas, one of the lowest in mainland Spain, and it was very difficult for electricity to compete in terms of price.

The gas industry began competing with electricity in 1883 with the Siemens intensive burners, but in 1891 it found its salvation with the gas mantle invented by Carl Auer von Welsbach, which gave rise to a new development of gas lighting. It had initially been developed in 1885, after which different variations were made, and it was patented in 1891. Auer received the gold medal for this invention in the 20th Congress of the Société Technique de l'Industrie du Gaz en France, held in Paris in 1893.

Figure 4.1 Advertisement for Auer lamp.

Source: La Vanguardia (21-11-1893).

The Sociedad Española de Electricidad (SEE) began the task of promoting the use of electricity at an economically adverse time, competing with the gas industry, which made every effort to counteract it. However, in 1896, the Compañía Barcelonesa de Electricidad (CBE) was created, promoted by Allgemeine Elektricitäts Gesellschaft (AEG), assuming the role that the SEE had undertaken. It was wound down when it had 120 subscribers. At that time, one of the two gas companies, the Sociedad Catalana para el Alumbrado por Gas had 26,000 subscribers (Alayo, 2007, p. 67).

AEG built a large steam power plant with an output of 5,000 CV and a direct current electricity distribution of 110–220 V. This change in scale alerted the two gas companies that competed with one another in public and private gas lighting. As a result, in 1897, they joined together to compete in the electricity market, creating the company Central Catalana de Electricidad (CCE), with a steam power plant of 2.800 CV, less powerful than that of CBE, but with a direct current distribution of 150-300 V in order to extend its scope of activity.

These were the two largest Spanish electricity plants during that period.

Madrid

The first electric lighting in Madrid was carried out under the initiative of the City Council for the wedding celebrations of Alfonso XII and María de las Mercedes in January 1878. Although there were only two streetlamps, Compañía Madrileña de Gas, which had complained that gas was not considered for lighting this festivity, began to contemplate electricity as a possible competitor. The two streetlamps continued to operate for another three years until they were removed as they suffered from frequent outages (*El Demócrata*, 6-4-1881).

But electricity advanced and Madrid was an interesting city in which to install electric lighting.

> The Catalan optician Mr. Dalmau has arrived in the capital with the objective of establishing electric lighting with the Gramme machine. This optician has the privilege to use this lighting system in Spain and its colonies.
>
> (*Diario de Avisos y Noticias*, 5-7-1878)

The Dalmaus' activity was reflected in the constitution of the Sociedad Matritense de Electricidad, which sought to advance the implementation of electricity, with more success than in Barcelona.

It was said that, in the case of Madrid, replacing gas lighting with electric lighting would save 200,000 pesetas (*El Correo*, 16-7-1893). Gas in Madrid costed 0.30–0.39 pesetas/m^3 for private individuals. This price favoured a greater development of electricity than in Barcelona, where gas was cheaper.

However, when electric lighting was installed in the Retiro gardens and the Prado museum, an unforeseen blackout generated disappointment in electricity and it was decided to ban electric lighting and return to gas until a commission clarified the origin of the blackout (*La Correspondencia de España*, 21-8-1883). One month later, electric lighting was restored to these places and was extended to other parts of the city.

For the Compañía Madrileña de Alumbrado y Calefacción por Gas, the situation became problematic. So much so, that in 1888, theatres were obliged to replace gas lighting with electric lighting for safety reasons due to fire risk. To do this, self-generation was necessary as there was no electricity distribution network that could meet the demand of all of the theatres. This situation gave rise to a profit for the gas company because to generate electricity gas motors were used which took up less space than the steam engine and were enough to move the small electric machines. Therefore, the gas factory increased its output for a few years until the electricity network was consolidated.

In 1889 the two electricity companies Compañía General Madrileña de Electricidad and Compañía Inglesa de Electricidad de Madrid were established in the capital. This caused the Sociedad del gas to believe that it could not compete with electricity and it opted to become the first shareholder of the Compañía General Madrileña de Electricidad, owned by the General Electric Company of Berlin. The project for the factory and the facilities was undertaken by AEG in the same way as those of the electricity plant in Berlin. Therefore, the profits from the electricity business would compensate the reduction predicted in gas consumption (García de la Infanta, 1986, p. 70).

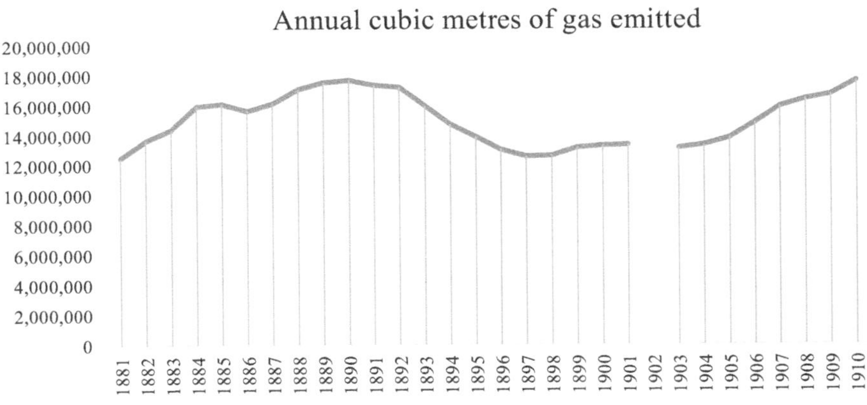

Figure 4.2 Gas output of the factory in Madrid 1881–1910.

Source: Simón Palmer (1989, p. 240).

In Figure 4.2 we can observe the influence exercised by the introduction of electricity in 1884, the increase in consumption in 1888–1891 and the reduction from 1891 due to the introduction of electricity. The gas production in 1890 was not reached again until 1910, with subscribers who used gas for cooking and heating.

4.2.2 Valencia

The creation of the Sociedad Valenciana de Electricidad (SVE) at the beginning of 1883, backed by the Sociedad Española de Electricidad, marked the start of the electrification process of the city. However, its trajectory was unsuccessful and it was eventually wound up.

José Campo, Marqués de Campo, the mayor of Valencia between 1843 and 1847, was the owner of the gas factory in Llano del Remedio, which had been constructed by Jules Pierre Lecocq and Charles Louis André Lebon in 1844. Despite the poor experience of SVE, the gas factory began producing electrical energy with a project of sixteen 75 CV steam generators connected with direct current dynamos to distribute a voltage of 150 V. Without abandoning gas, it began to produce electricity on 8 September 1886 with a facility with only four dynamos constructed by Planas, Flaquer y Cía.

Although it was awarded the contract to continue providing gas lighting, it also offered to provide electric street lighting, although this venture was never undertaken (Lastres, 1898, p. 7).

In fact, the competition was greater between the gas factories that coexisted in the city of Valencia than between gas and electricity, because after the creation of Compañía Central de Alumbrado y Calefacción por Gas - E. Lebon y Cia, in 1868, a new factory was constructed in Villanueva del Grao. However, it

Compañía Central de Alumbrado y Calefacción por Gas
Eugenio Lebon y C.ª—Valencia

Serie D — Núm. 8029

Recibimos de D. Maurice Luise la cantidad de seis ptas. 30 cénts. por el gas consumido en su domicilio P. Mirasol núm. 5 piso todo durante el presente mes.

593 m/c Indica en 31 de Mayo de 1905
581 » Indicaba en 30 de Abril de 1905
12 m/c á 0' 25.. . . | 3 |

Alquiler del contador..	3	
Id. de Mecheros Auer núm. ____, .		
Suma. . . .	6	
Imp.os gubernativos 10 °/o (ley 28 Junio 98).		30
Total Pesetas. . . .	6	30

Valencia 31 de Mayo de 1905
P. P. Eugenio Lebon y C.ª

Imp. Vda. de E. Pascual.

Figure 4.3 Invoice of the E. Lebon factory (1905).
Source: authors.

could not pipe or distribute gas in the city until October 1889, due to the pacts that the City Council had with José Campo (García de la Fuente, 1984, p. 100).

The gas factory of Eugéne Lebon y Cia installed its electricity plant in 1891 to distribute electricity in competition with gas.

The public street lighting of Valencia was powered with gas from 1844 until 1908, the year when the recently established Hidroeléctrica Española supplied hydraulic electricity through the distributing company Electra Valenciana by way of a contract with the City Council at very competitive prices with respect to those charged by the two gas lighting companies.

4.2.3 Bilbao

The streets of the city were lit with electricity with 10 arc lamps and 50 incandescent lamps.

> Electricity production is conducted by three Gramme dynamo-electric machines, moved by a locomobile which currently delivers 16 horsepower. Two of the dynamos feed each of the five arcs with 120 intense burners. The other feeds the incandescent lamps, whose bulbs each have a light intensity of 14 bulbs.
>
> (*La Electricidad*, 1883, p. 141, and *El Correo*, 3-5-1883)

However, in the city of Bilbao, on 15 October 1883, together with the works for the new port executed by the engineer Evaristo de Churruca y Brunet to facilitate sailing, the quays on the estuary were lit with electricity between

Portugalete and Sestao, a space of 6 kilometres, with 33 Brush arc lamps located on both sides of the estuary (*Revista de Obras Públicas*, 1885, p. 177).

> But between 1882 and 1885 the city council had installed in San Agustín, close to the site where the new Municipality was being built, a wooden building with an electricity plant, which lit several arc lamps in the Arenal district and a few in the Puente, Plaza Nueva and Plaza Vieja. Cinturería Street was lit with incandescent lamps.
>
> (De Orueta, 1929, p. 87)

Following the installation of this facility, which was damaged by a fire on 18 February 1890, electric public street lighting was introduced.

Bilbao had a gas factory before 1850, established by the Société pour l'éclairage de la ville de Bilbao, which provided public and private lighting. In 1865, it was acquired by the city council which undertook the task of producing gas for public and private lighting from 1886. It was the first municipal factory in Spain because, although a second gas factory called Gas Municipal operated in Barcelona from 1865, it was a private initiative although its management was controlled by the city council.

From 1890, the town council used the gas and electricity networks to light the city and private uses were supplied only by the gas network. After 1890, the thermal plant Electra-Compañía General de Electricidad also provided electricity to private individuals.

The creation, in 1901, of the company Hidroeléctrica Ibérica (HI) to develop hydroelectrical projects represented a significant change in Bilbao's society not only due to its strong emergence but also because in a few years a cluster of companies formed related to HI. This culminated in 1908 with the creation of the Unión Eléctrica Vizcaína, through the merger of the five companies in Bilbao including the Electra-Compañía General de Electricidad, which distributed the hydroelectrical energy produced by HI.

From then on, the days for the provision of public street lighting with gas were numbered.

4.2.4 Girona

This city had public and private gas lighting from 1861. The contract was to end after 25 years and included a clause whereby at the end of the contract all of the installations of the company would become property of the municipality. The factory was located outside of the walls in the neighbourhood of Mercadal where the city's industry was concentrated.

Due to the non-payment of the gas consumed in public lighting, the company began to suffer from liquidity problems. This situation prevailed for the whole of the period of the contract which expired in 1886. This translated into a reduction in the quality of the gas supplied and ended up facilitating the change of system.

Therefore, in 1886, the city switched to being lit by electricity, due to the poor quality of the gas lighting services which the city council had helped to worsen. Girona became one of the first cities in Europe to be completely lit with an AC mains network.

> In the dynamo room there two alternating current Zipernowsky and Deri systems. Only one is currently necessary for the public lighting demands which until now has been powered with electricity. A seven or eight horsepower Gramme dynamo is moved by the same transmission shaft. This machine has been working for almost a year to the satisfaction of the public and feeds five arcs or lamps of the same manufacturer.
>
> (*La Electricidad*, 1886, p. 177)

However, the gas factory was not municipalised and continued to distribute gas for public lighting until 1891 and also for private lighting. In 1908, it was acquired by another gas company, Alumbrado de Poblaciones, which continued the distribution.

4.2.5 Malaga

Electricity was introduced in Malaga in 1886, produced by the Compañía Andaluza de Alumbrado Eléctrico. A few years later, Fiat-Lux, emerged in the city and subsequently took over the Compañía Andaluza.

In those years, public lighting was provided by the Société pour l´Éclairage de Málaga, which had signed an exclusive contract in 1887 to provide gas lighting for 50 years at a fixed price for both public and private uses. This price had been lowered from 0.578 pesetas/m^3 to 0.375 pesetas/m^3. In 1881, public lighting represented only 17% of total lighting, although, in terms of consumption, it was four times that corresponding to private use (Fàbregas, 2003, pp. 55, 72).

This is perhaps why Malaga was a city that attracted electricity companies. In 1895, The Malaga Electricity Company Limited was established in the city, which built its coal thermal plant in Malagueta. In 1897, Siemens Elektrische Betriebe bought Fiat-Lux and built another coal thermal plant close to the River Guadalmedina and the English and German companies began to compete in providing lighting to private individuals.

At the end of the avenue we can observe the chimney of the electricity plant of The Malaga Electricity. In the foreground, one of the gas-lit lamp posts.

The introduction of electricity did not pose a great problem for the gas company, as it was guaranteed by the contract for the public service until 1929. However, part of the population stopped using it as the factory, which mainly served public lighting and retailers, did not provide gas at a sufficiently high pressure during the day. Electricity began to fill a space in the energy market that gas was not supplying suitably.

However, public lighting powered by gas was maintained beyond the 1940s (García de la Fuente, 1984, p. 116).

Figure 4.4 Fuente de las Tres Gracias (1906–1910).
Source: Colección Thomas / IEFC / Ref. ACM-3-2561

4.2.6 Burgos

Electricity was introduced in Burgos in 1892 with the facility constructed by the Compañía de Aguas de Burgos (Amigo, 2014, p. 12).

Despite the municipal interest, the gas company did not incorporate an electricity station in its factory. In 1897, electric lighting was installed in the Plaza Mayor and the Paseo del Espolón (*Diario de Burgos*, 28-7-1897), probably by the Compañía de Aguas. However, apart from this experiment, there was no further advancement in electric lighting and the gas factory continued to be the principal supplier of public lighting until 1925. This was when the company owning the factory at that time, Gas de Burgos, proposed the transfer of the factory and all of its assets to the city council, although the operation did not take place. However, an inventory was made which provides information about that time. There were 675 streetlamps and 23,400 metres of iron, asphalt and lead pipes (Archivo Municipal-Inventario del gas, 1925).

Much before, in 1905, a second electricity company had been created, El Porvenir de Burgos, with the objective of developing the use of electricity. However, it did not start operating until 1911 (Amigo, 2014, p. 12).

In this city, gas had a dominant position in public street lighting and also in the lighting of retail establishments. We do not know whether any action was taken to reduce the competition of electricity.

4.2.7 San Sebastián

In San Sebastián, in mid-1889, the gas factory installed an electricity plant, with a 65 CV Corliss steam engine connected to two 130 C Oerlikon dynamos with 200 A each (*La Electricidad*, 1889, Alumbrado eléctrico en San Sebastián, p. 186).

With this installation it began to provide electricity alongside gas and combined the supplies of each of them for public and private lighting.

4.2.8 Cadiz

When the gas factory was installed in Cadiz, it had two gasometers with 40,000 cubic feet each, and the chimney had a height of 100 feet. It was said that with its 6,500 square feet, it was the largest in the peninsula and that it could light up to 3,550 lamps (Madoz, 1846, p. 161).

In 1868, the Compagnie Centrale d'Éclairage par le Gaz, Lebon et Cie, bought the old factory and constructed a new one with a capacity to produce 12,000 m^3 per day.

The public street lighting contract expired on 4 January 1884, and, after much controversy, in November 1886, public lighting was awarded to the new company Sociedad Cooperativa Gaditana de Fabricación de Gas, created in January 1885 and which had built its gas factory in Cadiz (Fernández Paradas, 2015, pp. 104–113).

Electricity was introduced in Cadiz when the entrepreneur Francisco de la Viesca y de la Sierra proposed the installation of electric lighting in 1889. In response, the Sociedad Cooperativa Gaditana de Fabricación de Gas also came to an agreement for the installation of an electricity plant.

De la Viesca began operating his factory in May 1889 and started to distribute electricity in the city. The auction, at a price of 0.05 pesetas per hour and 16 bulb lamp, which should have been held on 25 November 1889, only had one bidder, as the Sociedad Cooperativa was slower and its electricity factory could not begin operating until 1898. Public lighting was provided by gas, supplied by Lebon et Cie and by electricity, supplied by La Viesca, until 1896 when the gas factory of Lebon et Cie bought the electricity facilities of Francisco de la Viesca.

In 1903, the average daily production of gas by Lebon et Cie was 6,189 m^3 and that of the Sociedad Cooperativa was 6,778 m^3 (Estadística del impuesto sobre el consumo de la luz de gas, electricidad y carburo de calcio-año de 1903, 1905, pp. 38–39), and the two competed against each other until 1918, when the gas factories had to stop production due to a shortage of coal. That of Sociedad Cooperativa did not open again, while that of Lebon et Cie resumed production in 1921.

4.2.9 Seville

Electricity was introduced in Seville in 1889 through the use of a locomobile to move electric machines. Two years later the facility was completed with fixed steam engines. However, it closed in March 1892 by municipal order (Madrid, 2007, p. 219).

Another initiative emerging in 1890 was that of Enrique Bonnet, who built a thermal plant in the city, which began operating in 1892 distributing electricity for private lighting (Madrid, 2007, p. 228).

Gas public lighting was provided by the company Catalana de Gas, which had a contract signed in 1883 for a term of 30 years.

In 1894, the Compañía Sevillana de Electricidad (CSE) was established, which, together with Allgemeine Elektricitäts Gessellschaft, constructed a 600 CV, direct current steam thermal plant. In 1902, it bought the Bonnet network with its 450 subscribers and 97 businesses (Bernal et al., 1994, p. 166).

> The first streets to have electric lighting, supplied by "Sevillana" with the fierce opposition of the company Catalana de Gas, will have this new light in the year 1905.
>
> (Madrid, 2007, p. 234)

The provision of public street lighting with electricity was one of the objectives of CSE, which it fulfilled in 1905, bypassing the contract of Catalana de Gas (González, 1981, p. 134).

This situation led Catalana de Gas to install a new gas and electricity factory in the city in 1912 with a 1.100 CV thermal station, which began competing with CSE with its own direct current electricity network (*Boletín Oficial de la Provincia de Sevilla*, 13-1-1912).

Sociedad Catalana para el alumbrado por Gas

Sección del Servicio Técnico Administración de Sevilla Calle San Roque núm. 13

En evitación de erróneas noticias que circulan por esta población, ponemos en conocimiento de nuestros abonados y del público en general, lo siguiente:

PRECIO COMPARATIVO DEL ALUMBRADO POR GAS Y POR ELECTRICIDAD EN SEVILLA

ELECTRICIDAD

10 BUJÍAS con las nuevas lámparas de incandescencia á filamento metálico consumen 15 watios ó sea 1,5 watios por bujia y hora. Siendo el precio del hectowatio ptas, 0,10, ó sea una peseta el kilowatio, el costo de las 10 bujias en una hora es $\frac{15 \times 0,10}{1.000}$ 0'015 Ptas.

GAS

Con los nuevos mecheros intensivos por incandescencia, las 10 bujías se obtienen con 10 litros de gas, ó sea: un mechero de 100 bujías, 100 litros por hora.

Siendo el precio del gas ptas. 0.25 el metro cúbico, el costo de las 10 bujias en una hora es $\frac{025 \times 10}{1.000}$ 0'0025 Ptas.

Figure 4.5 Propaganda on the price of gas and electricity.

Source: González (1981, p. 140).

4.2.10 A Coruña

The company that supplied gas to A Coruña, which also produced and distributed gas in Vigo, obtained a license in 1888 to distribute electricity to private individuals. Composed of a steam thermal station, this facility was located in the gas factory and began to distribute electricity in 1890 (Martínez López et al., 2009, p. 186).

The competition from electricity began in the year 1900 when two more companies appeared—Electra Industrial Coruñesa (1901) and the Cooperativa Eléctrica Coruñesa (1902) —which promoted electrification more intensely. The electricity was produced by thermal stations.

The concession for public street lighting that the gas company had held since 1880 expired in 1910, and by then a part of the lighting was provided with electricity. The new contract for the service, which was not signed until 1913 due to administrative reasons, was awarded to Cooperativa Eléctrica Coruñesa. Gas was no longer dominant in public street lighting (Martínez López, 2017, p. 6).

In 1918, when the company Fábricas Coruñesas de Gas y Electricidad was established, with facilities in Coruña and Vigo, it continued to distribute gas and electricity in the city in competition with the other two companies.

4.3 Conclusions

All of the gas factories in Spain that began operating throughout the nineteenth century and even in the twentieth century were constructed with the technology necessary to provide a gas with a good light power. However, the economic or technical circumstances meant that sometimes a lower-quality coal had to be used or even other fuels that could be gasified, giving rise to a gas with a lower lighting and heating power. This situation did not favour the development of the use of gas.

With the emergence of electricity in its first stages, until 1890, the gas companies were able to remain sufficiently competitive as electricity has still not been sufficiently technically developed and the majority of the electricity produced was thermal, using coal, in the same way as the gas factories, and, therefore, they were operating in the same conditions.

The European gas industry had responded to the competition from electricity by adopting the Auer burner, which was more powerful and economical than those that were lighting urban spaces, which is where the competition from electricity was most evident.

However, with the deployment of electrical technology after 1890, the gas factories adopted three strategies so as not to lose their business: (1) counteracting the emergence of electricity by enforcing the clauses relating to public lighting in their contracts; (2) reconsidering the sale prices of gas; (3) adopting the new technology with the installation of electricity stations moved by steam or gas motors, which they made themselves.

From the end of the nineteenth century, in light of the changes that were to take place with electricity and with the aim of increasing consumption, the gas factories began to promote the thermal uses of gas, with the introduction of cookers, heating and its industrial use.

Those gas factories that had very simple installations and lacked capital to undertake the reforms necessary to increase quality or performance ended up closing down. We should not forget that often the gas companies had debts generated by the city councils which did not pay for the public lighting. These debts had an impact on their finances and, ultimately, on the quality of the gas. This provided the city councils with an argument for not paying and a vicious circle arose that was difficult to resolve.

We have seen the extent to which gas survived after the introduction of electricity and how the gas companies acted. As a general rule, they adopted the production of electricity without abandoning the production of gas. Therefore, gas and electricity complemented each other until it became technically or economically unfeasible.

References

Alayo Manubens, Joan Carles. 2007. *L'Electricitat a Catalunya*. Lleida: Pages Editors.

Amigo Román, Pedro. 2014. *Las Empresas Gasistas de Castilla y León: La difícil relación con los Ayuntamientos de Valladolid y Burgos (c.1860-c.1935)*. Madrid: XI Congreso Internacional de la AEHE.

Barca Salom, Francesc X., Pont Estradera, Maria, Puig-Pla, Carles, and Bernat, Pasqual. coords. 2009. *Fàbrica, taller i laboratori. La Junta de Comerç de Barcelona: Ciència i tècnica per a la indústria i el comerç (1769-1851)*. Barcelona: Cambra de Comerç.

Bernal Rodríguez, Antonio Miguel et al. 1994. *Compañía Sevillana de Electricidad: Cien años de historia*. Sevilla: Fundación Sevillana de Electricidad.

De Orueta, José. 1929. *Memorias de un bilbaíno. 1870 a 1900*. San Sebastián: Talleres Tipográficos de Nueva Editorial, S.A.

Estadística del impuesto sobre el consumo de la luz de gas, electricidad y carburo de calcio-año de 1903, 1905. Madrid: Dirección General de Contribuciones, Impuestos y Rentas.

Fàbregas, Pedro A. 2003. *La Globalización en el siglo XIX: Málaga y el gas*. Sevilla: Ateneo de Sevilla-Universidad de Sevilla.

Fernández Paradas, Mercedes. 2015. *La industria del gas en Cádiz (1845-2012)*. Barcelona: Fundación Gas Natural Fenosa.

García de la Fuente, Dionisio. 1984. *La Compañía Española de Gas, S.A. "CEGAS". Más de cien años de Empresa*. Paterna: Artes Gráficas Vicent, S.A.

García de la Infanta, José María. 1986. *Primeros Pasos de la Luz eléctrica en Madrid y otros acontecimientos*. Madrid: Ediciones Fondo Natural.

González García, Antonio. 1981. *El gas en Sevilla – Cien años de historia*. Sevilla: Gráficas Salesianas.

Lastres y Juiz, Francisco 1898. *El Conflicto del Gas en Valencia y la fábrica del Sr. D. Georges Agustín Touchet Giblet*. Madrid: Imprenta de los hijos de M.G. Hernández.

Madoz, Pascual. 1846. *Diccionario Geográfico-Estadístico-Histórico de España y sus posesiones en Ultramar*. Tomo V. Madrid: Establecimiento tipográfico de P. Madoz y L. Sagasti.

Madrid, Rufino-Manuel. 2007. *Vencer la noche. La Sevilla Iluminada*. Sevilla: Universidad de Sevilla.

Martínez López, Alberte. 2017. La electrificación en la periferia: Galicia, 1883-1935. In *La electrificación y el territorio. Historia y futuro*, edited by Horacio Capel et al. Barcelona: Universidad de Barcelona.

Martínez López, Alberte, Mirás Araujo, Jesús, and Lindoso Tato, Elvira. 2009. *La industria del gas en Galicia: del alumbrado por gas al siglo XXI, 1850-2005*. Barcelona: Fundación Gas Natural.

Rojas y Caballero Infante, Francisco de Paula. 1879. *La luz eléctrica y sus aplicaciones*. Barcelona: Biblioteca Ilustrada de Espasa Hermanos.

Simón Palmer, María del Carmen. 1989. *El Gas y los madrileños*. Madrid: Gas Madrid-Espasa Calpe.

5 The rivalry between gas and electricity in France and Spain through advertising and marketing (1890–1936)*

Antonio Rafael Fernández-Paradas and Nuria Rodríguez-Martín

5.1 Introduction

In the 1880s and 1890s, the electricity industry began to expand throughout the western world. This gave rise to strong rivalry to replace its competitor, gas, as the primary source of energy. In order to increase the number of subscribers and consumption figures, and ultimately to push their competitors out of the market, the gas and electricity companies used different strategies. These included price and tariff wars and the implementation of technological improvements. The gas companies went to great lengths in order to safeguard at all costs the monopoly privileges with respect to their underground occupancy and frequently recurred to the courts. Another strategy adopted by the companies of both sectors was the use of advertising and other sales techniques, which were focused mainly on the domestic consumers.

This chapter scrutinises the sales activities of energy companies in France and Spain from 1890 to 1936, through the analysis of a selection of advertising materials, such as posters, printed advertisements, invoices, leaflets and catalogues. All of these items were created and distributed to promote a range of gas or electricity-powered appliances and products. The varied repertoire of the proposed documentary elements allows us to determine and establish the symbolic and iconographic values used as a means to attract and persuade. To some extent, through illustrations, design and art, an attempt was made to redirect the tastes of society, thanks to the beauty of these elements. We will also analyse in detail the messages and images of this marketing material in order to determine the ideas and arguments used by the advertisers and promoters who had the dual objective of selling gas and electric domestic appliances and increasing the consumer market.

The principal source used for elaborating the work are materials that are not highly valued in general by historiography, such as advertisements and other sales elements which, for our case, have a considerable artistic, symbolic and

* This research is part of the results of the R+D+I Research Project "Gas in Latin Europe: A comparative and global perspective (1818-1945)", PID2020-112844GB-I00, financed by the Ministry of Science and Innovation of the Government of Spain and ERDF Funds.

DOI: 10.4324/9781003428695-5

iconographic value. With a few exceptions, they are barely used as a primary source by contemporary historians, even in the fields of economic and business history and social history. It is also a field that has received little attention from the history of art and illustration. This is despite the important social and economic role played by advertising, which is a fundamental tool for observing and analysing consumption habits and also the social uses and customs of each historical moment, of which advertising is both a mirror and a reflection (Rodríguez Martín, 2021).

One of the principal obstacles for working with these types of documentary sources is that, for the historical period studied, there are quantitatively few examples that have been preserved and, therefore, few that can be used. Their ephemeral nature, as the materials were not made to last, means that they are relatively scarce. Furthermore, they are difficult to find due to their dispersion, except for printed advertisements, which can be drawn from the newspapers of the period.

5.2 The marketing and advertising strategies of the gas and electricity companies

Both in Spain and in France the companies selling energy and the manufacturers of appliances that used it as a source of energy, employed a whole series of advertising strategies. These strategies sought, on the one hand, to increase the number of subscribers to the gas supply and, on the other, to push out the competition from electricity, which had become a serious threat to the position of gas as the principal source of energy in the early years of the twentieth century.

5.2.1 Pavilions and stands in fairs and exhibitions

The strategies and promotional tools included, first, the participation of the gas companies and manufacturers of the appliances in different public events, such as the universal and international exhibitions and specialised trade fairs. They participated through pavilions and stands where they demonstrated the importance of the gas industry and the advantages and superiority of gas-run appliances. These types of events could receive thousands of visitors. Therefore, they constituted a highly important form of public visibility and also increased the social prestige of the exhibitors and were a means to attract new consumers.

During the Universal Exhibition of Paris in 1889, which was also the stage for celebrating the centenary of the French Revolution and for which the Eiffel Tower was built, the so-called *Pavillon du Gaz* showed the public all of the gas appliances in a "modern" home, exalting "the different advantages for the current living conditions which seek, most of all, a saving in time and also in money" (*Guide du consommateur de gaz. Gaz de Marseille*, 1891, p. 3). Furthermore, the gas companies wished to show their superiority in the energy field during this large global event with the illumination of the rest of the pavilions, rooms and accesses to the exhibition ground through thousands of lamps and candelabras, which earned Paris the title of "la Ville lumière" (*Gaz à tous les étages*, 2011). The *Pavillon du Gaz* was located in a privileged spot, close to one of the feet of the Eiffel Tower in an open area which could be seen from the Seine River. The objective of this exceptional location was to display the illuminations of the pavilion in all their glory. The pavilion had a Renaissance-inspired eclectic architecture designed by the French architect Pierre-Henri Picq (1833–1911).

Participation in fairs and exhibitions was a marketing resource also adopted by the electricity producing and distributing companies and the manufacturers of electrical appliances (Rodríguez-Martín and Mirás Araujo, 2021, pp. 201–203). In March 1927, the Modern City and Home Exhibition was held in Madrid. Among the exhibitors was the company Siemens Schuckert, which erected two large stands where, as well as showing visitors the different appliances for indoor and outdoor lighting, engines, electricity meters and light bulbs that it manufactured, it also installed a kitchen and living room to demonstrate how the different appliances worked, such as its PROTOS vacuum cleaner, electrical hobs, and an automatic washing machine. It also exhibited small kitchen motors for coffee grinders, meat mincers, ice-cream makers, knife cleaners and so on (*ABC*, 17/04/1927).

Another major manufacturer of that time which frequently participated in these events to promote its electrical appliances was Electrolux, showing primarily its star product, the vacuum cleaner. The company, which was founded in 1919 in Sweden by Axel Wenner-Gren, from the outset was renowned for its large investments in advertising. In Spain, it participated in all kinds of fairs and exhibitions in the 1920s and 1930s, such as the Trade Fair of Madrid of 1923, the First Fashion Fair of 1923, the Health and Hygiene Exhibition in 1924 and the General Exhibition of Construction and Rooms of 1925 (Ice Palace, Madrid). The National Library of France preserves a photograph dated in 1933 showing the visit to the Electrolux stand of the then French minister of trade. The stand was located in the wagon of an "exhibition train" in the railway station of Austerlitz, and in the photograph different electrical refrigerators and several Model V vacuum cleaners with their characteristic design can be seen.

5.2.2 Leaflets

The participation in fairs and exhibitions, which allowed companies to perform *in situ* demonstrations for the public, also enabled them to undertake direct advertising, that is, the handing out of printed materials, such as leaflets and catalogues to the visitors. Direct advertising, with the printing and distribution of leaflets and catalogues for individual consumers, was one of the most popular marketing strategies deployed by the Spanish and French gas companies. Some examples have been preserved, showing a high degree of sophistication and quality (in terms of advertising), embodied in their design and content. One of these is the leaflet edited by the Compañía Madrileña de Alumbrado y Calefacción por Gas in 1906 and titled *Curso de cocina por gas*.[1]

The number of copies of the document that were printed and how they were distributed is unknown. It is made up of 12 pages and was printed on low-quality paper in black and white, except the front and back covers which were in bright colours (red, green, yellow, etc.). The front cover featured a series of illustrations under the name of the company and the cities in which it had factories (Valladolid, Alicante, Burgos, Logroño, Jerez and Madrid). The back cover displayed a wilful and democratic advertising slogan of the company: "No home without gas", which was printed in capitals and framed with artistic edging.

The content of the leaflet is mostly dedicated to describing and advertising the course on cooking with gas organised by the company as a strategy to convince the public "of the positive advantages offered by the NEW GAS COOKERS in terms of cleanliness, easy, speed, hygiene and ECONOMY over all other cooking systems" (*Curso de cocina por gas*, 1906, p. 1). It was an innovative advertising tactic, based on offering the subscribers and potential clients of the company face-to-face demonstrations of the working, use and operation of the different models of gas cookers available for sale or hire on 52 Serrano Street, where the gas company had a store and showroom. Allowing the public to see and use the appliances stimulated their desire to own them and therefore to purchase them. Both the text of the leaflet and the activity carried out constituted comparative advertising, as they not only exalted the virtues of the gas cooker, but also indicated and insisted that its qualities were superior to the rest of the cooking systems, although they did not specifically mention any of them.

The cooking course was given by a prestigious chef of the day, Ignacio Doménech, who was also a food writer and journalist. The objective was to associate the name of the company with that of a prestigious figure in the culinary world, thereby highlighting the importance and superiority of using gas in the kitchen. The leaflet also contains images of the different appliances which the public could see and purchase in the company's showroom: heaters, irons, cookers, gas toasters and "bath heaters".[2] These images were accompanied by simple texts and slogans which used verbs and nouns referring to well-being and comfort in the home: "Instant, hygienic, adjustable heat"; "No sparks or ash. No smoke or soot". It also alluded to the economical use of these appliances, with exact data of the cost of gas.

Another example of the advertising leaflet designed to stimulate gas consumption through the use of domestic appliances is the 27-page leaflet printed by the Société du Gaz de Paris in 1913 with the title *Comment combattre la vie chère*.[3] The leaflet of the Parisian company was commissioned to an advertising agency, according to its back cover, the Agence Française de Publicité. It was printed in colour and included many eye-catching illustrations which reinforced the principal message of the texts, which revolved around the idea of savings and the economy of using gas in homes: "Le gaz économise SANTÉ, TEMPS, ARGENT" (Gas saves health, time and money).

From an artistic point of view, the front and back covers of the document have a striking design and the inside is abundantly illustrated with different types of images. The front cover of the document depicts a domestic scene with three female figures: an elegant lady sitting at a *bonheur de jour*, a purely feminine writing table, with a document in her hand, a maid with a shopping basket at her feet on the floor and a girl holding a doll. Two other things are worth noting regarding the front cover. The first is that it is aimed a priori at a female audience. The second is that there is no reference to gas or any appliance related to the gas industry. We have to wait until the next page to find LE GAZ printed in large letters within a bold box decorated with sepia-toned plant motifs. From this page onwards, the leaflet deploys all of its iconographic and symbolic values. The text is clear. Gas means "santé, temps, argent".

The rest of the pages are filled with different illustrations that reflect, with a comic style, the uses, virtues and benefits of gas, gas appliances, life with "gas", "cooking with gas" and other elements. Within the pages of the leaflet we can find many images that reflect a large catalogue of gas-run appliances for the home, but also the possibilities of gas for public establishments, such as hotels and restaurants. Moreover, exterior images are shown with paradigmatic places in Paris, such as the Place de la Concorde, lit by gas. The objective was to exalt the importance of public gas lighting. Finally, we can find a good repertoire of lightbulbs and lamps with their respective prices. While the front cover depicts an indoor scene, the back cover shows an outdoor scene in which we can see a gas operator, specifically a lamplighter, in a very busy square lit by gas. The lamplighter is doing the round at the established time to manually light the gas lamps.

The leaflet also includes a double-page calendar-almanac for the year 1914. The purpose of including it was no other than to ensure that the readers kept the leaflet for its practical use so as not to throw it away quickly considering as mere publicity. This type of publicity with the inclusion of gifts for the consumers was became a frequently used resource during the first third of the twentieth century (Prat Gaballí, 1934, pp. 85–87; Rodríguez Martín, 2015, pp. 335–343). These gifts could have a practical use, as in the case of a calendar inserted in the leaflet.

5.2.3 Promotional gifts

There were also marketing gifts in the form of Christmas greetings cards from the personnel of the gas companies (lamplighters and technicians responsible for lighting and putting out the gas lamps and opening and closing the shut-off valves, respectively), typical of popular Spanish culture. These objects were chromolithographs given to their clients in exchange for a bonus during the Christmas holidays. They were decorated with illustrations showing the tasks undertaken by these workers and the different types of subscribers and uses of gas, without referring to other energies. In the Archive of the Naturgy

Foundation (Barcelona, Spain), there are many examples of these greetings cards printed between the end of the nineteenth century and the mid-twentieth century by the companies Gas Lebon and the Sociedad Catalana del Gas (Oliva Pascuet, Oliva Sanosa and Fàbregas, 2013, pp. 18–49). These Christmas cards should be understood as small great sources of information which show us how the gas industry sought to introduce itself into families using daily life, traditional or religious images. They are also important visual icons reflecting the artistic styles from the end of the nineteenth century to well into the twentieth century.

Another interesting example of the promotional items given to the consumers is the map of Paris which the Société du Gaz de Paris gave in 1913, an almost essential element in a city of the size of the French capital. The map highlights in red the gas factories, and in the top-left part of the document, there is a box with a list of the 17 showrooms of gas appliances which the company had and the customer service offices with their location on the map. It also informed that the office located at number 92 of Boulevard Raspail ran gas cookery courses.

5.2.4 Books and press

The promotion of gas cookers was one of the main undertakings of the gas-producing companies at the end of the nineteenth century, when gas overtook the traditional fuels of coal and firewood, even though these had been used since the 1820s and 1830s (Fernández-Paradas and Rodríguez-Martín, 2022). As previously mentioned, in Spain, the gas companies used free cookery courses to promote the use of gas for cooking, although they also used other promotional strategies for this specific purpose. For example, they financed cookbooks, such as *La Cocina por Gas. Agenda de Cocina para 1897*[4] by the chef Ángel Muro, which was commissioned by the Compañía Madrileña de Alumbrado y Calefacción por Gas. This book highlighted the advantages of lighting, cooking and heating with gas in the home, assuring the hygiene, economy and comfort that having a gas supply in the home provided. The book also includes a series of news articles and reports published in different newspapers of the time which referred to the promotional activity of the gas company of Madrid, highlighting the concern that the company showed for the living conditions of the working classes, specifically labourers' homes and their kitchens. The rest of the pages were filled with recipes for every day of the year created by the chef. A total of 6,000 copies of this publication were printed and could be purchased in bookshops and in the company's shop on Alcalá street in Madrid.

The *Agenda de cocina de Ángel Muro* was not the only project of a publication with promotional purposes supported and financed by the Compañía Madrileña de Alumbrado y Calefacción por Gas. Another was the publication of a culinary magazine *El Gorro Blanco*, edited by the chef Ignacio Doménech, to whom we previously referred.[5] The magazine, which was sold as individual copies or by subscription, inserted advertising in its pages which, together with the sales, financed the publication. The majority of the advertisements in the issues of the magazine published between 1906 and 1913 promoted the gas cooker of the Compañía Madrileña de Alumbrado y Calefacción por Gas. The advertisements were simple texts in the form of panels which positively described the gas cooker: "Cocina simpática «La cocina por gas»" [Pleasant kitchen "Gas cooker"], "Cocina regularizable «La cocina por gas»" [Adjustable cooker "The gas cooker"], "Cocina elegante «La cocina por gas»" [Elegant cooker "The gas cooker"] … which were repeated on most of the pages of each issue.

With respect to the previously mentioned stores and showrooms of the gas companies, it should be noted that they were also used for other actions, such as conferences, according to news reports that we have gathered from the press of the day. According to a report published on 2 October 1896 in newspaper *La Correspondencia de España*, the director of the Compañía del gas de Madrid offered a series of theoretical and practical culinary conferences on "the many applications of cooking with gas, demonstrating its advantages over coal". While he spoke, a chef cooked in front of the audience "allowing them to taste the dishes which were prepared with astonishing speed with the blue gas flames". The event was primarily designed to attempt to convince the consumers that it was not costly to enjoy the comfort of gas in the kitchen, quelling the fear of the energy bill, as, according to the report, "A meter marked the cost of the gas and the public were amazed at how little it cost to cook food for a family with those simple and elegant machines" (*La Correspondencia de España*, 2/10/1896, p. 2).

Achieving this type of free advertising in the press was a huge success for the companies. In this respect, it should be explained that both the gas and electricity companies used camouflaged advertising in the form of unsigned news reports (individual) on the front pages of the newspapers which highlighted the advantages of the energy and usually included more or less concealed criticism of other energies. Their use increased as electricity began to gain ground.

In this respect, we should consider the fact that when its production began in the last third of the nineteenth century, electrical technology had certain shortcomings as there were problems to produce current on a large scale and transport it at a low voltage, which required the electricity companies to locate the small-scale power plants close to the centres of consumption. Furthermore, direct current was the most used, but it had the disadvantage of changing voltage, which caused continuous malfunctions which interrupted the service. This situation began to change at the beginning of the twentieth century, thanks to the development of alternating and high voltage current, which enabled the construction of high voltage power lines able to transport electricity across large distances, and turbines that enabled the exploitation of large waterfalls to generate hydroelectricity. All of this translated into the lowering of the prices of electricity. Hence, the gas companies doubled their efforts so as not to lose the privileged position that they had held until then in the energy sector, disseminating the use of gas, incentivising its consumption in the home, basically in the kitchen and as heating.

An example of this type of propaganda is the single piece published in the French newspaper *Le Figaro* on 16 July 1909 which, under the title "La cuisine au gaz à la portèe de tous" informed that the Société du gaz de Paris would give free of charge to its subscribers a gas cooker with two hobs and a grill in the showroom that the company had in the *rue* Condorcet. The advantages of the appliance were highlighted, together with its ease of installation and use, the little amount of space it occupied and its economical energy consumption.

5.2.5 Outdoor advertising

Artistic posters were a form of propaganda which reached their peak in terms of production and diffusion at the end of the nineteenth century throughout Europe. They were used by both gas and electricity companies and also the manufacturers of the appliances. Some of these elements were created by the most renowned graphic artists of the day, such as Jules Chéret. Posters constituted an advertising medium designed to be displayed in outdoor spaces in order to reach the highest possible number of people. They were pasted on walls, façades or specific urban furniture created for this purpose, such as the famous and historical Morris column.

The National Library of France possesses an exceptional collection of artistic posters relating to the energy sector. Among them are two beautiful examples promoting incandescent lights of the brands Westinghouse and Osram, both dating from 1912. The Westinghouse poster makes a statement of intent with its slogan, "Westinghouse lamp, the most elegant, the least fragile". This advertisement should be understood from a dual perspective. On the one hand, the consolidation of the electrical systems and the overcoming of their technological deficiencies and, on the other, the quality and durability that the Westinghouse brand provided with its products. It is a lithographed poster, designed by Jean-Marie Michel Liebeaux, who signed as Mich.

The Westinghouse poster[6] consisted of a design of a curious lamp in the form of a woman, whose trunk resembled a feminine form and the lower half a large electrical light bulb reminiscent of the old over skirts worn by the women in the modern age and the nineteenth century. Coloured in red and pink tones and topped with an elegant hat, the figure was truly "elegant". The second advertisement,[7] for the Osram brand, was designed by Eugène Ogé. It depicts a feminine allegory which illuminates the city of Paris throughout the night. She does so with a light bulb, held in one hand, with a dark background, lighting the emblematic building of the Opera. In Ogé's poster, the female figure, in the form of an allegory, takes the place and role that the moon would have on a clear night over the city of Paris.

These two posters show a broad reality of the period which prevailed in both gas and electricity advertising. In both cases, and from the end of the nineteenth century, an iconographic model was codified in which the light, either through gas or electricity, was personified as a woman. Although the reasons for choosing this model are not clear, the idea could be derived from the ancient cultural substratum in which the woman is a source of light and life.

Another type of printed advertising used by both gas and electricity companies was the inclusion of advertisements in the invoices sent to the subscribers. The front of the invoice was used for the details of the bill and the back for advertising the company, its services, etc. (Sintes, 1933, p. 827). For the case of gas, there is an extraordinary and representative example dated in 1913 which is preserved in the General Archive of the Complutense University of Madrid.

The invoice is an exceptional example which combines design, beauty and functionality in a single document. While on the front there is a breakdown of the items to pay, the back depicts several colourful indoor scenes, with an allegory and a box with text listing the possibilities of gas for inside the home. Both the three indoor scenes showing ironing, hair straightening and the bath and the box underneath with the text are framed with contours inspired by the modernist style. It is striking that the advertising message is, again, directed at women. The idea seems clear: it was women who had to be convinced of the need to have gas in the home.

Finally, in the scene at the top of the back of the invoice, there is a naked ephebus leaning against a type of sun and observing a gas streetlamp at night. This could be an allegory of the sun eclipsed by the new moon, the gas streetlamp, which lights the sky and shines brighter than the stars. We must point out that the composition is reminiscent of the legend of Narcissus who was fixated with his own beauty.

In addition to the artistic posters, designed to be fixed to walls and the façades of buildings to be seen by all passers-by, the gas companies also used another type of outdoor advertising. This consisted in placing advertising elements and supports that use gas to light them, thereby showing the possibilities that the energy offered for the promotion and visibility of retail establishments in the cities. Gas powered luminous advertising was fairly widespread in Spanish cities at the end of the nineteenth century, according to García de la Fuente (2006). The so-called luminous bombs were installed, replacing the glass boxes of the public streetlamps. They were hollow spheres made of glass or porcelain with the name of the establishment or brand imprinted on them (García de la Fuente, 2006, pp. 220–222).

It was also common for industrial businesses and advertising agencies to send applications to the local councils of the large cities and capitals requesting authorisation to use the gas-powered public streetlamps as advertising supports, hanging different types of advertising from them. However, in general, these requests were denied as they infringed the municipal bylaws that protected the urban décor and aesthetics. Therefore, despite the existence of gas-powered luminous advertisements, it was electrical energy that exploited this type of advertising. In the early years of the twentieth century, it began to be installed in the large cities using light bulbs that transformed the night-time urban landscape.

Although the boom in electric light signs occurred in all of the large western cities during the 1920s, they had already been installed before the beginning of the First World War. In Spain, in 1913, the manufacturer of electrical articles A.E.G. Thomson Houston Iberica was one of the first to install this kind of advertising, placing a huge electrical luminous sign in the Puerta del Sol of Madrid. This sign advertised its Egmar lamp and was located on the roof of a building in the central square. It was six metres tall and had the shape of a light bulb.[8] According to a description in a note published in the newspaper *El Imparcial*, it produced a "magic effect" and enabled Madrid to resemble the rest of the European capitals in terms of large luminous advertisements.

At first, given the strong establishment of gas in public lighting, electricity found its privileged space in the private, retail or domestic environments. In homes, shops and public establishments, such as theatres or cafés, electrical energy expanded rapidly, at first for lighting. In the case of Spain, we must consider the limited penetration of gas in homes, despite the efforts of the gas companies to promote its consumption in the domestic environment, and as we shall explain, the promotion of gas appliances. Therefore, until well into the twentieth century, gas was only present in the homes of the wealthiest, due to its high price, its dangerousness and other inconveniences inherent in its use in homes, as well as, of course, the low standards of living of the population (Arroyo, 2003). All of this favoured the introduction and expansion of electricity in homes, at first for lighting (Rybczynski, 1986, pp. 150–151).

5.2.6 Printed advertisements

This is confirmed by the multiplication of printed advertisements of different types and brands of light bulbs. Both in Spanish and French newspapers (particularly the dailies, but also the weeklies and also general and specialised journals), we can observe an increase from the beginning of the twentieth century of advertisements of different brands and manufacturers, such as Osram, Philips, Wotan, Sirius or Tantale.

In this way, the electrical lamps became a strongly advertised consumer article in the French and Spanish press, and their advertisements show the rapid technical improvements that they underwent, with this being one of the principal sales arguments used: "Nueva Lámpara Metal. Filamento trefilado irrompible" [New Metal Lamp. Unbreakable drawn steel wire filaments] claimed an advertisement of this brand in 1914.

As well as innovation and technical superiority, in the advertisements, the manufacturers and advertisers proclaimed the low sales price of their product, the quality in terms of the light provided by the lamps and, most of all, the saving in the electricity bill. These arguments, which were very similar, were repeated in the advertisements of the different brands and were practically the same in Spain and France. One example is an advertisement of 1909 for metallic filament Philips Lamp made by the manufacturer with the same name, in which it is presented as the "only lamp for the future. 75% saving in energy or four times more light for the same price. White and constant light. 1,000 hours duration".[9] The Nitra-Egmar lamp went even further, being advertised in 1914 with the slogan, "The almost free electric light". The Osram brand also used saving as its principal selling point, affirming in its advertisement at the end of 1911: "The consumption of the OSRAM lamp with 16 spark plugs is one cent per hour (a guaranteed consumption). Replacing ordinary lamps with OSRAM lamps gives better lighting and saves more than two-thirds of the electricity budget".[10]

Advertisements of these same brands also appeared in the French press, and it is not surprising that they used the same slogans and arguments, invoking, as previously explained, savings, quality and technical superiority. We have only found one difference with respect to these advertisements in that those published in the French press referred to national manufacture, even indicating the place in the country where the establishment that produced the lamps were located.[11] This was not the case in Spain, where, on the contrary, the argument of foreign manufacture was used as a guarantee of the superiority of the product.

In the years immediately following the First World War, the printed advertisements for incandescent lamps incorporated new sales arguments. As well as the economy, savings and the quality of the product, other intangible benefits for the consumers were also used, such as eye health. In Spain, in the mid-1930s, the Osram brand launched an advertising campaign titled "*Cuide su vista empleando mejor luz*" [Take care of your eyes by using better light]. This campaign included the design of a logo formed by the slogan surrounding a pupil to form a human eye, which was inserted in the newspapers in advertisements with different designs. We can also refer to the publication of a 32-page illustrated leaflet titled *De la buena visión con alumbrado artificial* [Good vision with artificial lighting] (Osram, 1936). This leaflet was sent free of charge to all interested consumers who sent a coupon inserted in the newspaper advertisements.

Apart from the electric lamp advertisements in the French and Spanish press, the advertising of electrical appliances for the home, including the first white goods launched on the market, was relatively scarce in the years preceding the First World War. According to Rodríguez-Martín and Mirás Araujo (2021) for the Spanish case, the emergence and multiplication of advertisements of apparatus such as vacuum cleaners, floor polishers, irons or electrical refrigerators took place in the 1920s and 1930s. However, we should highlight the advertising presence of certain retail establishments specialised in the sale of small electrical appliances, such as toasters, stoves, table fans or hairdryers. One example is the advertisements of Casa Ureña, located in Madrid, which, in 1900 offered a broad catalogue which included "electrical table and ceiling fans, electrical motors, electric arcs, incandescent lamps, electric heaters, electric coffee machines, electric water heaters, cigarette lighters, electric irons, electric rotisseries, telephones; all electricity applications can be found here".

However, it was in the 1920s when a quantitative and qualitative leap was made in the advertisements of electric products and appliances for the home. This growth in the advertising of electrical appliances coincided with the boom in the electricity market. In the mid-1930s, the variety of domestic electrical appliances in the market was enormous and practically covered all of the tasks and needs of the home: kitchen, lighting, ironing, heating, ventilation, refrigeration, cleaning, laundry and dishwashing, and so on. This led to an increase in the demand for electricity to the detriment of gas consumption.

The innovations in terms of sales and advertising, which had been created and implemented from the end of the nineteenth century by the gas companies, were then used, maximised and improved by those of the electricity sector, which had then won the battle with gas for the energy market. It was helped, to a great extent, by the strong and negative impact that the cataclysm of the First World War had on the industry (Fernández-Paradas, 2023).

5.3 Conclusions

At the end of the nineteenth century, the boom in the electricity industry began to threaten the dominance of the gas companies in the energy sector in Europe. The rivalry between the two energy sources until the First World War translated into the implementation by companies in both sectors of a whole series of strategies to increase the number of subscribers and consumption figures, and ultimately to push their competitors out of the market.

Among the newest business practices used was that of advertising and other sales tools which today we would call marketing. The analysis of a representative sample of advertising pieces (posters, printed advertisements, leaflets and catalogues, etc.), conceived, designed and distributed between 1890 and 1918 in Spain and France to promote the hire and sale of appliances and consumer articles run by gas or electricity, enables us to affirm that the hard competition between the two sectors was settled on a social and cultural level as well as on an economic and industrial level.

The gas and electricity companies operating in Spain and France in the chronological period analysed in this study gave advertising and sales propaganda a leading role within their business strategies which has not been fully addressed by the historiography. The gas companies, which were well established at the end of the nineteenth century, felt threatened by the electricity industry and attempted to stay a step ahead in this respect. They used direct advertising, the sponsorship of food publications, showrooms of domestic appliances and other innovative techniques which have been analysed in detail in the article and which were subsequently used by the electricity companies and manufacturers of electrical appliances. Although the battle was finally won by electricity, at the end of the First World War, the result of the struggle had still not been decided.

Notes

1 Gas cooker course. A digitised copy of this document is freely available on the Memoria de Madrid Digital Library website at: http://www.memoriademadrid.es/buscador.php?accion=VerFicha&id=346855&num_id=8&num_total=15
2 Water heaters placed in the bath to heat water for bathers. The one advertised in the leaflet was cylindrical; it was supported by three legs on the floor and provided between 10 and 25 litres of water per minute at a temperature of 35°C to 40°C.
3 *How to combat the high cost of living.* A digital version of this brochure is freely available at the City of Paris libraries website (Bibliothèques spécialisées et patrimoniales) at: https://bibliotheques-specialisees.paris.fr/ark:/73873/pf0002007012.locale=fr
4 *Gas cooking. Cooking Agenda for 1897.*
5 Access all digitised issues of this magazine through the National Library of Spain website at: https://hemerotecadigital.bne.es/hd/en/results?parent=14d2f1d9-d929-4547-a407-290946293566&t=alt-asc&c=1
6 A digital version of this poster is freely available on the website of the National Library of France at https://gallica.bnf.fr/ark:/12148/btv1b53127749v.r=Westinghouse?rk=21459; [1/09/2023].
7 A digital version of this poster is freely available on the website of the National Library of France at https://gallica.bnf.fr/ark:/12148/btv1b9011372d?rk=21459;2 [1/09/2023].
8 Archivo de Villa (Town Archive) of Madrid. Secretariat. File 18-272-1.
9 Philips Lamp advertisement, *El Porvenir Segoviano*, 16 October 1909.
10 Osram Lamp advertisement, *La Época*, 30 December 1910.
11 An example is the advertisement for the Lampe Sirius, "à Filament 'trèfilè' INCANSSABLE Lumière éclatante Très grande Économie", which specified: "Fabrication Française". *Le Journal*, 25 September 1912.

References

Arroyo, Mercedes. 2003. Gas en todos los pisos: el largo proceso hacia la generalización del consumo doméstico del gas. *Scripta Nova. Revista electrónica de geografía y ciencias sociales*, 146: http://www.ub.edu/geocrit/sn/sn-146(135).htm [Accessed 25 May 2022]

Fernández-Paradas, Mercedes. 2023. Gas in the First World War in Latin Europe. In *The Gas Industry in Latin Europe. Economic Development During the 19th and 20th Centuries*, edited by Jesús Mirás-Araujo and Andrea Giuntini, 107–131. Palgrave Macmillan.

Fernández-Paradas, Mercedes and Rodríguez-Martín, Nuria. 2022. Abrazar la felicidad a través del confort. Un estudio socioeconómico de la promoción del uso del gas en la cocina en España, Francia y Portugal hasta los años 1930. In *El Happiness Management. Un cisne amarillo que vuela hacia el marketing social, la inteligencia empresarial y el bienestar*, edited by Rafael Ravina Ripoll et al., 281–302. Valencia: Tirant Lo Blanch.

García de la Fuente, Dionisio. 2006. *Una historia del gas en Alicante*. Madrid: LID.

Guide du consommateur de gaz. Gaz de Marseille 1891. 1891. Marseille: Typographie et Lithographie Barlatier et Barthelet.

Oliva Pascuet, Víctor, Oliva Sanosa, Oriol, y Fàbregas, Pere A. 2013. *Publicidad para una historia. 170 años de compañía*. Sabadell: Fundación Gas Natural Fenosa

Prat Gaballí, Pedro. 1934. *Publicidad racional*. Barcelona: Labor.

Rodríguez Martín, Nuria. 2015. *La capital de un sueño. Madrid en el primer tercio del siglo XX*. Madrid: CEPC.

Rodríguez Martín, Nuria. 2021. *La publicidad y el nacimiento de la sociedad de consumo. España, 1900-1936*. Madrid: Catarata.

Rodríguez-Martín, Nuria, and Mirás Araujo, Jesús. 2021. La más útil joya del hogar. La promoción de los primeros electrodomésticos en España, 1900-1936. *Aportes*, 107, 183–213.

Rybczynski, Witold. 1986. *Home. A short history of an idea*. New York: Viking.

Sintes, Francisco F. 1933. *La industria eléctrica en España*. Barcelona: Montaner y Simón.

Gaz à tous les étages. La naissance du confort. 1850-1920. 2011. *Catalogue de l'exposition du même titre*. Paris: Montag Éditions

Osram. 1936. *De la buena visión con alumbrado artificial*. Madrid: Osram.

Curso de cocina por gas. 1906. S. l. S. n.

6 The withdrawal of foreign capital from the gas industry in Spain in the first third of the twentieth century*

María Vázquez-Fariñas, Mariano Castro-Valdivia and Juan Manuel Matés-Barco

6.1 Introduction

In a free market economic system, foreign investment in a territory is usually determined by its development. This prominence of foreign capital in national economies has generated much controversy. There have been diverse interpretations. In some cases, the academic literature criticises international loans. On the one hand, it talks of "domination", "foreign control" and even "colonialism" and some refer to a "loss of sovereignty to foreign encroachment". Others cite David Landes (1999) when he says that "over time I have come to better understand that capitalism means movements of capital". Within this context, different theories have emerged that applaud or undermine the investment of foreign capital in a certain country. Sometimes, foreign direct investment is identified with multinational companies, but this connection is not always exact. At other times, the positive or negative aspects are assessed according to personal convictions, although more recently a more objective view has become predominant that perceives foreign investment as an aid to growth (Tascón, 2008). It is important to note that one of its undeniable properties is that it substitutes the lack of capital in less developed countries and enables projects to be carried out that would otherwise be unviable. Furthermore, this foreign capital is usually accompanied by modern technology, often unattainable for the receiving country through its own means.

The objective of this chapter is to analyse the evolution of the presence of foreign companies in the Spanish gas industry in the first third of the twentieth century and how they disappeared from the sector during this period. To do this, based on the 1901 edition of *Estadística del Impuesto sobre el consumo de luz de gas, electricidad y carburo de calcio*, a census has been made of the foreign companies that owned gas factories at the beginning of the twentieth century. To complement this information, the *Anuario Financiero y de Sociedades Anónimas* and the *Gaceta de Madrid* have been consulted, which provide

* This research is part of the results of the R+D+I Research Project "Gas in Latin Europe: A comparative and global perspective (1818-1945)", PID2020-112844GB-I00, financed by the Ministry of Science and Innovation of the Government of Spain and ERDF Funds.

DOI: 10.4324/9781003428695-6

information about the presence of foreign companies in Spain and data referring to the capital invested. In some cases, the names of the people forming part of the governing bodies are mentioned. This is relevant in order to learn about the family and economic relationships of these directors. Another important source for this study has been the *Estadística de la Contribución de Utilidades sobre la Riqueza Mobiliaria*, which has enabled us to determine the base capital declared for taxation, the type of shares, data on income, expenses, profits and so on.

The chapter is structured into two blocks. After this introduction, the first block addresses the characteristics of foreign investment in Spain in three sections which analyse the boom, the predominance of French and English companies during the second half of the nineteenth century and the withdrawal of foreign capital in the first third of the twentieth century (second, third and fourth paragraphs). The second block, made up of the firth section, analyses the presence of foreign companies in the gas industry in Spain in the period of study; specifically the French companies Lebón y Compañía; Alumbrado, Calefacción y Fuerza Motriz de La Coruña y Vigo; Compañía de Gas de Málaga; Compañía del Gas de Zaragoza; and Gas Franco-Belga Robert Lesage & Compagnie; the German company Gaswerk Santa Cruz de Tenerife A.G.; and the English companies The Huelva Gas Electricity Company Limited and Anglo-Spanish Gas Company; ordered by capitalisation.[1] The article ends with some brief conclusions and the references consulted.

6.2 Boom of foreign investment

During the nineteenth century, foreign investment in Spain was present in almost all of the sectors of economic activity. This was pointed out in a pioneer study by Teresa Tortella (1997). Until the middle of the century, the data indicate that the majority of the capital invested was for government loans, while between 1850 and 1890, the investments were focused on companies. Although initially it was public debt that attracted foreign investors, later on the interest from the banking and finance sector became evident, followed by the retail, transport (rail), mining, public services, food and chemical industries. This type of investment was characterised by several features, including the fact that it was not exclusive to the Spanish capital, but extended to the principal cities and provinces and to a considerable number of companies, many of which were large Spanish companies of the twentieth century (Tortella, 1997).

The railways, mining and banking are the sectors that have been most studied and in which the majority of foreign capital was invested. However, these were not the only sectors as there were other branches of industrial activity that also received this foreign investment: the automobile, ceramics, cork, naval construction, electricity, gas, water, wood, chemical, insurance, tobacco, telephone, telegraph, winemaking, iron and steel, mechanical and glass industries (Tortella, 1997). Therefore, there was a long list of sectors that received foreign investment in Spain throughout the nineteenth century.

6.3 French primacy

This process of investing abroad was led by the most developed countries. The classic work by Rondo Cameron (1971) revealed France's dominance throughout the nineteenth century, which became one of the largest capital exporters, even to a greater extent than that corresponding to its level of development (Tortella, 2008). In nineteenth-century France, entrepreneurs, particularly bankers, were regarded as the champions of industrialisation and those responsible for disseminating the achievements of the new society throughout Europe. The railway became the symbol of this process. These perspectives were inherited from the ideas of the Duke of Henri de Saint-Simon and were adopted by individuals such as Michel Chevalier, who was a good friend of the Péreire brothers and also influenced by the ideas of Utopian socialism (Castro, 2007).

Spain then became a destination for French investments (Broder, 1976). From early on, the French entrepreneurs built a network of personal interests which converted them into a dominant group within the Spanish economy. These actions date back to the first trips made by French mining engineers to analyse the feasibility of the mines. From the mid-nineteenth century, the *Revista de Obras Públicas* was already reporting the relevance of these professionals and their influence in many of the construction projects of the day (bridges and railway lines), mines, and so on.

Other prominent players were the tobacco commission agents who maintained continuous relations with the Inland Revenue and the Rothschild family. Due to the economic difficulties of the Spanish governments, this family asserted their financial dominance in order to obtain the monopolies of the production of the mercury mines of Almadén and tobacco leasing. Bribes and privileges in the form of subsidies formed part of the political and economic scene of Spain in the mid-nineteenth century, where some French entrepreneurs played a prominent role. The Bank of Issue Act and the Building Societies Act, both of 1856, are related to the creation of the banking entities by the Rothschilds and the Péreires, among others, and the granting of large loans to the government. On the other hand, their interaction with relevant figures of the social and political life of the country was one of the distinctive features: noblemen, bankers and ministers became visible faces of the economic interests of the French companies in Spain. The management model was very similar and had a common characteristic: the relevance given to the general director, who had little weight in decision-making but was the true representative of the company on Spanish soil. The Rothschilds placed their trust in Eduardo Maristany for managing the Madrid-Zaragoza-Alicante rail company, better known as MZA, in Jules Aron for the mines of Peñarroya and in the Germans Bauer and Weisweller for banking businesses. Similar forms of action were taken by the Péreires and the Banco Paribas. This model lost popularity in the final decades of the nineteenth century due to the competition from German and Spanish investors and due to the growing suspicion of foreign investment (Castro, 2007).

France brought technological, organisational and capital advantages. The cultural and language differences were not excessively large and were mitigated by the proximity between the two countries, which reduced risks and information costs. Moreover, the French influence within the legislative framework was evident and the Spanish laws were inherited from the models established in France. Therefore, it was relatively easy for these investors to enter the peninsula and invest in banking, railway construction, mines and the implementation of new public water, gas, electricity and tram services, and so on in many of the cities (Cameron, 1971; Castro, 2007). Within this investment framework, an illustrative case of this scenario was the figure of Charles Lebon, who will be analysed later.

In the mid-nineteenth century, the Railway Acts (1855) and the Banks and Building Society Acts (1856) enabled the entrance of foreign capital into Spain. Castro (2007) identifies the principal actors of this French investment. On the one hand, a bank of issue such as Paribas and, on the other, three families, such as the Péreire brothers (Émile and Isaac), the Prost-Guilhous and the Rothschilds, which, in turn, created the financial entities Crédito Mobiliario Español, Compañía General de Crédito de España and Sociedad Española Mercantil e Industrial, respectively. The latter switched from public financing to industrial investments. The principal mission was to finance the large rail companies, specifically Caminos de Hierro del Norte de España, the MZA; the Ferrocarril de Cádiz a Sevilla, which subsequently became Ferrocarriles Andaluces; and that of Lérida-Reus-Tarragona. Furthermore, they also became involved in promoting mining operations, such as those of Río Tinto, the gas industry (Gas Madrid), insurance (La Unión y El Fénix) or the supply of drinking water.

Foreign investment in the nineteenth century was broad and distributed across different sectors, although the French dominance was notable, particularly in the railways and banking. The second most important country was Great Britain, which directed its investments towards the mines, the trams and the short-distance railways for the transport of minerals. Belgium, meanwhile, invested in mining and trams, while Germany (the last country to invest in Spain at the end of the nineteenth century) played a relevant role in the electricity, chemical and transport (trams) industries (Tortella, 2008). In the final decades of the century, British and French investors turned their attention towards urban services such as gas, water and trams, electricity, insurance, chemical products, explosives, communications and public works in general.

The differences between them resided in the size of the business and their resilience over time. Family-run companies were predominant with a great capacity to adapt to the Spanish ways of life. Access to finance facilitated the creation of endogamic networks with industrial and commercial interests. Furthermore, the foreign investors showed interest in relatively new businesses, such as gas, chemicals or beer.

6.4 The withdrawal of foreign capital

In the twentieth century, particularly from 1914, a change in trend took place that interrupted this investment process. There were different reasons for this. On the one hand were the problems caused by the outbreak of the First World War. On the other, the new "nationalising" direction taken by the Spanish governments facilitated the entrance of greater own contributions and promoted the acquisition of foreign companies by native entrepreneurs. Furthermore, it is worth noting the emergence of new competitors within a difficult context, replete with problems generated by the war and the bankruptcy of certain emblematic companies, which led to a high level of prevention and a mistrust of foreign investors (Castro, 2007). Factors related to the gradual diversification and growth of the Spanish economy occurred simultaneously. Capital repatriation, caused by the loss of the last colonies, gave rise to the entrance of investors in some of these businesses. Moreover, the reinforcement of the peseta with the reforms introduced by Minister Fernández Villaverde, generated an expansive wave. The First World War accelerated this process, and some companies were taken over by Spanish capital. Gabriel Tortella (2008) refers to the training efforts and the creation of business networks financed by foreign capital in the peninsula in the previous decades: training of employees, transmission of organisational and business practices and so on.

In summary, from 1918, the reduction in the foreign presence was due to two basic factors: first, the trend of "nationalising" foreign companies and second, the desire to strengthen the Spanish economy. However, this withdrawal or reconversion of foreign investment can also be explained from a market perspective. Some companies decided to abandon the country due to the emergence of new competitors which reduced their profits. The retreat of the French banks (generated by the bankruptcy of some entities) led to the withdrawal of a good part of the business conglomerate. This situation gave rise to the incorporation of Spanish business groups which began to acquire different companies. The harsh competition that electricity represented for gas led to the gradual withdrawal from these activities. For example, as it was not a large financial corporation, Lebón y Compañía sought refuge in its possessions in the north of Africa and prioritised its interests in Egypt and the Maghreb over continuing to commit to a country where there was a constant emergence of new entrepreneurs.

Other companies became profitable when the French had sold their shares. These actions indicated that Spain was no longer an attractive country for French investment. This seems to be the principal reason why assets related to the railways, banking, gas, water and electricity were liquidated and sold to Spanish entrepreneurs. A modern banking sector was taking shape during these decades, which explains why they took over many of these businesses. Furthermore, the bankruptcy of Casa Bauer in the 1920s, after almost

100 years with a presence in Madrid as representatives of the Rothschilds, generated a certain level of mistrust (Castro, 2007).

From 1920, the legislation was more restrictive for foreign companies. The Royal Decree of 30 April 1924 limited the proportion of foreigners who could form part of a board of directors of a company to one third. It also stipulated that the chairman and directors could not be foreign. It also laid down another series of restrictions: foreign capital could not exceed 25%, and native personnel were established at 80%. This legislation oriented the Spanish companies towards the acquisition of technology and human capital in detriment to that of financial capital (Tortella, 2008). In short, all of these factors generated a gradual withdrawal of foreign capital from Spanish economic activity (Castro-Valdivia and Matés-Barco, 2020).

6.5 Foreign gas companies

The history of gas in Spain as an industrial activity began in 1842, when the Sociedad Catalana para el Alumbrado por Gas, directed by the Frenchman Charles Lebon, started to light the Ramblas de Barcelona. Foreign investment played a fundamental role in the beginnings and introduction of gas. In addition to Lebón y Compañía, British, Belgian, Dutch and Swiss capital also participated, although to a lesser extent. Of the 72.6 million pesetas that were invested in the Spanish gas industry in the second half of the nineteenth century, 82.6% was French (Costa, 1983).

The predominance of foreign capital was due to the fact that in the beginnings of the gas industry, there was little experience in how to finance sectors such as this one, which needed large amounts of capital. Back then, there was no banking system in the "modern" sense. On the contrary, in other European countries, mainly France and Great Britain, there were large amounts of accumulated capital waiting to be invested. Furthermore, there was also interest in these countries to favour the construction of the factories and supply of equipment (Fernández-Paradas, Martínez and Mirás, 2017; Fàbregas, 2017).

Charles Lebon participated with local partners in the expansion of gas in Spain after obtaining the concessions for gas public lighting in Barcelona (1842), Valencia (1843) and Cadiz (1845). Shortly afterwards, Lebon briefly abandoned Spain, mainly due to disagreements with his Spanish partners and to the change in the economic cycle in France caused by the crisis of 1848. However, on 23 March 1847, he created the Compagnie Centrale d'Éclairage par le Gaz, Lebon et Cie. in Paris, into which he incorporated gas factories in Spain. By the end of the nineteenth century it had eight gas factories in Almeria, Barcelona, Cadiz, Granada, Murcia, El Puerto de Santa María, Santander and Valencia (Fernández-Paradas, 2009).

In 1901, Spain had 79 gas factories and had produced 136,853,231.2 m^3.[2] Moreover, at that time there were eight foreign companies operating in the Spanish gas industry: Alumbrado, Calefacción y Fuerza Motriz de La Coruña y Vigo; Anglo-Spanish Gas Company; Compañía de Gas de Málaga; Gas

Franco-Belga Robert Lesage & Compagnie; Gaswerk Santa Cruz de Tenerife A.G.; Lebón y Compañía; Compañía del Gas de Zaragoza and The Huelva Gas Electricity Company Limited.[3]

On the other hand, the calculation of the 3rd Tariff of the *Contribución sobre las utilidades de la riqueza mobiliaria* obliged the Ministry of Finance to establish an "equity value" (capital) for each of the companies considered as foreign with the objective of calculating their taxation in Spain during the second decade of the twentieth century. These data were published in the *Gaceta de Madrid* between 15 December 1911 and 22 November 1924. With regard to the gas sector, seven foreign companies were identified, one less than at the beginning of the century. The French company Lebón y Compañía, leader of the sector, accounted for around 82% of the capital declared in the sector. This was followed in the ranking by Compañía de Gas de Málaga, also French, representing around 5%. The French company Compañía del Gas de Zaragoza was the next largest, accounting for 3% of total capital. The rest of the companies, ordered from the highest to lowest capitalisation were the French company Alumbrado, Calefacción y Fuerza Motriz de La Coruña y Vigo, the English company The Huelva Gas Electricity Company Limited, the German company Gaswerk Santa Cruz de Tenerife A. G. and the French company Gas Franco-Belga Robert Lesage & Compagnie. None of them exceeded one million pesetas of capital at the end of the period studied, except for the first, which declared 1,036,849.02 pesetas for the financial year 1918, the last available data for this company. Table 6.1 shows the evolution of the capitalisation of the foreign gas supplying companies for the second decade of the twentieth century. Next, we will analyse these companies in accordance with the year in which they finalised their activity.

The first foreign gas company that was liquidated in the twentieth century was Anglo-Spanish Gas Company, constituted in London in 1886 with a nominal capital of 200,000 pounds. This company had the objective of supplying gas to different Spanish cities, although it only obtained the concessions of Denia and Xátiva, both in 1887 (Martínez-López, 2017b, p. 82). In the company's extraordinary general shareholder's meeting of 30 December 1909 it was agreed to voluntarily wind down the company and in 1910, the factories of Denia and Xátiva were sold to the Spaniards Pablo Ballester and Ricardo Sanz, respectively (Martínez-López, 2017b; Martínez-López and Mirás, 2021; Vázquez-Fariñas et al., 2023).

The next company to cease operations in Spain was the British enterprise The Huelva Gas Electricity Company Limited, established in 1878 with a social capital of 25,000 pounds in Glasgow (Scotland). The contract of the public gas lighting concession was signed on 2 May 1877, and the factory began to operate in 1879 or 1880. On 17 November 1896, the company modified its statutes in order to be able to supply electricity and expand to other cities, although it did not obtain new concessions. The problems derived from the First World War led it to bankruptcy. The gas factory closed on 10 December 1917 and was sold two years later to Antonio Mora Claros

Table 6.1 Capitalisation values of the foreign gas companies in Spain between 1911 and 1920 (in pesetas)

	1911	*1912*	*1913*	*1914*	*1915*	*1916*	*1917*	*1918*	*1919*	*1920*
Sociedad alemana Gaswerk Santa Cruz de Tenerife A. G.	883.475,10	924.777,01	1.275.035,44	1.406.433,98	1.279.931,43	1.155.424,05	1.014.206,93	905.933,03	682.228,69	
Sociedad francesa Alumbrado, Calefacción y Fuerza Motriz de La Coruña y Vigo	2.989.021,37	3.277.425,57	3.472.947,73	3.661.217,55	3.328.232,39	3.234.693,49	3.025.544,41	1.036.849,02		
Sociedad francesa Compañía del Gas de Zaragoza	1.233.240,00	1.233.420,00	1.419.340,00	1.419.340,00	1.419.340,00	1.388.140,00	1.277.620,00	1.277.620,00	1.277.620,00	1.546.237,05
Sociedad francesa Compañía de Gas de Málaga	1.209.674,60	3.624.246,60	1.979.216,60	1.979.216,60	1.979.240,00	1.979.240,00	2.249.440,00	2.249.440,00	2.249.440,00	2.357.886,93
Sociedad francesa Gas Franco-Belga Robert Lesage & Compagnie	266.063,77	233.695,53	256.778,67	257.779,16	256.071,21	256.839,63	256.783,54		308.357,09	
Sociedad francesa Lebón y Compañía	35.159.563,00	36.178.360,66	31.351.639,22	38.708.553,63	40.314.021,63	32.722.041,60	32.163.894,74	30.992.205,80	30.678.961,66	29.857.091,68
Sociedad inglesa The Huelva Gas Electricity Company Limited	1.358.983,31	1.467.320,54	1.311.723,03	1.295.214,73	1.230.629,23	1.069.917,45	987.163,93			
TOTALES	43.100.021,15	46.939.245,91	41.066.680,69	48.727.755,65	49.807.465,89	41.806.296,22	40.974.653,55	36.462.047,85	35.196.607,44	33.761.215,66

Source: Own elaboration based on the data drawn from the 3rd Tariff of the *Contribución sobre las utilidades de la riqueza mobiliaria* published in the *Gaceta de Madrid* between 15 December 1911 and 22 November 1924.

(Martínez-López, 2017a; Martínez-López and Mirás, 2021; Vázquez-Fariñas et al., 2023). The capitalisation of this company in 1911 was 1,358,898.31 pesetas. In 1912 it reached its maximum value, 1,467,320.54 pesetas, and, from that moment and until the termination of its activity in 1917, the equity fell to 987,163.93 pesetas, representing a decapitalisation of over 30% in only five years.

The French company Alumbrado, Calefacción y Fuerza Motriz de La Coruña y Vigo sold its factories to Spanish entrepreneurs in 1918. It began its trajectory in 1853, when a French entrepreneur, Louis Laty, obtained the concession from the City Council of A Coruña to light the city with gas. The local government created the Sociedad para el Alumbrado de gas de la ciudad de A Coruña with this objective and began lighting the city in 1855. This company obtained the contract to light Vigo in 1883. The company was restructured and the Société Anonyme d'Éclairage, de Chauffage et de Force Motrice de La Corogne et Vigo was created. In 1894, the Société de Gaz et Eléctricité du Sudest, directed by Maurice Piaton, took control and direct the company until 1918, when the factory in A Coruña was sold to Fábricas Coruñesas de Gas y Electricidad and the one in Vigo to Electra Popular de Vigo y Redondela (Martínez-López, Mirás and Lindoso, 2009). The capitalisation of this company in 1911 was 2,989,021.37 pesetas and in 1914 it reached its maximum value of 3,661,217.55 pesetas. From that moment and until the termination of its activity in 1918, the equity fell to 1,036,849.02 pesetas, representing a decapitalisation of over 70% in only four years.

The next company to cease its activity in Spain was the French enterprise Gas Franco-Belga Robert Lesage & Compagnie, founded in Belgium in 1880 and which obtained the concession from the Town Council of Sanlúcar to light the streets with gas in 1882. This company lit the town from 1883 until 1917, finalising its activity on 30 October 1919, as the business of supplying private individuals was insufficient to maintain the factory open and the payment defaults by the local government of Sanlúcar rendered the business unviable. On 18 December 1926, a ruling of the Dispute Tribunal acknowledged the debt that the town had with the company which amounted to 203,811.63 pesetas (Bartolomé Rodríguez and Girón Sierra, 2018). The capitalisation of this company in the period was small, growing from 260,063.77 to 308,357.09 pesetas between 1911 and 1918.

The French company Lebón y Compañía was the undeniable leader of the sector in the period analysed. In 1911, its capital amounted to 35,159,563 pesetas and it ended the second decade of the twentieth century with an equity of 29,857,091.68 pesetas, the lowest value in the period studied. The company experienced a decapitalisation of 15% in this decade, although the evolution was uneven. Between the financial years 1911 and 1915, the capital of the company grew by around 15% and the firm reached its maximum value of capitalisation in 1915 with 40,314,021.63 pesetas. However, during these five financial years there were three differentiated periods. In the first, between 1911 and 1912, the capital grew at a moderate pace of 3% per year. Between 1912 and

1913, the company suffered a decapitalisation of 13%, while in the two-year period 1913–1915 it grew by around 28%, particularly in 1914, when it experienced a recapitalisation of 24% per annum. The entrenchment of the war and the progressive implementation of electric lighting in the cities, which was preferred over gas, affected this company and generated a change in the trend of its value. During the last five years of the period studied, 1916–1920, the decapitalisation was significant and the equity declared decreased by more than 10 million pesetas, representing a reduction of 26%. The first financial year, that of 1916, was the worst of all, with a loss of almost 8 million pesetas, almost 19%. In the following years, the company continued to decapitalise at an average annual rate of 2%. At the end of the war, the context for the French company was not favourable and it opted to relocate by selling its equity to other companies in the sector formed with Spanish capital. In 1921, it sold the gas and electricity factories in Almeria to Fuerzas Motrices del Valle del Lecrín and the electricity plant of Valencia to Electra Valenciana e Hidroeléctrica Española. In 1923, the rest of the company was acquired by the same banking group, led by Arnús-Garí, that had acquired Aguas de Barcelona in 1920. On 31 December 1923, this group founded the Compañía Española de Electricidad y Gas Lebón S. A. with the capital paid of 24 million pesetas in order to buy the gas factories of Granada, Malaga, El Puerto de Santa María and Valencia and the gas and electricity factories of Cadiz, Santander and Murcia (Fernández-Paradas, 2015).

The next company to be analysed is the Compañía de Gas de Málaga. On 4 September 1852, the City Council of Malaga granted Louis-Jean Gosse the exclusive privilege to supply gas to the city for thirty years, although subsequently it reduced the concession to twenty years and established the gas prices according to use, either public lighting or private consumption. This entrepreneur left for Paris in the same year and founded a company to manage his gas business: Gosse, Constant et Cie., which transferred the Malaga concession to a group of French businessmen on 12 July 1854. This group constituted the Société Civile pour l'Éclairage de Málaga in Lyon on 1 March 1859, with an initial capital of 1,200,000 francs (Arroyo, 2006). According to the statistics consulted for this study, the company was called Compañía de Gas de Málaga for the financial year 1911. In 1912, it appeared as Compañía de Alumbrado y Calefacción de Málaga. From 1913 to 1916, the name of the company was the same as that in 1911. Between 1917 and 1920, the company appeared under the name Compañía Lyonesa del Gas de Málaga. On the other hand, with respect to the evolution of its capital, at the beginning of the period studied, the company had a capital of 1,209,674.60 pesetas and ended the second decade of the twentieth century with an equity of 2,357,886.93 pesetas. The company increased its value by 95% in this decade, although the evolution was heterogeneous. For several years it declared the same equity: between 1913 and 1916 it declared a capital of 1,979,216.60 pesetas, and between 1918 and 1919 the value of the company was 2,249,440 pesetas. Therefore, the variations only affected four financial years. In 1912, the company published a capital of

3,624,246.60 pesetas, which was almost double that of 1911 and was the maximum value of capitalisation of the company during this period. In 1913, it suffered a capital reduction of around 45%. In 1917, its capital increased by 14% with respect to 1916. In the last year, 1920, it accumulated an annual increase of 5%. The political situation of Spain at the beginning of the second decade of the twentieth century and the poor business expectations led the French owners to sell the company. In November 1923, the company was sold for 1,040,000 pesetas to the bank Arnús-Garí, which subsequently incorporated it into the Compañía Española de Electricidad y Gas Lebón S. A. (Arroyo, 2006).

Meanwhile, the origin of the Compañía del Gas de Zaragoza dates back to October 1864 when Crédit Lyonnais established a gas factory in Zaragoza, which was acquired in 1870 by the Genin family from France, who founded the Société pour l´éclairage des villas de Biarritz et Saragosse in 1893. In the statistics consulted for this study, the company appeared with the original name from 1911 to 1913. From 1914 until the end of the period analysed, the company was given a Spanish name which was published as Compañía del Gas de Zaragoza. With respect to the evolution of its capital, this increased from 1,233,240 to 1.546.237.05 pesetas between 1911 and 1920. The company increased its value by 26% in this decade, although the evolution was not homogeneous. The data published show that the capital did not change in five periods: from 1911 to 1912, with 1,233,240 pesetas; from 1913 to 1915, with 1,419,340 pesetas and from 1917 to 1919, with 1,277,620 pesetas. There was decapitalisation in two periods: 1915–1916 and 1916–1917 with a variation rate of −2% and −8%, respectively. The company's capital increased by 15% in 1913 with respect to the previous year and by 21% in 1920 compared to 1919. This company was not unaffected by the historical context, and, in 1925, it restricted its activity to Zaragoza and became known as Société pour l´éclairage de Saragosse. However, this French company could not withstand the political pressure in favour of the nationalisation of the foreign companies, and in 1927 it was sold to Eléctricas Reunidas de Zaragoza, S.A., which created the Compañía del Gas de Zaragoza, S.A. on 27 December 1927 with a social capital of 2 million pesetas. It was incorporated into ENDESA Gas in 1997.

Finally, the German company Gaswerk Santa Cruz de Tenerife A.G. was the last foreign company in the gas sector. On 18 February 1906, the German entrepreneur Carl Francke requested the local council of Santa Cruz de Tenerife the concession for lighting the city with gas for a period of 75 years. The proposal was accepted in April of the same year, and in September, the company was constituted and its representative on the island was Jacob Ahlers. The service began a year later, at the end of 1907. Due to the impact of the First World War, the factory located in Llano de los Molinos had to close from the end of 1917 until March 1920, for 30 months, due to a shortage of coal. This situation led the owner to sell the company to the German-Swiss finance company Aktiengesellsllschatt für Gasunternehmungen in 1919. On 15 October 1931, the company's extraordinary general shareholders' meeting held in Zurich agreed for the liquidation of the gas factory in Santa Cruz de Tenerife, which was sold to Unión Eléctrica de Canarias S.A. (UNELCO) on 30 June 1932 (Matos, 2005). The capitalisation of this company in 1911 was 883,475.10 pesetas. In 1914, it reached its maximum value of 1,406,433.98 pesetas, and from this moment, its capital reduced for the rest of the period to 682,228.69 pesetas in 1919, representing a decapitalisation of around 23% in the second decade of the twentieth century.

6.6 Conclusions

The study of foreign investment in Spain, particularly in the gas industry, reveals interesting elements. The first is how important this sector was, with the installation of distribution networks. A second element of note was the public service nature of gas and its connection with the municipal domain. Finally, it was unique in that it provided a service under a monopoly regime.

However, in the interwar period of the twentieth century, different factors arose that limited the expansion of foreign capital. The first is related to the rupture of the traditional supply circuits of the material used, specifically the pipes of the supply networks manufactured in the countries of origin of the foreign companies. Second, the period between 1914 and 1922, the First World War and the subsequent economic crisis brought about financial alterations that gave rise to large capital reductions and the companies attempted to disengage themselves from these investments. In this situation it was logical that certain foreign companies sought to liquidate their shares as soon as possible and foreign capital was replaced by national capital. This is what happened in the Spanish gas industry. Furthermore, it experienced a process of business concentration, which was particularly relevant in the cases of the Compañía Española de Electricidad y Gas Lebón and Catalana de Gas y Electricidad, which bought small companies.

Notes

1 With respect to the company names, those most repeatedly mentioned in the *Gaceta de Madrid* between 1911 and 1924 have been used. These were the years when the value or capital used as the base for liquidating the contributions due from the foreign companies in accordance with the *Contribución sobre las utilidades de la riqueza mobiliaria (Contribution from real estate revenue and profits)* were published.
2 *Estadística del Impuesto sobre el consumo de luz de gas, electricidad y carburo de calcio. Año 1901*. Dirección General de Contribuciones, 1902, pp. 140–141.
3 *Estadística de la Contribución sobre las utilidades de la riqueza mobiliaria. Año 1901*. Dirección General de Contribuciones, 1903.

References

Arroyo Huguet, Mercedes. 2006. Actitudes empresariales y estructura industrial. El gas de Málaga, 1854-1929. *Scripta Nova. Revista electrónica de geografía y ciencias sociales* X (215): 1–35.

Bartolomé Rodríguez, Isabel, and Girón Sierra, Álvaro. 2018. ¿"Privilegio" o condena? La compañía de gas y el Ayuntamiento de Sanlúcar de Barrameda (1882-1919). *Revista de Historia Industrial* 71: 55–85.

Broder, Albert. 1976. Les investissements étrangers en Espagne au XIXe siècle: Méthodologie et Quantification. *Revue d'Histoire Economique et Sociale* 54 (1): 29–63.

Cameron, Rondo E. 1971. *Francia y el desarrollo económico de Europa, 1800-1914. Conquistas de la paz y semillas de guerra*. Madrid: Tecnos.

Castro Balaguer, Rafael. 2007. Historia de una reconversión silenciosa. El capital francés en España, c.1800-1936. *Revista de Historia Industrial* 33: 81–82.

Castro-Valdivia, Mariano, and Matés-Barco, Juan Manuel. 2020. Los servicios públicos y la inversión extranjera en España (1850-1936): las empresas de agua y gas. *Historia Unisinos* 24 (2): 221–239. https://doi.org/10.413/hist.2020.242.05

Costa Campí, María Teresa. 1983. *La financiación exterior del capitalismo español en el siglo XIX*. Barcelona: Universidad de Barcelona.

Dirección General de Contribuciones. 1902. *Estadística del impuesto sobre el consumo de luz de gas, electricidad y carburo de calcio. Año de 1901*. Madrid: Imprenta de la sucesora de M. Minuesa de los Ríos.

Dirección General de Contribuciones. 1903. *Estadística de la contribución sobre las utilidades de la riqueza mobiliaria. Año 1901*. Madrid: Imprenta de la sucesora de M. Minuesa de los Ríos.

Fàbregas Vidal, Pere-A. 2017. La estrategia de la implantación de la industria del gas en España (1826-2010). In *Globalización, nacionalización y liberalización de la industria del gas en la Europa latina (siglos XIX-XXI)*, edited by Isabel Bartolomé Rodríguez, Mercedes Fernández-Paradas, and Jesús Mirás Araujo, 21–44. Madrid: Marcial Pons.

Fernández-Paradas, Mercedes. 2009. Empresas y servicio público de alumbrado en España (1842-1935). *TST. Transportes, Servicios y Telecomunicaciones* 16: 108–131.

Fernández-Paradas, Mercedes. 2015. *La industria del gas en Cádiz (1845-2012)*. Sabadell: Lid Editorial / Fundación Gas Natural Fenosa.

Fernández-Paradas, Mercedes, Martínez López, Alberte, and Mirás Araujo, Jesús. 2017. Changes and Strategies of the Spanish gas companies in the long run. In: *Annual Congress of the European Business History Association, 21st, Vienna, 2017. Transformation in Business and Society: The Historical Approach.* Vienna: Institute for Economic and Social History, Vienna University of Economics and Business.

Landes, David. 1999. *La riqueza y la pobreza de las naciones: por qué algunas son tan ricas y otras son tan pobres*. Barcelona: Crítica.

Martínez-López, Alberte. 2017a. Transición energética y capital extranjero: Huelva, 1878-1919. In *Globalización, nacionalización y liberalización de la industria del gas en la Europa latina (siglos XIX-XXI)*, edited by Isabel Bartolomé Rodríguez, Mercedes Fernández-Paradas, and Jesús Mirás Araujo, 215–236. Madrid: Marcial Pons.

Martínez-López, Alberte. 2017b. La Anglo-Spanish Gas y su actuación en España, 1886-1910. *TST. Transportes, Servicios y Telecomunicaciones* 32: 78–100.

Martínez-López, Alberte, and Mirás-Araujo, Jesús. 2021. British investments in the gas industry in Spain: the role of the free-standing companies. In *Business History in Spain (19th and 20th centuries)*, edited by Mercedes Fernández-Paradas, and Carlos Larrinaga Rodríguez, 113–129. Berlin: Peter Lang. https://doi.org/10.3726/b17988

Martínez-López, Alberte, Mirás-Araujo, Jesús, and Lindoso Tato, Elvira. 2009. *La industria del gas en Galicia: del alumbrado por gas al siglo XXI, 1850-2005*. Barcelona: Lid Editorial / Fundación Gas Natural.

Matos, Rafael. 2005. L'industrie gazière à Tenerife (Canaries). Le rôle des capitaux allemands et helvétiques (1906-1933). In *L'industrie du gaz en Europe aux XIXe et XXe siècles. L'innovation entre marchés privés et collectivités publiques*, edited by Serge Paquier, and Jean-Pierre Williot, 373–379. Bruxelles: P.I.E.-Peter Lang.

Tascón Fernández, Luis Julio. 2008. Los últimos cien años de inversión extranjera en España. Volviendo la vista atrás… Europa. In *La inversión extranjera en España*, edited by Luis Julio Tascón Fernández, 11–30. Madrid: Minerva.

Tortella Casares, Teresa. 1997. Una guía de fuentes sobre las inversiones extranjeras en España entre 1780 y 1914. *Revista de Historia Económica - Journal of Iberian and Latin American Economic History* 15 (3): 607–623. https://doi.org/10.1017/S0212610900006728

Tortella, Gabriel. 2008. El capital extranjero en la formación del capitalismo español. In *La inversión extranjera en España*, edited by Luis Julio Tascón Fernández, 31–48. Madrid: Minerva.

Vázquez-Fariñas, María, Castro-Valdivia, Mariano, and Matés-Barco, Juan Manuel. 2023. The Internationalisation of the British Gas Industry in Latin Europe in the Nineteenth Century. In *The Gas Sector in Latin Europe's Industrial History. Lighting and Heating the World*, edited by Ana Cardoso de Matos, Alexandre Fernandez, and Antonio Jesús Pinto Tortosa, 13–24. Cham: Springer. https://doi.org/10.1007/978-3-031-36674-1_3

7 Pre-war and war energy market in Latin Europe

Gas and electricity in Spain and France in the 1930s*

Mercedes Fernández-Paradas, Carlos Larrinaga Rodríguez and Antonio Jesús Pinto Tortosa

7.1 Introduction

In the 1930s, Spain and France experienced an increase in gas and electricity consumption, in the middle of the global crisis that the Wall Street 1929 Crash and the subsequent Great Depression generated (Matés-Barco, 2023, pp. 1–37). As a result of the crisis, the political and social atmosphere in Europe turned more tense and complicated during the decade. For example, on 14 April 1931 the Spanish 2nd Republic was proclaimed, and in May 1936 the Popular Front won the elections in France. Such events talk about a convulse period in which the social divide, not only between the rich and the poor, but also between opposed ideologies, grew, too. Besides, on 18 July 1936 the Spanish Civil War exploded: the conflict would last until the 1 April 1939, when the triumph of the nationalist army inaugurated Franco's dictatorship. Only five months later, on 1 September 1939, Nazi troops occupied the Polish city of Gdansk, motivating France's war declaration against Germany, which in a few weeks unleashed the Second World War (1939–1945). The German army marched quickly towards France and occupied most of it. In June 1940 an armistice declared Germany's victory over the French, starting a four-year German domination over the country, either directly or indirectly.

We have chosen Spain and France as a case study for this research because they share a border, as well as a common cultural, political, and economic background, which goes back to the nineteenth century, but was especially strengthened during the First World War (1914–1918). In the nineteenth century, France was one of the major foreign investors in Spain's take-off, namely in the gas sector.[1] Considering their extension, both countries are similar, too: Spain covers an area of 505,9544 km^2, and France 552,000 km^2, not including colonial possessions at the time. Yet, there are relevant differences between them: firstly, in terms of population, in 1928 Spain had 22,977,000 inhabitants,

* We thank Jean-Pierre Williot for his help with French gas and electricity statistics in the period that we study in this chapter. This research is part of the results of the R+D+I Research Project "Gas in Latin Europe: A comparative and global perspective (1818–1945)", PID2020-112844GB-I00, financed by the Ministry of Science and Innovation of the Government of Spain and ERDF Funds.

DOI: 10.4324/9781003428695-7

whereas France's population was 1.8 times as higher, amounting 41,050,000 people. Therefore, population density was different in Spain and France: 45.4 inhabitants/km^2 in the former, and 74.4 inhabitants/km^2 in the latter. So were the figures of urban population, too: 4,664,617 Spaniards lived in cities (villages of over 10,000 inhabitants), which represented 20.3% (one fifth) of the country's population (INE, 1927–1928); and around 13,869,765 French were included under the title "urban population" in the 1920s, which represented 36% of the country's people, and escalated to over 40% in the 1930s (Chatel et al., 2017, pp. 1021–1040).[2] Likewise, French economy was much more powerful: in 1928, French Gross Domestic Product (GDP) grew up to 181,912 million Geary-Khamis 1990 dollars, whereas the Spanish GDP only amounted 59,371 million Geary-Khamis 1990 dollars (3.1 times lower than the French one). Raw domestic income per habitant also evidenced relevant differences: 4,432 Geary-Khamis 1990 dollars in France, and 2,584 Geary-Khamis dollars in Spain (1.7 times lower) (Maddison, 2003, pp. 38–68). The data provided are crucial to study network infrastructures, namely of gas and electricity, which are linked to population density and energy demand. That is how we can explain, for instance, a major progress of such infrastructures in France.

In this chapter, we study gas and electricity production and consumption in France and Spain, assuming a comparative scope, and including other Latin European countries in the research. Given the limitations imposed by a limited corpus of documentary sources, and considering the research topics that other scholars have previously covered, we will compare France and Spain to Portugal and Italy, in electricity production and consumption; and to the latter country, in the case of gas. Two main factors brought a turning point to competition between gas and electricity after the First World War: on the one hand, the building of waterfalls and long-distance transportation of electricity by companies; on the other hand, coal scarcity and increase in cost. Combined, they favoured the conquest of most lighting market by electricity. Gas companies tried to react by proposing new uses of this energy source, at home and in factories. Statistical studies used in the following pages start in 1928, with the aim of assessing the impact of the Great Depression on France's and Spain's energy market.

7.2 Electricity

Table 7.1 shows Spanish and French production of electricity between 1928 and 1940, distinguishing between hydraulic and thermic energy. In 1928, electricity production in France rose 12,976 million kWh, 4.8 times Spain's production (2,714 million kWh). Considering both countries' population, GDP and per capita income, which we have analysed in the previous section, Spain's production level was lower than expected. It is probably due to the remarkable fact that evolution of electricity production and consumption behaved differently from general national economic development (Table 7.3). Between 1929 and 1938, in Spain both indicators stayed over the 1928 figures, in an ever-growing trend that was only interrupted in 1935. The year 1931 registered the biggest

Table 7.1 Electricity production in Spain and France (1928–1940), expressed in million kWh (1928 represents 100%)

	Spain						*France*					
Year	*Hydraulic*		*Thermic*		***Total***		*Hydraulic*		*Thermic*		***Total***	
1928	2,428	100	285	100	**2,714**	**100**	5,598	100	7,378	100	**12,976**	**100**
1929	2,584	106	556	195	**3,140**	**116**	6,142	110	8,210	112	**14,352**	**111**
1930	2,884	119	270	95	**3,154**	**116**	6,876	123	8,463	115	**15,339**	**118**
1931	2,921	120	299	105	**3,221**	**119**	5,851	104	8,381	114	**14,232**	**110**
1932	2,920	120	315	110	**3,234**	**119**	5,884	105	7,708	105	**13,592**	**105**
1933	3,112	128	250	88	**3,362**	**124**	6,665	119	8,241	112	**14,906**	**115**
1934	3,296	136	263	92	**3,559**	**131**	7,195	128	7,977	109	**15,172**	**117**
1935	3,365	138	279	98	**3.365**	**124**	8,164	146	7,654	104	**15,818**	**122**
1936	3,366	138	279	98	**3,644**	**134**	8,836	158	7,823	108	**16,659**	**128**
1937	2,305	95	166	58	**2,645**	**97**	9,872	176	8,290	113	**18,162**	**140**
1938	2,236	93	512[a]	180	**2.749**	**101**	10,200	182	8,800	121	**19,000**	**146**
1939	2,844	117	267	94	**3,111**	**115**	12,174	217	9,800	133	**21,974**	**169**
1940	3,353	138	264	93	**3,617**	**133**	11,833	211	6,850	93	**18,683**	**144**

Source: in the Spanish case, Bartolomé Rodríguez (2007, p. 131) for the years 1928–1936, and the Ministerio de Industria y Comercio (1949) for 1937–1940. In France, Vidal Burdils (1946, p. 10) for 1928–1938, and in the figures provided by Williot for 1939–1940. The latter does not include data for the MosPielle, Haut-Rhin, and Bas-Rhin departments. Author-designed.

Note:
[a] The 1938 production figures in thermoelectricity seem anomalous. We have taken them from Vidal Burdils (1946) and the Ministerio de Industria y Comercio (1949). There is no way to explain such a relevant increase in production, compared to 1937.

downfall in industrial production of energy since 1929: 13.5%. Nevertheless, electricity production then was 19% higher than in 1928, and 2.6 times higher compared to the 1929 levels. GDP in 1931 was 93.9% of the one in 1929, a value that the country did not reach again until 1935 (Carreras and Tafunell, 2005, pp. 251–269; Martín Aceña, 2011, p. 61). In 1936, electricity production was 36% higher than in 1928. All in all, in the whole period only in 1937 was it 3% lower than in 1938; in fact, in 1939 and 1940 production surpassed again the 1928 levels. And during the Spanish Civil War, electricity production grew in both sides, though growth was more acute in the nationalist one (Fernández-Paradas and Rodríguez Martín, 2023, pp. 159–184).

French electricity production evolved in a very similar way: it stayed over the 1928 levels between 1929 and 1938. It lowered a bit in 1932, but it did not stop increasing ever since: in 1939 it was 69% higher than in 1928. In 1940 it decreased, showing figures that were slightly below the pre-war levels. As in Spain, too, electricity production data do not go hand in hand with France's general economic situation: GDP kept on decreasing until 1932, when it reached its lowest peak, 85.3% the GDP of 1929. The latter year's level was not reached by French economy until 1939 (Aldcroft, 2003, pp. 107–107).[3] Therefore, we can conclude that the evolution of the electric sector was more positive than the economic context in both countries, where departure electrification levels were low, so there was room for growth in the sector, even in the Great Depression context. We do not mean that the crisis had no impact in the energy market of both countries: a close analysis of the data provided shows how electricity production, for example, stayed stuck in Spain in 1929–1932, and in France in 1929–1933.

Hydroelectricity dominated the Spanish electric market:[4] it represented 89.5% of the overall electricity production in 1928, and it increased 38% in 1935. In 1937–1938 it dropped dramatically, staying 5%–7% under the 1928 level, but it grew again since the end of the Spanish Civil War in 1939, when it was 17% higher than in 1928. In 1940 it reached figures similar to 1935–1936. On the opposite side of the electric market, thermoelectricity always stayed under levels lower than the 1928 ones, with the exception of 1931–1932, and 1938. In 1940, hydroelectricity was even more relevant, taking 92.7% of the electric market, whereas thermoelectricity only represented 7.3%. The advance of hydroelectric plants, which overpassed the number of thermic plants, made it possible for the substitution of public gas lighting with public electric lighting. Among other reasons, higher coal prices and lower electricity prices favoured the trend (Otero Carvajal, 2020, pp. 10–11).

France counted on more hydrological resources than Spain, but two factors determined the lower impact of hydroelectricity in the electric market (43.1% of overall electric production): on the one hand, it had higher coal reserves than Spain; on the other hand, Spain's hillier landscape favoured the building of waterfalls (Espejo and García Marín, 2010, pp. 107–129).[5] Hydroelectricity always stayed over the 1928 figures, showing a trend to grow safe for the years 1931–1932, though even in this period levels stayed higher than four years before. Growth was more intense than in Spain: by 1938, it had increased 82%. Thermoelectricity played a more relevant role than in Spain, but it stayed behind hydroelectricity. It kept growing along the decade, too, and in 1938 its production was 21% higher than ten years before.

Table 7.2 shows how power capacity also increased, faster than electric production in both countries, which led to power overflow, with regard to existing demand. It might be possible to explain this because of the long-term investment cycle in the electric sector: years went by between the making of the decision to invest in a new plant, and the actual moment when the plant started to operate. In the period that we have chosen, investment characterised the late 1920s financial euphoria, but many plants did not start working until the first years of the Great Depression. In France, there is information until 1936, a year when power capacity was 60% higher than in 1928, whereas it was 53% higher in Spain. Operating hours stayed below the 1928, due to the aforementioned overflow, and to the economic recession, a context that did not favour energy consumption. The decay in the use of the plants was higher in France during the Depression, but it was also dramatic in Spain during the Civil War. The loss in generated electricity was relevant in both countries, though Spain's figures doubled those of France, which indicates poor efficiency in plants and networks.

Table 7.2 Power capacity and usage hours in Spain and France (1928–1940), expressed in million kWh (1928 represents 100%)

	Power capacity				*Usage hours*			
Year	*Spain*		*France*		*Spain*		*France*	
1928	1,020	100	6,980	100	2,400	100	1,912	100
1929	1,100	108	7,474	107	2,375	99	1,939	101
1930	1,200	118	7,920	113	2,330	97	1,645	86
1931	1,144	112	8,653	124	2,335	97	1,409	74
1932	1,256	123	9,643	138	2,240	93	1,495	78
1933	1,338	131	10,160	145	2,165	90	1,459	76
1934	1,353	133	10,420	149	2,240	93	1,459	76
1935	1,480	145	10,846	155	2,215	92	1,490	78
1936	1,565	153	11,200	160	1,789	74	-	-
1937	1,566	153	-	-	1,579	65	-	-
1938	1,568	153	-	-	1,755	73	-	-
1939	1,553	152	-	-	2,010	84	-	-
1940	1,554	152	-	-	2,325	97	-	-

Source: Vidal Burdils (1946, pp. 4, 21), for power capacity and usage hours. Author-designed.

Another element that helps explain the growth of electricity in France is the development of high power and low power transportation. The lower network grew from 2,800 in 1926, 4,000 km, in 1929, 5,200 in 1931, 7,400 in 1934 to 10,600 km in 1937. In this year, according to Vidal Burdils (1946, p. 27), French transportation network was the largest in the world. The French Ministry of Agriculture contributed to the process, financing new networks in the countryside (Sintes and Vidal Burdils, 1933, p. 699). Concerning high power wire, in 1933 France had more than 225,000 km; two years later,[6] Spain had around 33,000 km. At the same time that in Spain there was a majority of production-consumption point lines, "in France they had started to integrate charges, creating interconnection networks between different electric markets, which diversified the production forces, as well as potential consumers" (Bartolomé Rodríguez, 2005, 2007, pp. 25–26; Aubanell, 2019, p. 53).

Table 7.3 displays the evolution of electric consumption, which evolved in a very similar way to electric production: it increased along the decade, but became stuck, or even dropped, in the Great Depression and the Spanish Civil War, respectively. In the Spanish case, we count on consumption figures provided by Bartolomé Rodríguez (2007) for 1928–1936; for 1937–1940, we have deduced 21% losses from the data given by the Ministerio de Industria y Comercio (1949). In France, we have used the data included in Table 7.1, deducing 12.7% losses from them, for 1928–1938; for the years 1939–1940, we count on the figures of the Institut National de la Statistique et des Études Économiques (1966), from which we have deduced the same percentage. Consumption decayed in Spain in 1937–1938, in the middle of the Civil War, whereas in France it reached its highest peak in 1939–1940, though in 1940 production was a bit lower than in 1939.

Table 7.3 Electricity consumption in Spain and France (1928–1940), expressed in million kWh (1928 represents 100%)

	Spain		*France*	
Year				
1928	2,415	100	11,328	100
1929	2,433	101	12,529	111
1930	2,609	108	13,391	118
1931	2,681	111	12,424	110
1932	2,802	116	11,866	105
1933	2,953	122	13,013	115
1934	3,158	131	13,245	117
1935	3,402	141	13,809	122
1936	2,743	113	14,543	128
1937	1,953	81	15,855	140
1938	1,958	81	16,587	146
1939	2,458	102	19,467.9	172
1940	2,857	118	16,674.3	147

Source: Bartolomé Rodríguez (2007, p. 133), for electric consumption in Spain in 1928–1936; Ministerio de Industria y Comercio (1949) for 1937–1940; data included in Table 7.1. Author-designed.

We have studied several relevant indicators about electrification. For example, Table 7.4 shows the number of people with access to electricity: in early 1930s, 88% of Spanish people,[7] and 97.6% French people (close to British numbers in the latter case). Italy and Portugal were at an intermediate point,[8] with 93.4% and 90% people with access to electricity, respectively. Seeger (1936, p. 18) states that, in European context, the last two countries were among the ones with a higher electrification level; Switzerland and Denmark led the rank, with almost 100% of its population granted electricity access. At the end of the list were eastern European countries, namely Romania, with 21.7%, and Bulgaria, with 24.8%.

Per habitant and km^2 kWh production, expressed in millions, was 28,750 in France, and 4,3 times lower in Spain (6,845) (Vidal Burdils, 1946, p. 13). Therefore, electricity was indeed more spread in France than in Spain, in terms of population with access to it, and considering the extension of the network, too.

Table 7.5 displays per habitant production in 1928, 1935, and 1938: respectively, the year before the Wall Street Crack, the year prior to the start of the Spanish Civil War and the year before the beginning of the Second World War. The data included in it confirms the previous assumption. Besides, we add other Latin European countries, such as Italy and Portugal, as well as information from Sweden and Norway, the latter with higher production ratios. In 1928 France's per habitant production was 2.1 times higher than Spain's; Italian figures positioned between the two, but closer to France. Portugal had much lower ratios than Spain. In all the countries analysed, per habitant production grew significantly in 1935–1938, with the sole exception of Spain, due to the war context. For instance, France's production in 1938 was 43% higher than one decade before, and the gap between this country and Spain increased.

Table 7.4 People (%) with access to electricity, and with the chance to consume gas, too; percentage of gaslight and electricity points in European lighting, Madrid and Paris by early 1930s

Country	*People with access to electricity (%)*	*People with access to gas (%)*	*Gaslight points, related to total light points (%)*	*Electric light points, related to total light points (%)*
Germany	87.7	51.5	46.2	53.8
Austria	n.d.	40.4	27.5	72.5
Belgium	98.7	58.4	n.d.	n.d.
Bulgaria	24.8	n.d.	n.d.	n.d.
Czechoslovakia	72.0	18.2	n.d.	n.d.
Denmark	100	50.4	n.d.	n.d.
Spain	88.0	23.6	27.5	72.5
Estonia	27.3	n.d.	n.d.	n.d.
Finland	66.4	9.7	27.5	76.9
France	97.6	52.2	n.d.	n.d.
Great Britain	97.4	n.d.	n.d.	n.d.
England	n.d.	n.d.	54.0	46.0
Greece	n.d.	n.d.	n.d.	n.d.
Netherlands	96.3	69.0	12.0	88.0
Hungary	61.4	53.5	34.1	65.9
Ireland	29.0	n.d.	n.d.	n.d.
Italy	93.4	28.2	n.d.	n.d.
Lithuania	n.d.	n.d.	n.d.	n.d.
Luxembourg	90	n.d.	n.d.	n.d.
Norway	69.0	10.5	6.7	93.3
Poland	32.3	14.5	n.d.	n.d.
Portugal	90.0	n.d.	n.d.	n.d.
Romania	21.7	n.d.	n.d.	n.d.
Sweden	91.7	25.9	14.5	85.5
Switzerland	100	53.4	2.3	97.7
Madrid	n.d.	n.d.	81.1	18.9
Paris	n.d.	n.d.	67.7	32.3

Source: Seeger (1936, pp. 18, 25, 27); Union Internationale de l'Industrie du Gaz (1949). Author-designed. N.d.: no data.

Table 7.5 Per habitant electricity production in Spain, France, Italy, Portugal, Sweden and Norway, in 1928, 1935 and 1938, expressed in kWh (1928 represents 100%)

Country/ Year	*1928*		*1935*		*1938*	
Spain	118.1	100	137.0	116	108.7	92
France	316.1	100		119	452.8	143
Italy	261.7	100	n.d.		343.3	131
Portugal	31.5	100	n.d.		51.9	165
Sweden	758.0	100	n.d.		1,256.8	166
Norway	2,496.1	100	n.d.		3,154.2	126

Source: For Spain and France, Table 7.1. Population figures are included in Maddison (2003, pp. 38, 44). In the rest of the countries, but for 1935, Bartolomé Rodríguez (2007, p. 18). Author-designed.

In relation to GDP, kWh production shows big differences between countries. In 1928, Spain registered a 0.031 production and France 0.076 (more than twice the Spanish level). In 1937 production grew, up to 0.035 and 0.1111 respectively. Portugal and Spain had similar figures in those years, as happened to France and Italy (Bartolomé Rodríguez, 2007, p. 18).

Distribution of consumption is also relevant. In Spain, in 1936, 49.1% went to the industry; 23.8% to losses; 19.2% to lighting and domestic uses; and 7.9% to traction.[9] It is remarkable that electric light points represented 75.5% of all light points, so gaslight points were still used: Madrid had 81.8% of them (Table 7.4). In France, in 1937, 46.5% of electric production went to industrial driving force; 18.5% to electrochemistry and electrometallurgy; 12.7% to losses; 11.9% to lighting and domestic uses; 6.1% to electric traction; and 4.3% to small driving force (Vidal Burdils, 1946, p. 20; Bartolomé Rodríguez, 2007, p. 17). We need to emphasise the bigger industrial consumption in France, higher-level lighting and domestic use in Spain, and bigger losses in the latter, too. We can explain France's figure thanks to the combination of different factors: a bigger population, a more powerful economy, higher per capita income and a larger development of transportation network for electric fluid. Moreover, the industrial sector, stronger in France, was a major consumer of electricity.

7.3 Gas

Table 7.6 describes gas production in Spain and France between 1928 and 1940,[10] in order to compare the figures of both countries. Spain grew in a sustained way between 1928 and 1935: in the latter year gas production was 63%

Table 7.6 Gas production in Spain and France, expressed in thousands of m³ (1928–1940) (1928 corresponds to 100%)

Country/ Year	*Spain*		*France*	
1928	115,843	100	1,897,000	100
1929	127,488	110	1,996,000	105
1930	152,082	131	1,996,000	105
1931	163,255	141	2,023,000	106
1932	173,925	150	1,996,000	105
1933	179,218	151	2,007,000	105
1934	183,484	158	1,980,000	104
1935	189,047	163	1,754,211	92
1936	177,842	154	1,913,000	100
1937	135,381	117	1,914,000	100
1938	142,183	123	1,722,867	90
1939	168,196	145	1,532,753	80
1940	205,926	178	1,405,779	74

Source: For Spain, Fernández-Paradas and Larrinaga (2018, p. 32), for the years 1928–1934, and Fernández-Paradas (2019, p. 29), for 1936–1937. In the French case, data for 1935, and 1938–1940 can be found in Fernández-Paradas, Martínez-López, and Mirás-Araujo (2023); for the rest of the years included in the series figures provided by Williot. Author-designed.

higher than in 1928. It decreased since 1936, with ups and downs, but it always stayed way over the 1928 level. In 1939 it increased again, starting a trend that was confirmed in 1940, when production was 78% higher than in 1928, thus recovering and overpassing the pre-war figures. The 1936 downfall was due to the drop in production in the Republican side, especially in Catalonia and Madrid, the latter being the main gas-producing centre in the country. Moreover, problems in coal supply, together with the dismantling of the board of many companies, contributed to the negative context. The split of the companies' actives was also more harmful for the interest of the Republican side (Fernández-Paradas, 2019, pp. 25–50; Fernández-Paradas and Rodríguez Martín, 2023, pp. 159–184). In France, though bigger coal reserves made it possible for gas production to reach much higher levels than in Spain (more than ten times), it experienced a discrete growth until 1932, when it dropped (from 106% to 105%, with regard to 1928), probably as a consequence of the economic recession provoked by the Great Depression, as well as the advance of electricity. In 1933 it recovered slightly, but it stayed only 5% higher than in 1928, the same proportion as the previous year. Since then, the drop accelerated, and in 1940 gas production was on 74% of the one reached in 1928. In only five years, between 1935 and 1940, it had decreased 19.9%.

Table 7.7 reports gas consumption in Spain and France between 1928 and 1940. Taking 1928 as a reference, consumption only dropped in both countries in war context: in 1937 and 1938 in Spain, and in 1939–1940 in France. In this field, the Spanish gas sector grew continuously and significantly until 1935, but for 1934, in which growth was only 3%. The year 1936 marked a turning point, when the trend reverted, with special attention to 1937, when it dropped 47%.

Table 7.7 Gas consumption in Spain and France (1928–1940), in thousand m³ (1928 represents 100%)

Year/Country	*Spain*		*France*	
1928	90,820	100	1,722,465	100
1929	99,950	110	1,865,465	108
1930	118,767	130	1,865,225	108
1931	127,496	140	1,890,438	110
1932	137,312	151	1,865,604	108
1933	143,701	158	1,875,427	109
1934	146,387	161	1,850,443	107
1935	153,033	168	1,801,887	105
1936	144,146	158	1,788,313	104
1937	101,607	111	1,789,176	104
1938	108,903	119	1,769,691	103
1939	132,549	145	1,574,410	91
1940	171,018	188	1,443,985	84

Source: For Spain, 1928–1929, Fernández-Paradas and Larrinaga (2018, p. 32). For the rest of the years, and for the French case, Union Internationale de l'Industrie du Gaz (1949). Author-designed.

In France, though gas consumption always stayed over the 1928 level until 1940, growth pace was slower than in Spain, but in 1937–1938, when Spain levels dropped dramatically, as previously stated. The year 1940 marked the highest peak in gas consumption in Spain: 48% higher than in 1928; in France, it was the year 1931, when consumption was 10% higher than in 1928.

It is relevant to highlight the meaningful contrast between the accelerated growth in gas consumption in Spain in the said period, and its slower rhythm in French territory, where increase was almost non-existent. Among other reasons, one might mention the different departure point of the two countries in gas production: whereas French gas sector was already consolidated, Spanish take-off in the field came later, so in the 1920s and 1930s there was still room for improvement and growth.

With regard to the uses of gas, by 1930 in Spain most of it (77.6%) was consumed at home, followed by public lighting (19.1%), and industries (3.3%).[11] The situation had not changed in 1935: 79.9% was consumed at home, 16.8% in public lighting, and 3.3% in industries; figures for 1937 were 86.40%, 7.90%, and 5.7%, respectively (Union Internationale de l'Industrie du Gaz, 1949). In France, in 1938 distribution of uses differed from the Spanish case: 53% at home, 36.7% in industries, 7.45% for commercial uses and 2.8% for public lighting (Institut National de la Statistique et des Études Économiques, 1966). As we can see, domestic use was much higher than industrial use in Spain, and public gas lighting still resisted in the 1930s. In contrast, French public gas lighting was half the Spanish; it devoted most gas produced to domestic uses, too, but in a much lower percentage than in Spain. All in all, France showed a more diversified use of gas, which explains its broader diffusion in the country, given a bigger demand by factories, main gas consumers. A late development of the Spanish gas sector, together with a later industrial take-off, explains lower consumer rates here, and a bigger advance of the new energy source: electricity.

Industrial uses of gas started in France in 1818, and in 1842 in Spain: a reason why French gas sector was one of the most powerful ones in Europe. French companies, engineers and investors arrived in Mediterranean countries, playing a crucial role in the sector's take-off in them. This is one of the reasons why electricity found so much resistance by gas companies in France, no matter how small the village in which they operated, but in Spain it found an open market of opportunities, but for medium- and large-size cities, where gas companies operated in monopolistic conditions.[12] However, at the beginning of the twentieth century, there were around 1,000 gas factories in France, and only 81 in Spain (Sudrià, 1983, pp. 97–118).

Table 7.8 depicts gas diffusion in Spain and France in 1937. French subscribers amounted to 4,833,275, and the Spanish ones to only 378,973 (12,7 times below). Given the different dimension of both markets, France was one of the European countries where most people had access to gas supply: half its population were subscribers. The lead in the rank corresponded to the Netherlands, with 69% of its inhabitants subscribed to gas supply. The Spanish

Table 7.8 Indicators of gas diffusion in Spain and France in 1937

Indicator/Country	*Spain*	*France*
Population	25,043,000	41,930,000
Inhabitants in supplied areas	5,923,822	22,025,336
% inhabitants with gas access	23.6	52.2
Inhabitants per km^2	49	76
Subscribers	378,973	4,833,275
Subscribers per km^2	0.7	9.0
Pipeline extension	2,426	41,979[a]
Pipeline km per km^2	0.0048	0.0760
Gas consumption	101,607	1,789,176
Gas consumption per capita, m^3	4	42
Gas consumption per subscriber, m^3	268	370
Gas consumption per capita in supplied areas, m^3	17	81

Source: Union Internationale de l'Industrie du Gaz (1949).
Note:
[a] The figure refers to 1947.

percentage, 23.6%, was similar to the Italian (28.2%) and the Swedish (25.9%). All of them were higher in the rank than northern European nations (Finland, 9.7%; Norway, 10.5%) or central-eastern European countries (Poland, 14.5%; Czechoslovakia, 18.2%).

Concerning the extension of gas pipelines, and their density per km^2, in 1940 France counted on 38,000 kilometres, including distribution and transportation networks (the 1937 data is missing). In 1937, Spain had 2,246 kilometres of pipelines built, 15.7 times below the French one. Consequently, France had more pipeline km per km^2, 0.0760, whereas Spain was way further: 0.0050. If we consider the data, together with the surface area of each country, we will understand the higher figures of subscribers per km^2 in France, compared to Spain: 9 and 0.7, respectively (12.8 times lower in the Spanish case).

Gas consumption levels per capita are also relevant: 42 m^3 in France, more than ten times higher than in Spain (4). Differences persist in the analysis of gas per capita consumption in areas with gas supply: 81 m^3 per capita in France, and 17 m^3 per capita in Spain. Nevertheless, gas consumption per subscriber is not that different: 370 m^3 per capita in France and 268 m^3 per capita in Spain. Hence, we can conclude that differences in gas consumption between both countries were caused by the diffusion of pipeline networks in the territory, and by social penetration of that energy source.

7.4 Conclusions

Though France and Spain covered an area of similar extension, there were not that many similarities between them, in terms of energy (electricity and gas) consumption. In fact, the only common feature between them is that energy consumption grew in both territories, despite the negative context provoked by the Wall Street Crack and the Great Recession. Such behaviour emphasises that the energy market evolved independently from global economic context. In contrast, there were two main differences between the Spanish and the French case: firstly, the Spanish Civil War had a deeper negative impact on electricity and gas consumption in the country. Secondly, the Spanish gas sector experienced a 48-year delay compared to the French, which not only conditioned the late evolution of the Spanish market, but also an insurmountable breach between the latter and the French market. Consequently, when electricity appeared in France, the gas sector was already powerful and consolidated, whereas in Spain it still operated within certain limits.

Thirdly, the last assertion cannot make us deduce that there is a correlation between development level of the gas industry and evolution of electricity. Considering the previously described characteristics of the Spanish gas market, one might think that electricity found it difficult to progress in France, given the resistance by the gas companies, and that Spain was "garden of Eden" ready for the success of electricity. However, things did not work that way: Spanish people with access to electricity were always below the French levels (88% vs. 97.6%, respectively), as were per capita production levels (137 kWh vs. 377.1 kWh). Therefore, dissimilarities between the two cases of study were due to other factors, namely consumption patterns, and diffusion of distribution and transportation networks. With regard to the former, in France most energy (gas and electricity) was consumed in factories, major energy consumers, and at home; in Spain, industrial uses of energy showed lower values. Concerning the latter, the gas and electricity networks were far more extended in France than in Spain, as a consequence of the configuration of a much more integrated French market.

Notes

1 Due to Spanish protectionism since the early twentieth century, French investors left the country gradually. The tendency accelerated as a consequence of British and French capital repatriation during the Great War and after it, as well as of the strong economic nationalism that Miguel Primo de Rivera's dictatorship exercised between September 1923 and January 1930 (Castro-Valdivia et al., 2019, pp. 51–74).
2 To know more about French urban demography and its evolution in the historical period that we study, see Pinol (1996, pp. 11–12).
3 In order to study French economy in the 1930s, see Borne and Dubief (1989, pp. 20–33), and Berstein (1993, pp. 25–51).
4 Hydroelectricity estimates can be seen in Maluquer de Motes (1987, p. 58). According to him, by 1930 it represented 23% of the overall Spanish electric sector.
5 Despite the lesser capacity of French hydroelectricity compared to Spain, France's hydroelectric production was one of the highest in world terms: it was the first in 1914. (Bairoch and Toutain, 1991, p. 22). For further details about hydroelectricity and thermoelectricity in the period that we study, see Morsel (1987, p. 102) and Barjot (1991, pp. 22–23).

6 To know more about electricity transportation and network connections in France, see Boune (1994, pp. 777–852).
7 In 1934, 5,086 Spanish villages had electricity, and only 48 had still gas energy supply (Martínez-López and Mirás, 2018, p. 91).
8 In 1937, Lisbon and Porto together accounted for 30% of Portuguese electric consumption, and 26% of the country's overall population in 1940 (Bartolomé Rodríguez, 2021, p. 68).
9 For a further analysis on electricity and gas consumption for lighting in Spain between 1926 and 1934, see Martínez-López and Mirás (2018, p. 93).
10 To study gas consumption in Spain between 1842 and 1935, see Fernández-Paradas (2009, pp. 108–131). For France, between 1840 and 1930, see Williot and Paquier (2005).
11 See Martínez-López and Mirás (2018, p. 97).
12 To study the advance of gas and electricity in Spain between the 1900s and the 1930s, considering the population of the villages, see Martínez-López and Mirás (2018, pp. 87–111).

References

Aldcroft, Derek H. 2003. *Historia de la economía europea 1914–2000*. Barcelona: Crítica.

Aubanell Jubany, Anna Maria. 2019. La industria eléctrica durante la Guerra Civil. In *El impacto de la Guerra Civil española en el sector terciario*, edited by Mercedes Fernández-Paradas, and Carlos Larrinaga, 51–76. Granada: Comares.

Bairoch, Paul, and Toutain, Jean-Claude 1991. *World Energy Production 1800–1985. Production mondiale d'énergie*. Paris: Centre National de la Recherche Scientifique.

Barjot, Dominique (1991). *L'énergie aux XIXe-XXe siècles*. volume 2. Paris: Presses de l'École Normale Supérieure.

Bartolomé Rodríguez, Isabel. 2005. La red nacional y la integración de los mercados eléctricos españoles durante los años de entreguerras. ¿Otra oportunidad perdida? *Revista de Historia Económica* 2: 269–297.

Bartolomé Rodríguez, Isabel. 2007. *La industria eléctrica en España (1890–1936)*. Madrid: Banco de España.

Bartolomé Rodríguez, Isabel. 2021. Tan solo algunos distritos iluminados. El espejismo de la electrificación portuguesa hasta 1944. *Ayer* 122: 67–97.

Berstein, Serge 1993. *La France des années 30*. Paris: Armand Colin.

Borne, Dominique, and Dubief, Henri. 1989. *La crise des années 30. 1929–1938*. Paris: Éditions du Seuil.

Boune, Charles. 1994. Le transport d'energie et l'interconnexion. In *Histoire de l'électricité en France, Tome deuxième. L'interconnexion et le marché, 1919–1946*, directed by Maurice Lévy-Leboyer and Henri Morsel, 777–902. Paris: Fayard.

Carreras, Albert, and Tafunell, Xavier. 2005. *Historia Económica de la España Contemporánea*. Barcelona: Crítica.

Castro-Valdivia, Mariano, Fernández-Paradas, Mercedes, and Matés-Barco, Juan M. 2019. Las empresas extranjeras de agua y gas en España (circa 1900–1923). In *Los servicios públicos en España y México (siglos XIX-XXI)*, edited by Juan M. Matés-Barco, and Alicia Torres Rodríguez, 51–74. Madrid: Sílex.

Chatel, Cathy, Morillas-Torné, Mateu, Esteve, Albert, and Martí-Henneberg, Jordi. 2017. Patterns of Population and Urban Growth in Southwest Europe: 1920–2010. *Journal of Urban History* 43 (6): 1021–1040.

Espejo Marín, Cayetano, and García Marín, Ramón. 2010. Agua y energía: producción hidroeléctrica en España. *Investigaciones geográficas* 51: 107–129.

Fernández-Paradas, Mercedes. 2009. Empresas y servicio de alumbrado público por gas en España (1842–1935). *TST. Transportes, Servicios y Telecomunicaciones* 16: 108–131.

Fernández-Paradas, Mercedes. 2019. El sector del gas en la Guerra Civil. In *El impacto de la Guerra Civil española en el sector terciario*, edited by Mercedes Fernández-Paradas, and Carlos Larrinaga, 25–50. Granada: Comares.

Fernández-Paradas, Mercedes, and Larrinaga Rodríguez, Carlos. 2018. L'industrie du gaz en Espagne dans le période de l'entre-deux-guerres. *Histoire Économie & Société* 3: 30–46.

Fernández-Paradas, Mercedes, and Rodríguez Martín, Nuria. 2023. The gas industry in Madrid during the Civil War (1936–1939). In *The Gas Sector in Latin Europe. Economic Development During the 19th and 20th centuries*, edited by Jesús Mirás-Araujo, and Andrea Giuntini, 159–184. Cham: Palgrave Macmillan.

Fernández-Paradas, Mercedes, Martínez-López, Alberte, and Mirás-Araujo, Jesús. 2023. The Impact of World War II on Gas Production in Latin Europe. In *The Gas Sector in Latin Europe's Industrial History*, edited by Ana Cardoso de Matos, Alexandre Fernández, and Antonio Jesús Pinto Tortosa, 147–174. Berlin: Springer.

Institut National de la Statistique et des Études Économiques. 1966. *Annuaire Statistique de la France. Résumen Rétrospectif*. Paris.

Instituto Nacional de Estadística. 1927–1928. Padrón Municipal. https://www.ine.es/inebaseweb/pdfDispacher.do?td=82148&ext=.pdf (accessed July 12, 2023).

Maddison, Angus. 2003. *The World Economy: Historical Statistics*. Berlin, Mexico, Tokyo, and Washington: OECD Publishing.

Maluquer de Motes, Jordi. 1987. L'électricité, facteur de développement économique en Espagne: 1900–1936. In *Un siècle d'électricité dans le monde, 1880–1980*, edited by Fabienne Cardot, 57–67. Paris: Association pour l'histoire de l'électricité en France.

Martín Aceña, Pablo. 2011. *Pasado y Presente: de la Gran Depresión del siglo XX a la Gran Recesión del siglo XX*. Bilbao: Fundación BBVA.

Martínez-López, Alberte, and Mirás-Araujo, Jesús. 2018. Difusión y consumo de gas y electricidad para el alumbrado en las urbes españolas durante la segunda transición energética (1901–1934). *Revista de Historia Industrial* 71: 87–111.

Matés-Barco, Juan M. 2023. The Great Depression of 1929. In *The Age of Global Economic Crises (1929–2022)*, edited by Juan M. Matés-Barco, and María Vázquez-Fariñas, 1–37. London and New York: Routledge.

Ministerio de Industria y Comercio. 1949. *Electricidad. Datos y previsiones*. Madrid.

Morsel, Henri. 1987. Panorame de l'histoire de l'électricité en France dans la première moitié du XXe siècle. In *Un siècle d'électricité dans le monde*, 85–117. Paris: Association pour l'histoire de l'électricité en France.

Otero Carvajal, Luis Enrique. 2020. Introducción. Los cimientos de la modernidad: las infraestructuras que impulsaron la ciudad moderna. In *Las infraestructuras en la construcción de la ciudad moderna. España y México, 1850–1936*, edited by Luis Enrique Otero Carvajal, 9–17. Madrid: Catarata.

Pinol, Jean-Luc. 1996. Un sistema urbano con veinticinco siglos de historia. In *Atlas Histórico de ciudades europeas Francia*, edited by Manuel Guàrdia, Francisco Javier Monclús, and José Luis Oyón, 1–24. Barcelona: Salvat.

Seeger, Bruno. 1936. *El consumo de energía eléctrica para alumbrado en Europa*. Madrid: Gráf. Administrativa.

Sintes Olives, Francisco Faustino, and Vidal Burdils, Francisco. 1933. *La industria eléctrica en España. Estudio económico-legal de la producción y consumo de electricidad y material eléctrico*. Barcelona: Montaner y Simon S.A.

Sudrià, Carles. 1983. Notas sobre la implantación y el desarrollo de la industria del gas en España, 1840–1901. *Revista de Historia Económica* 2: 97–118.

Union Internationale de l'Industrie du Gaz. 1949. *Les Statistiques Européennes de l'industrie du Gaz*. Union Internationale de l'Industrie du Gaz: London.
Vidal Burdils, Francisco. 1946. *Estado comparativo de las industrias francesa y española de producción y distribución de energía eléctrica*. Barcelona: Industrias Gráficas Seix y Barral Hermanos S. A.
Williot, Jean-Pierre, and Paquier, Serge. 2005. Stratégies entrepreneuriales et évolution des marches des années 1840 aux années 1930. In *L'industrie du gaz en Europe aux XIXe et XXe siècles*, 53–64. Bruxelles: Peter Lang.

8 How did the Second World War affect gas consumption in Western Europe?*

Mercedes Fernández-Paradas, Alberte Martínez-López and Jesús Mirás-Araujo

8.1 Introduction

Every war gives rise to disruption (also an opportunity) in industrial activity. For networked industries, an armed conflict generally generates critical difficulties, especially in the contending nations, although non-combatant countries also face considerable turmoil. This was the case in Europe during WWI and during the period under study, WWII, when many problems occurred simultaneously. On the production side, the following stands out. First, in countries at war, such as the United Kingdom, France and Italy, facilities were damaged by attacks. Moreover, the geographical evolution of the conflict, distorted the organisation of transport and communications and the movement of goods and people and the mobilisation of workers to the front, particularly skilled staff, generated serious perturbations. Finally, both in Europe at war and in the rest of the continent, the conflict severely disrupted the supply of the main raw material for the production of gas, coal, as well as that of other materials and equipment. The prices of all of these elements increased dramatically as a result of the scarcity and the direct impact on transportation systems.[1]

The chapter analyses the impact that the Second World War had on gas consumption in several Western European countries, specifically the two leaders of the gas industry (France and the United Kingdom) and Mediterranean countries such as Italy, Spain and Portugal. The hypothesis to be tested is that this impact was highly conditioned by two variables. First, the development of the industry prior to the war, that is, the different levels of territorial, sectoral and social penetration of the gas industry in those countries, which were highly dependent on their long-term trajectory, degree of industrialisation, per capita income and coal availability. Second, their position in the conflict as warring or

* This research forms part of the results of the R+D+I Research Project "Gas in Latin Europe: A comparative and global perspective (1818-1945)", PID2020-112844GB-I00, financed by the Ministry of Science and Innovation of the Government of Spain and ERDF Funds. Likewise, it has benefitted from the research stay that was carried out in 2015 by Mercedes Fernández-Paradas at the Centre for Contemporary Spanish Studies, European Institute, London School of Economics and Political Science, devoted to "The gas industry in Great Britain and Spain: historiography and sources (circa 1800-1950)".

DOI: 10.4324/9781003428695-8

neutral countries. The text is based on the current literature, statistics, business documentation and the leading journal for the sector in continental Europe, the *Journal des usines à gaz*.

8.2 Gas consumption: A general approach

The levels and the chronological dynamic of gas consumption in Latin Europe and the United Kingdom displayed important differences between countries, which were mainly influenced by their income levels, accessibility to coal and their involvement in the war. According to the data, on the whole, a clear contrast can be seen between the nations that had historically been leaders in the gas industry (the United Kingdom and France) and the Mediterranean countries. Within the latter, in turn, a descending tendency can be observed, from Italy to Portugal, which was underscored by their degree of economic and industrial development and urbanisation level, since access to gas continued to be limited to urban centres in those countries. These contrasts dated back a long way, as they were evident when the sector formed in the nineteenth century (Williams, 1981; Paquier and Williot, 2005).

Total gas consumption in the period 1935–1947 (Table 8.1) displayed enormous differences between the United Kingdom, with an annual average of about 10 billion m^3, France 1.9 billion, Italy 0.6 billion, Spain 0.15 billion, and Portugal (Lisbon) 0.02 billion. These differences were caused, as we will see, by the population with access to gas and by consumption per head. Chronologically, the evolution was largely marked by the differential impact of the war in the different countries on variables such as the availability of coal, the destruction of gas factories and facilities, the differential structure of energy prices and the level and income distribution.

Table 8.1 Gas consumption in Spain, France, Italy, Portugal and the United Kingdom, in thousands m^3 (1935–1947)

Year/ countries	*Spain*	*France*	*Italy*	*Portugal (Lisbon)*	*United Kingdom*
1935	153,033	1,801,887	536,616	9,346	8,372,753
1938	108,904	1,769,691	605,706	11,155	9,155,034
1939	132,549	1,574,410	609,381	11,406	9,094,148
1940	171,018	1,443,985	666,784	12,444	8,845,646
1941	95,957	1,845,735	806,096	13,940	9,303,851
1942	122,257	2,024,297	800,214	15,371	10,143,257
1943	157,802	2,064,426	539,069	15,783	10,262,372
1944	165,199	1,563,569	466,230	21,985	10,736,982
1945	165,252	1,989,047	260,065	24,187	11,045,247
1946	164,111	2,516,923	515,753	25,689	12,155,812
1947	176,118	2,645,700	757,652	29,249	12,624,234

Source: Companhias Reunidas Gás e Electricidade (1936 and 1939–1948), Sindicato Vertical de Agua, Gas y Electricidad (1948), Union Internationale de l'Industrie du Gaz (1949), Associazione Nazionale Industriali Gas (1950). Author's elaboration.

In Spain, consumption, which was initially already low, fell by almost 30% during the Civil War (1936–1939), and its quality deteriorated (Fernández-Paradas and Martykánová, 2019, pp. 38–39). The downturn continued throughout the early years of the Second World War, due to the destruction of facilities and the difficulty of importing British coal. Later, the figures gradually recovered, but barely exceeded those of 1935 due to Franco's autarkic policy (Fernández-Paradas and Martykánová, 2017).

In France, consumption had already stagnated in the pre-war years, perhaps due to the 1930s depression and also to competition from electricity and continued to fall at the beginning of the war as a result of the German occupation. Restrictive measures on gas consumption were introduced in 1940 in Paris and were extended during the following year.[2] However, despite the restrictions on consumption, it increased strongly between 1941 and 1943, exceeding pre-war figures.[3] In 1944 a significant contraction took place, when the conflict in the northern coal zone intensified (Mackowiak, 2006). In the post-war period, consumption finally recovered vigorously.

In Italy, during the war period, 1939–1945, the share of fossil fuels (coal, gas and oil) in total energy consumption fell drastically, from 47% to 18.4%, while wood increased from 17.2% to 32.6% (Malanima, 2006, p. 97). This country behaved quite similarly to France, although with a higher growth rate until 1943, when the Allied forces landed, causing a severe drop in consumption, which recovered after the war, although without exceeding the previous maximum figures. At the beginning of the war, the gas was distributed for only four hours a day, and later at a very low pressure. Subsequently, the distribution hours were extended.

In Portugal in the 1930s there was a dual urban energy model, led by the cities of Lisbon and Porto. In both of these cities, electricity had replaced gas in public lighting. However, the capital city finally became a unique case in the country, maintaining a strong presence of gas for other domestic uses, due to the more favourable prices compared to electricity. In Porto, on the other hand, lower electricity prices progressively reduced gas consumption until it ultimately disappeared during the war, which accentuated previous trends (Bussola, 2005, p. 60).

The government decision to maintain gas prices in Lisbon and the decreasing electricity tariffs in the cities of the centre and the north, together with the scarcity of traditional fuels such as coal and firewood, stimulated their substitution during the war in private urban homes, particularly for cooking and heating water. This new pattern of modern energy consumption consolidated after the war (Madureira, 2005, pp. 137–138).

Prices in Lisbon of both gas and electricity, remained stable between 1930 and 1942. Domestic and commercial consumption was also stable, except in the case of gas, which began to grow significantly from 1939. In the period 1943–1945, gas prices, which were subject to ministerial authorisation, almost doubled, which did not prevent its consumption from tripling with respect to 1939.[4] This was triggered, in part, by a substitution effect, since electricity consumption (lighting) fell by almost half in those years while its price almost doubled, and by the restrictions on electricity consumption, which were imposed between 1942 and 1947. This also suggests a higher price elasticity of electricity compared to gas in this usage, since in the other uses electricity consumption also increased greatly.[5] At the end of the war, the situation returned to normal, as both tariffs fell somewhat and electricity consumption partially recovered, while gas consumption resumed its previous upward trend.

In short, the pre-war pattern of domestic energy consumption, which displayed a tendency towards the progressive substitution of gas by electricity, was temporarily altered during the war. This was the result of the state promotion of gas, using the stagnation of the tariffs as the main tool, allowing gas to resist. Nonetheless, after the war the previous dynamic was resumed, albeit slowly (Bussola, 2005, pp. 68–73).

The United Kingdom was affected in the hardest early moments of the war, although to a small extent. But as early as 1941, pre-war figures were exceeded, and grew progressively but incessantly from that moment on.

The year in which consumption fell the most during the war varied from country to country, depending on when the conflict had the greatest impact. In France and the United Kingdom, it was in 1940, the year of the German occupation of France and the intense German bombing of British cities. In Spain it occurred in 1941, due to the sharp drop in imports of British coal. In Italy it was 1945, when the Allied occupation was at its peak. Consumption in Lisbon, an atypical case, was seemingly not greatly affected by the war due to the aforementioned specific circumstances of its energy market.

Regarding the intensity of the impact of the war on consumption, measured by the percentage drop in consumption between 1938 (1935 for Spain, the year before the start of its Civil War) and the year of lowest consumption, significant differences can be observed. Apart from the exceptional case of Lisbon, where consumption even increased by 2%, the least affected country was the United Kingdom, with a reduction of 3%, probably due to its coal self-sufficiency and the lesser physical impact of the war on its gas infrastructure. In France, the fall was more remarkable, 18%, and was caused by the greater incidence of the war in its northern coal regions. In Spain, the decrease was high, 37%, due to the concatenation of the Civil War, the world war and the autarkic policy of the government, and its traditional dependence on British coal. The most affected country, by far, was Italy, where consumption dropped by half as a result of the war destruction, the disruption of supply and the dependence on foreign coal.

In comparative terms, consumption increased in Spain by only 15% in the period as a whole, compared to 41% in Italy, 47% in France, 51% in the United Kingdom and 213% in Lisbon.

With respect to consumption levels, it is necessary to contemplate both quantitative (m^3 of gas consumed) and qualitative aspects (gas quality, measured in calories per m^3, that was served to the population). In this sense, the scarcity of soft coal – with the exception of the United Kingdom – during the war forced the use of other fuels (lower quality coal, wood, various by-products) which resulted in a progressive and significant loss of the calorific value of the gas produced in these countries. The only exception was probably the United Kingdom, a large producer of soft coal, whose production was not unduly affected by the conflict. On the contrary, in France the quality of the output dropped significantly, from 4,700 calories per m^3 in 1939 to 3,500 in 1943, that is, a reduction of 25.5%. In Italy, which already had lower levels of calorific power, it dropped gradually from the start of the war, being more noticeable in 1941 and 1942, probably due to the interruption of the British supply. It fell from 4,115 calories in 1938 to 3,144 in 1945, a reduction of 23.6% (Table 8.2). This low calorific value continued in the post-war period, since it was only 3,331 calories in 1947 or 3,512 in 1949, still very much lower than pre-war levels.

Another important issue to take into account when analysing gas consumption is its sale price to the consumer. In general, nominal tariffs rose considerably during the war, especially during the later years, and the post-war period, in parallel with the high inflation of the time. However, the consideration of gas as a basic necessity for citizens led governments to regulate its prices. Therefore, gas prices increased to a much lesser extent than prices in general, which accelerated a reduction in real terms of gas tariffs during the war, especially in its late and post-war years.

In France, gas tariffs increased substantially during the war (multiplying by 2.7 in 1939–1946), although at a much lower level than wholesale industrial prices, due to authorities' reluctance to authorise higher increases in order to protect the small consumers (Beltran and Williot, 1992, p. 41). In Lisbon, the government kept gas tariffs steady until 1942, doubling them in 1943–1945, although the strong increase in consumption suggests that they rose much less than global inflation. In Italy, gas prices increased sixfold during the war, but at a level similar to wage growth and well below inflation. Despite the reduction in calorific value, the greater drop, in real terms, in tariffs caused the price of calories to drop significantly in the latter years of the conflict and immediately after the war (Table 8.2).

Table 8.2 Calorific power, in calories/m^3, and prices, in lire/m^3, of gas in Italy, 1938–1947

Year	*Calorific power*	*Tariff, in current lire*	*Tariff, in 1938 lire*	*Price of 1,000 calories, in 1938 lire*
1938	4,115	0.82	0.82	0.20
1939	4,052	0.84	0.79	0.19
1940	3,980	0.91	0.68	0.17
1941	3,501	0.91	0.58	0.17
1942	3,282	0.91	0.51	0.15
1943	3,248	0.92	0.30	0.09
1944	3,182	1.30	0.07	0.02
1945	3,144	5.44	0.03	0.01
1946	3,204	11.37	0.03	0.01
1947	3,331	15.53	0.02	0.01

Source: see Table 8.1 and Istituto Nazionale di Statistica (2011). Author's elaboration.

8.3 The structure of consumption

The structure of consumption also differed across countries (Table 8.3). The gas that was earmarked for public lighting was already insignificant (except in Spain), due to its widespread substitution by electricity during the first third of the century. During the world war, its importance was further reduced, due to restrictions and destruction, recovering somewhat in the post-war period, but without reaching pre-war figures.

Industry was the second largest consumer sector, based on the weight of this activity in the different economies and the spread of gas engines (Table 8.4). The figures for Spain are very low and stagnant, both in absolute values and in percentages, especially until 1942. But later they increased rapidly due to the focus of the industrialist policy of the dictatorship and the deterioration of

Table 8.3 Gas consumption for public lighting in Spain, France and the United Kingdom, in percentage (1935–1947)

Year/Countries	*Spain*	*France*	*United Kingdom*
1935	16.8		4.5
1938	7.9		4.7
1939	9.4		3.1
1940	10.9		0.3
1941	10.7	0.24	0.5
1942	4.9	0.02	0.5
1943	3.3	0.02	0.3
1944	3.2	0.03	0.5
1945	2.3	0.18	1.4
1946	2.1	0.43	1.9
1947	3.1	0.58	1.2

Source: see Table 8.1. Author's elaboration.

Table 8.4 Gas consumption for industry in Spain, France and the United Kingdom, in percentage (1935–1947)

Year/Countries	*Spain*	*France*	*United Kingdom*
1935	3.4		
1938	6.5		
1939	5.6		
1940	4.3		
1941	5.2	24.9	
1942	4.4	27.3	
1943	13.1	28.8	38.4
1944	18.9	25.2	34.3
1945	23.0	23.5	31.0
1946	20.2	22.8	29.8
1947	19.5	25.0	30.1

Source: see Table 8.1. Author's elaboration.

living standards in domestic consumption. For the period 1943–1947, the annual industrial consumption was barely 31 million m^3, compared to 538 million m^3 in France or 3,694 million m^3 in the United Kingdom.

The United Kingdom, which started from figures much higher than those of the other two countries, displayed a distinctly downward trend during the war, in both absolute and relative values. This was possibly due to the destruction of manufacturing facilities and/or the deindustrialisation trend, although the pace slowed down in the post-war period. In France there was small growth in the early years of the war, caused by a reorientation in the structure of consumption, although this process was later readjusted. In the Paris area, despite not exceeding 20%, industry also increased its overall weight, since sales to this sector multiplied by 2.5 in 1938–1943 (Williot, 2006). In reality, this trend began as far back as 1937, when a reduced rate for these activities was approved, based on their volume of consumption. Moreover, it was reinforced when the gasoline supply was interrupted.

The industrial branches with the greatest weight in the structure of French industrial consumption were mechanical construction, automobile manufacturing, aviation and metallurgy, that is, energy-intensive capital goods industries, which were emblematic of the second industrial revolution (Table 8.5). On the contrary, the activities with the least weight were traditional industries,

Table 8.5 Gas sold for industrial uses in France, 1944–1945

Industry	*Consumption, average 1944–1945 (%)*	*No. of establishments (%)*	*Consumption growth 1944–1945 (%)*	*Consumption, average 1944–1945 (m^3)*
Food	10.4	8.8	21.2	5,810
Chemical	5.5	6.9	29.4	3,915
Paper	4.2	6.0	31.8	3,424
Textile	6.0	24.4	33.6	1,218
Packaging and conditioning	1.4	1.5	76.6	4,698
Glass and ceramic	8.8	2.5	-14.7	17,266
Metallurgy	10.9	2.0	-5.9	26,909
Metal working and mechanics	19.6	11.3	13.0	8,573
Automobile and aviation	18.3	2.5	9.0	35,716
Electrical constructions	7.5	2.2	19.3	16,633
Various industries	7.3	31.9	32.6	1,119
Total	100	100	13.2	4,916
Total, thousand m^3	155,023 (1944) 175,431 (1945)	33,610		

Source: Journal des usines à gaz, August 15, 1946. Author's elaboration.

consumer goods and low energy intensity manufacturing, such as textiles, paper or packaging.

After the slump of 1944, which was a consequence of the escalation of the war in French territory, industrial consumption increased by 13%, although with strong intra-sectoral differences. The most intense growth occurred in traditional industries, probably due to their greater facility to resume activity and their higher elasticity to the evolution of demand. On the contrary, those industries experiencing a drop were glass and ceramics and metallurgy. In number of establishments, the most numerous were "various industries" and textiles, which were characterised by their fragmentation and which represented 56% of the total, but only 13% of consumption. In terms of consumption per customer, three types can be established: the large consumers, with unit consumption between 16,500 and 35,500 m^3, such as automobiles and aviation, metallurgy, glass and ceramics, and electrical constructions; the medium ones, 3,500–8,500 m^3, such as mechanical constructions, food, packaging, chemicals and paper; and small consumers, less than 1,200 m^3, such as textiles and various industries.

The interruption in the supply of gasoline forced the use of gas for traction, so that in 1942, 13,000 compressed gas vehicles circulated throughout the streets of Paris. In the country as a whole, 117 million m^3 were sold for traction in 1945, almost all (116,5 m^3) was compressed gas, for a total of 24,202 vehicles.

The bulk of consumption corresponded to residential users (Table 8.6), with a greater and growing weight until 1942, in Spain due to the weakness of industrial consumption. In the United Kingdom this type of consumption recovered strongly from the middle of the war. In the post-war period there was a convergence between the countries. This consumption was focused on cooking and heating.

Table 8.6 Gas consumption for standard users in Spain, France and the United Kingdom, in percentage (1935–1947)

Year/Countries	*Spain*	*France*	*United Kingdom*
1935	79.9		
1938	85.7		
1939	85.0		
1940	84.8		
1941	84.0	74.8	
1942	90.7	72.7	
1943	83.5	71.2	61.2
1944	77.9	74.8	65.2
1945	74.7	76.3	67.6
1946	77.8	76.8	68.3
1947	77.4	74.4	68.6

Source: see Table 8.1. Author's elaboration.

In France, the objective was to not allow the conflict to excessively affect essential consumption such as heating in winter, although it was not achieved in critical situations such as that of 1944.[6] Gas appliances, especially stoves, were quite widespread in France in those years (Table 8.7), since almost half of homes had one.[7] In fact, the coverage of gas stoves reached no less than 98.8% of homes with gas in 1945, while the different heating devices, mainly water heaters, only 18.1% and refrigerators 0.3%.[8]

The level of consumption of commercial establishments was similar to that of industry. It was distributed mainly among large kitchens and bakeries, which represented almost 70% of total consumption (Table 8.8). The most numerous establishments were the large kitchens, which accounted for a little over half. The main customers were bakeries, with almost 12,000 m^3 per establishment. Intermediate-level consumers, 2,000–5,000 m^3, included those that heated large premises, the collective distribution of hot water and large kitchens. Finally, with a modest consumption, 800–1,400 m^3, were butcher's, pastry makers and varied establishments.

Table 8.7 Number of gas appliances in the home in France in 1945

Gas appliances	*Number*
Kitchen	4,618,544
Water and bath heater	574,526
Radiators	250,681
Central heating	18,869
Refrigerators	12,166
Special meters for heating	39,206

Source: Journal des usines à gaz, August 15, 1946. Author's elaboration.

Table 8.8 Gas sold for commercial and similar uses in France, 1944–1945

Establishment	*Consumption, average 1944–1945 (%)*	*No. of establishments (%)*	*Consumption growth 1944–1945 (%)*	*Consumption, average 1944–1945 (m^3)*
Large kitchens	45.2	51.0	24.7	2,135
Bakeries	23.3	4.7	88.1	11,816
Pastry shops	1.0	2.8	34.7	848
Butcher's	2.8	4.8	41.4	1,369
Heating of large premises	9.9	5.0	17.0	4,729
Collective hot water distribution	0.9	0.5	20.1	3,826
Various	17.0	31.0	18.3	1,322
Total	100	100	35.2	2,408
Total, thousand m^3	129,133 (1944) 174,641 (1945)	63,083		

Source: Journal des usines à gaz, August 15, 1946. Author's elaboration.

Commercial consumption recovered to a greater extent than industrial consumption, from autumn 1944, indicating the ease with which the consumers could start up their small and simpler facilities. However, here too there were strong contrasts, between the very strong growth of businesses that covered basic needs such as bakeries and the modest growth of large facilities for collective use.

8.4 Consumers

There were substantial differences in the number of subscribers between countries (Table 8.9). The United Kingdom had an average of 11 million, compared to 4.7 in France, 1.5 in Italy, 0.4 in Spain or 0.03 in Lisbon. In Spain, there was a decreasing trend during the world war (17%), peculiarly, with a greater negative impact than during the Civil War. However, it rose again in the post-war period, although without reaching the former highest levels. In France there was also a fall, but less pronounced (7%) at the beginning of the Nazi occupation, and then a slow initial recovery took place that accelerated in the post-war period. Italy exhibited an increase of 8% up to 1941, with an expected fall in the final years of the conflict and a new recovery in the post-war years. Lisbon showed the best and most continuous results. Finally, the United Kingdom suffered a slight decrease of 4% in the early years of the war, recovering progressively afterwards.

In general, the reduction in the number of users between 1938 (1935 in Spain and France) and the year with the lowest number of users was small, ranging from 2% in the United Kingdom to 13% in Spain, with 3% in Italy, 7% in France and an increase of 4% in Lisbon. This seems reasonable since this variable would not have to be excessively affected by a war. The high drop in Spain, a non-warring country, suggests the importance of the sharp

Table 8.9 Number of users in Spain, France, Italy, Portugal and the United Kingdom (1935–1947)

Year/Countries	*Spain*	*France*	*Italy*	*Lisbon*	*United Kingdom*
1935	378,270	4,833,275	1,303,483	23,499	10,516,759
1938	379,332		1,474,129	26,343	11,215,104
1939	383,931		1,493,383	27,388	11,347,775
1940	392,653	4,472,800	1,556,186	28,621	11,231,451
1941	379,838	4,559,668	1,604,475	29,707	10,991,760
1942	365,815	4,616,294	1,603,811	32,451	10,972,480
1943	364,592	4,630,189	1,578,268	36,375	11,199,880
1944	369,097	4,539,756	1,508,657	37,993	11,166,565
1945	328,347	4,772,129	1,431,617	40,422	11,299,911
1946	359,249	4,898,985	1,536,652	42,165	11,462,010
1947	382,726	4,971,700	1,590,121	44,737	11,612,658

Source: see Table 8.1. Author's elaboration.

socioeconomic deterioration of its population as a consequence of Franco's economic policy.

In comparative percentage terms for the period as a whole, the growth in the number of users was basically moderate, except in Lisbon, which was 90%, compared to 1% in Spain, 3% in France, 10% in the United Kingdom and 22% in Italy.

In geographical terms, consumption was very unevenly distributed in these countries. In France and, above all, the United Kingdom, a high proportion of the small towns and practically all the cities had gas. On the contrary, in Italy and, principally, Spain and Portugal, the medium-sized (but not all) and large cities enjoyed it. In Italy, the highest gas density was found in the urbanised and industrialised regions of the north, in Spain in Catalonia, and in Portugal around the only two large cities (Lisbon and Porto). In these three countries, the factories were located mainly on the coast so as to receive British coal more easily. In the French case, the Parisian region concentrated almost half of the gas consumed in the whole of France, and Paris accounted for 23%. The second largest consuming area was the northern coal zone, with just over a third of the total, with only 20% remaining for the rest of the country.[9]

The degree of social penetration of gas was also very different between nations (Table 8.10). The main contrasts were between the Mediterranean countries, in which it ranged between 1% and 3.5%, compared to leaders such as France with 11–12%, and the United Kingdom with 23–25%. If we estimate about 3.5 people per subscriber, and given that the overwhelming majority of them were domestic users, this means that, on average for the entire period, in Portugal only 3% of the total population had gas at home, in Spain 5%, and Italy 12%, in contrast to 41.5% in France, and 85% in the United Kingdom. In

Table 8.10 Percentage of subscribers (users) over the total population in Spain, France, Italy, Portugal and the United Kingdom (1935–1947)

Year/Countries	*Spain*	*France*	*Italy*	*Lisbon*[a]	*United Kingdom*
1935	1.5	11.6	3.0	0.3	22.4
1938	1.5		3.4	0.4	23.5
1939	1.5		3.5	0.4	23.8
1940	1.5	10.9	3.5	0.4	24.8
1941	1.4	11.6	3.6	0.4	24.5
1942	1.4	11.9	3.5	0.4	24.9
1943	1.4	12.0	3.5	0.5	25.6
1944	1.4	11.8	3.4	0.5	25.5
1945	1.2	12.2	3.2	0.5	25.0
1946	1.3	12.2	3.4	0.5	23.3
1947	1.4	12.1	3.5	0.5	23.3

Source: see Table 8.1. Author's elaboration.
Note:
[a] The data for Lisbon are calculated on the total population of Portugal. They would have to be doubled if we estimate that Lisbon users would represent around half of those in the country as a whole.

Table 8.11 Consumption per subscriber (user) in Spain, France, Italy, Portugal and the United Kingdom, in m^3 (1935–1947)

Year/Countries	*Spain*	*France*	*Italy*	*Lisbon*	*United Kingdom*
1935	404.6	372.8	411.7	397.7	796.1
1938	287.1		410.9	423.5	816.3
1939	345.2		408.1	416.5	801.4
1940	435.5	322.8	428.5	434.8	787.6
1941	252.6	404.8	502.4	469.2	846.4
1942	334.2	438.5	498.9	473.7	924.4
1943	432.8	445.9	341.6	433.9	916.3
1944	447.6	344.4	309.0	578.7	961.5
1945	503.3	416.8	181.7	598.4	977.5
1946	456.8	513.8	335.6	609.2	1.060.5
1947	460.2	532.2	476.5	653.8	1.087.1

Source: see Table 8.1. Author's elaboration.

the medium term, the situation exhibited insignificant variations. In Spain there was a slight decline, in contrast to the moderate increases in France, Italy and the United Kingdom, and the most notable growth was experienced in Lisbon.

With regard to the average consumption per user for the period as a whole, the main contrasts are observed between the United Kingdom, with 907 m^3, and Latin Europe: Lisbon 499 m^3, France 421, Spain 396 and Italy 391 (Table 8.11). The explanation for the high British consumption most likely lies in the lower price of gas, especially in terms of income and the greater weight of large industrial consumers. In Portugal, the figures for the country as a whole would probably be closer to the Spanish ones, given that per capita consumption in the large capitals was higher than in smaller towns. The French figures are somewhat distorted due to the incomplete time series.

The variation in time primarily reflects the impact of the war vicissitudes. In Spain, consumption per user fell during the Civil War and the early years of the world war, in France in 1940 and 1944, in the United Kingdom in 1940 and in Italy it fell dramatically at the end of the conflict. Only Lisbon saw an atypically sustained growth. In percentages, consumption per user throughout the entire period increased by 14% in Spain, 16% in Italy, 37% in the United Kingdom, 43% in France and 64% in Lisbon.

8.5 Conclusions

In the 1930s, in Western Europe there was a sharp difference in the levels of the implementation and development of the gas industry between the United Kingdom and France, on the one hand, and the Mediterranean countries, principally Portugal, on the other hand. On this basis, the war had also a differential impact, depending on its aftereffects on the physical and human capital of this industry, access to coal, and national regulations referring to this activity (coal quotas, tariffs, rationing, etc.).

In principle, it would be possible to distinguish between the situation of the countries at war (France, Italy, the United Kingdom) and the neutral nations (Spain and Portugal). It would be reasonable to say that the former would have faced greater difficulties, although the neutral nations would have too, as they depended on the external supply of coal, which was now more difficult to obtain. The situation in reality was complex and nuanced.

In general terms, the results, in terms of both production and consumption, were less negative than expected, although the reliability or scope of the statistics, especially for some countries such as Italy or Portugal, is limited. In fact, in all of them, except for Italy, the data for 1945 exceeded those for 1939. However, it is true that throughout this period there were relatively important decreases in the most critical moments of the war for each country: 1940 and 1944 in France, 1944–1945 in Italy or 1940 in the United Kingdom.

The impact on the consumer was more severe due to the notorious loss of quality and calorific power of the manufactured gas. This was caused by the shortage of coal, which forced the gas factories to use less efficient raw materials such as water, wood and olive pomace. Moreover, the consumption of coal in the gas industry fell significantly, especially in the countries that were most dependent on foreign supply such as Italy or Spain.

Gas tariffs increased significantly in the later years of the war and the immediate post-war years, due to the high inflation of the period. However, these increases were well below the level of inflation because of the government's consumer protection policy. The structure of gas consumption was also affected. The decline of gas in public lighting was accentuated, due to restrictions and destruction. Private consumption continued to account for the majority of total consumption, even though it fell slightly due to restrictions and to the priority given to industrial consumption. The number of users and their average consumption decreased during the worst years of the war in every country, but consumption did so to a much greater extent than the number of users.

Notes

1 Archives Nationales (1977).

2 The firm *Gaz de Paris* established a selective rationing based on previous consumption levels. In the Paris region consumption fell from 612 to 560 million m^3 in 1939–1940 (Williot, 2006, p. 401).

3 Also in the Paris region, which went from 612 to 900 million m^3 in 1939–1943.

4 The tariffs had not changed since the concession contract signed with the city council in 1928. Companhias Reunidas Gás e Electricidade, *Relatório do Conselho de Administração*, 1935-1947, Lisboa.

5 The Lisbon company attributed it to changes in energy consumption patterns, by causing a reduction in domestic lighting and the removal of electrical appliances.

6 *Journal des usines à gaz*, November 22, 1939. To this end, at least in some cities such as Arras and Amiens, a specific strategy of tariff increases was designed, smaller for

this use. This resulted in a lower impact of the conflict on the use for heating, at least during the early years. However, in the same city of Arras, daily consumption was only 10,000 m^3 in November 1944, compared to 34,000 m^3 in the winter of 1938 (Mackowiak, 2006, pp. 412, 414).

7 Calculating about ten million homes, with roughly four people per home.

8 Central heating systems would benefit several homes, but it is also true that the same home could have several heating devices, such as water heaters and radiators.

9 *Commission du plan d'équipement et de modernisation gaz, Rapport sur le Plan d'équipement de l'Industrie du Gaz*. Paris, 1948, pp. 111–122.

References

Archives Nationales. 1977. *Dommages de guerre des enterprises de gaz et d'électricité (1922-1965)*. Pierrefitte-sur-Seine: Archives nationales (France).

Associazione Nazionale Industriali Gas. 1950. *Compendio dei dati statistici relative alle officine del gas d'Italia dal 1938 al 1949*. Roma: Stabilimento Tipografico Fausto Failli.

Beltran, Alain, and Williot, Jean-Pierre. 1992. *Le noir et le blue. 40 ans d'histoire de Gaz de France*. Paris: Belfond.

Bussola, Diego. 2005. *A modernização dos lares lisboetas: consumo de energia e electrodomésticos na Lisboa de após guerra (1947-1975)*. Lisboa: Mestrado em História social contemporânea, Instituto Superior de Ciências do Trabalho e da Empresa.

Companhias Reunidas Gás e Electricidade 1936 and 1939-1948. *Relatório do Conselho de Administração e Parecer do Conselho Fiscal. Balanço e conta de ganhos e perdas*. Years 1935, 1938-1947. Lisboa: Topografia Gráfica.

Fernández-Paradas, Mercedes, and Martykánová, Darina. 2017. La industria del gas en España en los años 1940 en el contexto de Europa. In *Globalización, nacionalización y liberalización de la industria del gas en la Europa latina (siglos XIX–XXI)*, edited by Isabel Bartolomé Rodríguez, Mercedes Fernández-Paradas, and Jesús Mirás Araujo, 258–278. Madrid: Marcial Pons.

Fernández-Paradas, Mercedes, and Martykánová, Darina. 2019. El sector del gas en la Guerra Civil. In *El impacto de la Guerra Civil española en el sector terciario*, coordinated by Mercedes Fernández-Paradas, and Carlos Larrinaga, 25–50. Granada: Comares.

Istituto Nazionale di Statistica. 2011. *L'Italia in 150 anni: sommario di statistiche storiche 1861–2010*. Roma: Istat.

Mackowiak, Florence. 2006. Les compagnies gazières du Nord de la France sous l'Occupation: La Société artésienne de force et lumière et son activité à Arras. In *Les entreprises du secteur de l'énergie sous l'Occupation*, edited by Denis Varaschin, 407–418. Arras: Artois Presses Université.

Madureira, Nuno L., coord. 2005. *A História da energia: Portugal 1890-1980*. Lisboa: Livros Horizonte.

Malanima, Paolo. 2006. *Energy Consumption in Italy in the 19th and 20th Centuries. A Statistical Outline*. Napoli: Consiglio Nazionale delle Ricerche e Istituto di Studi sulle Società del Mediterraneo.

Paquier, Serge, and Williot, Jean-Pierre, dirs. 2005. *L'industrie du gaz en Europe aux XIXe et XXe siècles. L'innovation entre marchés privés et collectivités publiques*. Bruxelles: Peter Lang.

Sindicato Vertical de Agua, Gas y Electricidad. 1948. *Datos estadísticos técnicos de las fábricas de gas españolas, 1930-1947*. Madrid: Sindicato Vertical de Agua, Gas y Electricidad.

Union Internationale de l'Industrie du Gaz 1949. *Les Statistiques Européennes de l'industrie du gaz*. London: Union Internationale de l'Industrie du Gaz.

Williams, Trevor I. 1981. *A History of the British Gas Industry*. Oxford: Oxford University Press.

Williot, Jean-Pierre. 2006. Les entreprises gazières de la région parisienne sous l'Occupation: Contraintes apparentes et opportunités nouvelles. In *Les entreprises du secteur de l'énergie sous l'Occupation*, edited by Denis Varaschin, 381–405. Arras: Artois Presses Université.

9 More an Iberian Island than a Peninsula

Gas pipelines between France and Spain since c. 1955: Failures and achievements

Jesús María Valdaliso Gago, Patricia Suárez Cano and Carlos Alvarado-García

9.1 Introduction

Despite the European policies to create a single energy market implemented since the end of the 1990s, the Iberian Peninsula continues to be a separate gas market from the rest of Europe, both geographically and commercially speaking (Heather, 2015 and 2019). The connection of Spain's gas network to the rest of Europe has been at the forefront of the news since February 2022 as the result of the Russian invasion of Ukraine. In the new energy supply scenario in Europe, with a sharp drop in natural gas imports from Russia, Spain—currently with the largest liquefied natural gas (LNG) regasification capacity of the whole European Union and two gas pipelines operating with Algeria—could become the natural gas gateway for Europe. However, that opportunity is in contrast with the Spanish gas network's poor connection to Europe through France, which is limited to the Larrau-Irun double interconnection in the western Pyrenees (and which has proven to be much more important for gas imports than exports). Despite this new scenario, the MidCat gas pipeline project, joining the Spanish Mediterranean coast with France through Girona, has been shelved for good.

The first gas pipeline interconnection between France and Spain came into service in 1993; it connected the Lacq gas field in south-west France to the Spanish network along a pipeline running through Larrau to Calahorra. Subsequently, in 2006 a second gas pipeline also came into service in the western Pyrenees and joined the French Lussagnet gas field to the regasification plant at the port of Bilbao through the Irun-Biriatou link. There were other failed projects before and after those two connections, with the most recent the aforementioned MidCat gas pipeline in the eastern Pyrenees. This chapter will examine the achievements and failures of the French–Spanish gas pipelines, and we will try to extract the most important lessons learnt.

The paper has four sections. The first examines the evolution of the natural gas supply in Spain and the relative importance of the French–Spanish gas interconnection for the gas in- and out-flows in Spain. The first unsuccessful

DOI: 10.4324/9781003428695-9

interconnection attempts in the 1960s and 1970s and the reasons for their failure are then analysed. The development of the two operational interconnections between France and Spain in the western Pyrenees are then outlined. The fourth section analyses the failure of the last project in the eastern Pyrenees. The chapter then concludes.

9.2 Transnational gas pipelines and energy supply: The Spanish case

Gas pipelines in general and the transnational ones in particular are large infrastructures whose construction requires—along with large technical and project implementation capacities in construction companies—different geostrategic, political and economic factors to be combined and balanced in the countries and governments in question, and which are closely interrelated. The energy mix of the countries in question and their energy supplies, the life cycle and the prices relating to the available energies, and the cost and profitability of the investment required, along with the availability of capital, should be highlighted among the first factors; the second include the interests and the relative power of the stakeholders associated to each energy source in each country, along with the energy policy of each country affected; finally, the security of the energy supply in each country and the commercial and diplomatic relationships not only between the countries through which the gas pipeline passes, but also with third parties and the global geopolitical context, come into play. The relative price of gas and other competing energies is an important variable, as a substantial variation can alter the cost-benefit analysis, along with giving impetus to or putting investment decisions on the back burner. However, geostrategic and/or political variables are usually those that, ultimately, explain the success or failure of the project.[1]

In the most recent case, the Russian invasion of Ukraine marked the end of a long period of good diplomatic relations between Russian and Germany, which underpinned the development of the Nord Stream 1 and 2 gas pipelines (Russell, 2021); it has contributed to drive up the natural gas price on the international market and has led to the European Union reconsidering its gas supply alternatives, along with decisions regarding investments in infrastructures such as regasification plants or gas pipelines with other possible suppliers (Di Bella et al., 2022). In a case closer to home, the growing tensions between Algeria and Morocco led to the end of Algerian gas exports along the Maghreb gas pipeline (from 31 October 2021), which forced Spain to increase its gas supply by importing LNG from other countries. The diplomatic crisis between Spain and Algeria, triggered in March 2022 after the Spanish government's sudden change in position regarding the Western Sahara, altered the natural supply sources in Spain; that reduced Algeria's importance and led to rise in LNG from countries such as the United States and even Russia (Guasch, 2022).

Until the end of the 1990s, all the natural gas imported in Spain was LNG transported in gas carriers; after its regasification at the Barcelona, Huelva and Cartagena plants, it was distributed through a gas pipeline network to the rest

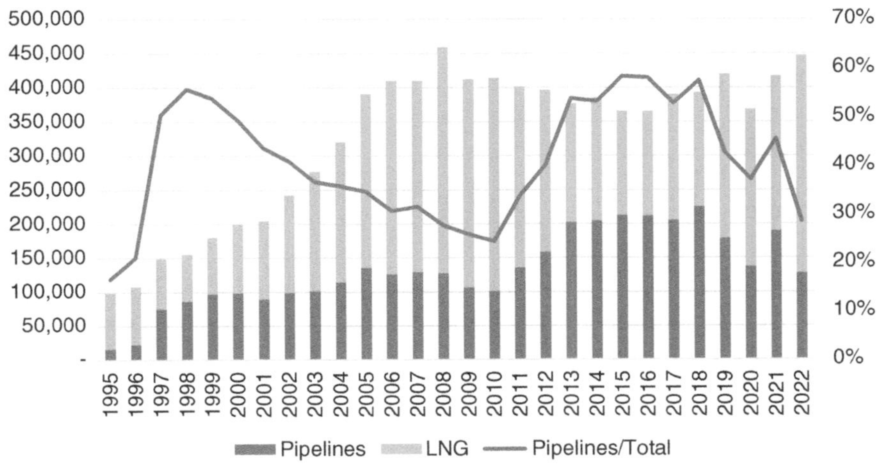

Figure 9.1 Natural gas imports in Spain, 1995–2022 (GWh).

Source: SEDIGAS, Annual Reports, and Enagás, The Spanish Gas System, Annual Reports, several years.

of the country (Ballestero, 2017, pp. 135–36). After the Calahorra-Lacq gas pipelines came into service in 1993 and the Maghreb one in 1996, the natural gas pipeline imports experienced strong growth to the point that they accounted for half or even more of the total gas imports (see Figure 9.1). The growth in gas consumption in the first decade of the twenty-first century was particularly down to LNG imports, which were subsequently converted into natural gas at different regasification plants brought into operation at different Spanish ports. The coming into service of the Medgaz gas pipeline in 2011, which entered Spain through Almeria, led to a rise in natural gas pipeline imports, at the expense of LNG, up to 2015 and 2016; at that time, they accounted for 58% of all imports and that figure remained steady until 2018. The closure of the Maghreb gas pipeline in 2021 was followed by a further drop in natural gas pipeline imports, which only accounted for 29% of total imports in 2022.[2]

Until the Maghreb gas pipeline came into service in November 1996, the French–Spanish pipeline was the only way for natural gas to enter Spain, from Norway and distributed through the French network. Between 1997 and 2003, the gas supplied by the Pyrenean connection accounted for nearly 30% of the natural gas coming into Spain; it then fell down to a percentage of around by 20% by the end of the period (see Figure 9.2). Therefore, this connection has allowed the supply of natural gas to be diversified in Spain and led to greater energy security.

Even though the first French–Spanish connection was not a reality until 1993, two types of projects to connect the gas networks of both countries emerged from the mid-1950s onwards. On the one hand, those aimed at accessing the Lacq natural gas field (which began to be exploited in 1957; Fernandez,

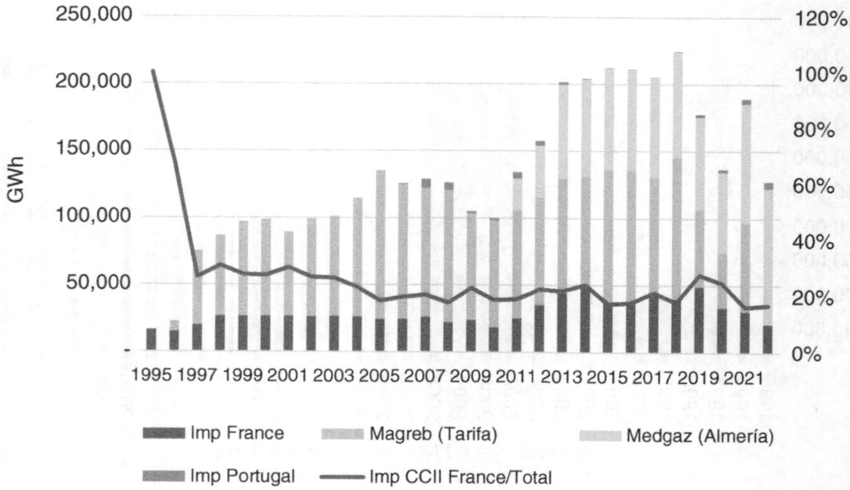

Figure 9.2 Natural gas pipeline imports in Spain, 1995–2022 (GWh and %).
Source: SEDIGAS, Annual Reports, and Enagás, The Spanish Gas System, several years.

2018) in the south-west of France; the aim was to supply industry in northern Spain by means of a gas pipeline that would connect both networks in Irun. On the other hand, there were the different projects for a transnational gas pipeline that would link different North-African gas sites with Central Europe along a route along the Spanish Mediterranean coast from Almeria to Barcelona and would enter France through the eastern Pyrenees. In the first case, the goal was to import French natural gas to Spain; in the second, to import Algerian (or Nigerian) gas to be used in Spain and to transport it from our country to France and, as applicable, to other European countries.

9.3 The first failed attempts at the two ends of the Pyrenees (1955–1983)

The first attempt to import French natural gas to the north of Spain took place in 1958 and was headed by the Bilbao and Vizcaya banks, the electricity company Iberduero and the city gasworks of the Basque Country and Asturias. The original project envisaged bringing natural gas from Lacq to the provinces of Guipuzcoa and Biscay, one of the regions with the highest energy consumption in Spain. The gas would be brought by pipeline connecting the French city of Bayonne, which was already supplied by natural gas, and Bilbao; the gas would be taken along a stretch of 200 kilometres with a 350-millimetre diameter pipe, a capacity to transport 2 million m^3 (0.2 bcm) of gas, and involving an estimated investment of 250 million pesetas (which was subsequently expanded to 400 million pesetas). The imported gas would be used by Basque industry and the Iberduero Pasajes and Burceña thermal power plants, and would account for 20% of the gross energy consumption of both provinces. In the summer of 1959, executives from Basque industry and the Basque and Asturian gasworks visited the Lacq facilities. However, the project would end up not being approved due to the strong opposition that emerged among the Oviedo Provincial Fuel Trade Union (which represented the interests of Asturian coal mining, the most important of Spain); the large investment to be made in the infrastructure required and the high annual payments for gas imports in a context of serious difficulties in the international position of the Spanish economy; the risk of depending on a supply monopoly controlled by a foreign government; and the differences of opinion within the Government of Spain regarding the authority tasked with managing the business (the Ministries of the Treasury or of Industry) (Valdaliso et al., 2024).

The project was taken up again in 1966 by Petrogas, a company set up by the Bilbao and Vizcaya banks to solve the problem of supplying oil and natural gas to the Basque Country; however, it was again shelved once the contract to supply Spain with LNG from Libya to Barcelona had been signed. In 1968, Petrogas managed to revive the project by setting up a working group made up of the company, the National Institute of Industry (the holding of the Spanish business state-owned sector) and the French company Société Nationale des Pétroles d'Aquitaine. The connection with the French network would be in Irun and the gas pipeline would continue first to San Sebastián and Bilbao, and, subsequently, to Vitoria. In July 1970 and after different dealings and conversations between the Spanish Ministry for Industry and the French authorities, the Sociedad du Gaz du Sud-Ouest (in charge of the transport and distribution of the gas from Lacq) and the engineering firm of the National Institute of Industry Auxiesa, were commissioned to produce the preliminary study for the Irun-Bilbao gas pipeline, with its different branch lines, and the distribution of gas to 100 major industrial customers in the region; it was also asked to prepare a corporate organisational chart, an investment plan and a budget with the annual operating costs. However, and yet again, the project did not come to fruition due to the misgivings of the gas company and the French Government in that regard and to the trade-offs required from the Spanish side in the negotiation (the concession of the new oil refinery in Tarragona), which the Spanish Government eventually did not granted (Valdaliso et al., 2024).

As regards the transnational gas pipeline projects, the first attempt to connect Algeria, Spain and France was the Eurafrigas project in 1955, a pipeline measuring 2,600 kilometres in length and with a supply capacity of 10,000 bcm a year; it would connect the Hassi R'Mel gas field in Algeria to France and Germany along a route that would enter Europe via Cartagena and from there to Barcelona, crossing the French border across the eastern Pyrenees, then on to Lyon, Paris and finally the German city of Essen. The project developer was Association Eurafricaine Minière et Industrielle (ASSEMI), and its purpose was to drive the integration between Africa and Europe; however, once the Algerian gas field had been discovered, it mainly focused on exploiting and distributing that resource. ASSEMI was the driving force behind the setting up of a Committee to study the use of Algerian gas in Europe, whose members were different gas companies and some financial institutions, which included, on behalf of Spain, the Sociedad Catalana de Gas (Pere Duran) and the Banco Urquijo (Juan Lladó), but it never got beyond the study phase (Ballestero, 2017, pp. 22–23). After Algeria gained independence, from 1963 onwards, there were other proposals to channel Algerian gas to Spain and France, driven by French companies and with the support of its government, but they did not come to fruition due to the technological challenges of the underwater connection project between North Africa and southern Europe (Hayes, 2004, pp. 26–27).

In 1973, the recently created Sociedad de Estudio del Gasoducto del Mediterráneo Occidental (Segamo)—owned by the Algerian company Sonatrach (50%), the French Gaz de France (25%) and the Spanish Enagás (25%)—proposed a new connection project between the gas fields of the Algerian Sahara and France, by means of a gas pipeline that would enter Spain in Almeria, and from there to Barcelona and the border with France (García Alonso and Iranzo, 1988, pp. 336; Hayes, 2004, pp. 27–28; Ballestero, 2017, p. 87). Segamo commissioned an engineering firm from the United States, Williams Brothers, to produce the feasibility study; in 1975, it discarded Almeria as the entry point for technical reasons and put forward an alternative route that meant going into Morocco and then entering Spain through Gibraltar. Enagás proposed an alternative route for the Spanish section, with an interconnection with the French network at Irun in the Basque Country, instead of through Barcelona. The project was finally shelved in 1979, mainly due to the political and diplomatic problems between Algeria and Morocco, and between Morocco and Spain due to the Western Sahara, but also to the technical problem of laying underwater pipelines at great depths (Vela, 1995, pp. 365–66; Hayes, 2004, pp. 27–28; Ballestero, 2017, pp. 88 and 178).

In 1983 the Spanish Government proposed a new gas pipeline project that would connect the African gas fields of Algeria and Nigeria with Europe through Morocco and Spain. The project would offer Europe a natural gas supply alternative to avoid the growing dependency on natural gas from the USSR; it had the support of Germany and Belgium in Europe, but France was reluctant, as it was negotiating the purchase of Siberian gas at that time. On the African side, the tensions between Algeria and Morocco, on the one hand, and Nigeria's decision to opt for exporting LNG, on the other hand, prevented the project from going ahead (Hayes, 2004, p. 29; Ballestero, 2017, p. 179).

The failure of all those projects can also be explained by the very low demand for natural gas in Spain in the 1970s and the political weakness of the players and stakeholders associated with that industry and, on the contrary, by the strength of the oil industry interests (Ballestero, 2017, pp. 40–55; Tortella, 2022); however, it also meant that gas needs were met by importing LNG, regasified at the Barcelona plant and then distributed to a predominantly regional market (Hayes, 2004, pp. 29–30; Fernández-Paradas and Sudrià, 2018). The supply of natural gas to the rest of the country would use two gas pipelines connecting Barcelona to two of the main markets of the rest of Spain: Basque Country and Valencia, whose construction began at the end of the 1970s, and it would then reach the third, Madrid, in 1987 (Vela, 1995, pp. 265–66; Ballestero, 2017, pp. 89–92).

9.4 The connection through the western Pyrenees: The Calahorra–Larrau (1993) and the Euskadour (2006) pipelines

The first connection between the Spanish and French gas pipeline networks was approved in the 1988 Spanish Gas Plan, one of whose goals was to lower supply dependency on the Barcelona LNG regasification plant and to diversify the supply sources of natural gas for the successive Spanish governments in the 1980s and 1990s (Vela, 1995, pp. 481, 495 and 510–14). That same year a natural gas purchase agreement was signed between Enagás, the state-owned company that held the monopoly for transporting gas in Spain, and the consortium that exploited the Norwegian gas field in Troll, led by Statoil, for an initial 30-year period, to begin in 1996 (subsequently, in 1989, the supply was brought forward to 1993, which could be extended to 2030), with an annual supply amount set at between 7,000 and 16,000 GWh. The seller would pay the cost of transporting the natural gas through the European network to the French–Spanish border (Vela, 1995, pp. 316, 349–350 and 365). The connection between the Spanish and French networks would initially be along a route that would connect the Spanish gas pipeline between Barcelona and the Basque Country in Zaragoza to the French network and the Lacq natural gas field in Aquitaine from the Serrablo field in Huesca, which had been operating since 1984. However, the project was amended in 1989 for the connection point to be Calahorra through the Larrau mountain pass in Navarra. The new route, even though it was longer, meant the network was very stable as the entry of Norwegian gas was separated from that produced in Serrablo. The cost of constructing the Spanish section (145 kilometres from Villar de Arnedo to Larrau), paid by Enagás, was estimated to be 8,500 million pesetas at 1993 prices (51 million euros, around 100 million euros at today's prices). The works were conducted faster than initially envisaged and the Calahorra–Larrau gas pipeline came into operation in October 1993, with an initial capacity to import up to 2,000 million m^3 (2 bcm). Subsequently, thanks to a new compression station being set up in Lumbier, in 2007, and an increase of its power, in 2013, the import capacity was increased up to 3.1 bcm and 5.3 bcm in both regards, respectively.[3] After the pipeline came into service, gas supply security in Spain increased, although it was still lower than countries such as France, Germany and Italy due to Spain's very low storage capacity (Terzian, 1998, pp. 6 and 179).

In 2006 a second gas pipeline, the Euskadour, came into service connecting the Bahía Bizkaia Gas regasification plant at the Port of Bilbao to the Lussagnet gas underground storage facility—the largest of Europe—through Irun-Biriatou (see Figure 9.3). The total investment initially estimated for that gas pipeline, with a total length of 318 kilometres, was €180 million, which was

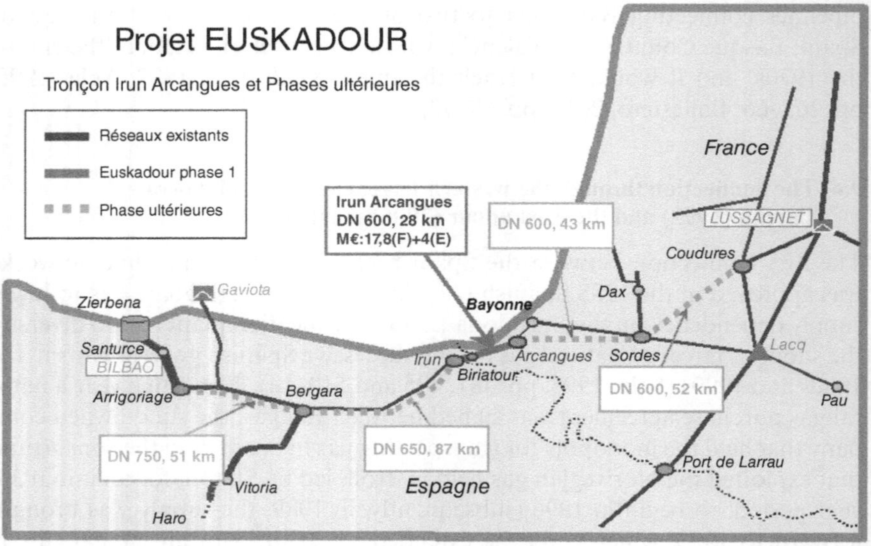

Figure 9.3 The Euskadour project in 2004.
Source: Commission de Régulation de l'Energie, 2004.

increased to €250 million after the twinning of the pipeline in 2010. It was constructed during a period of a strong growth in the demand for natural gas in Spain and of the European Commission striving for greater integration of the EU energy market; the aim was to diversify the gas supply sources by allowing gas to be exchanged between the north and south of Europe; it also meant that the Bilbao regasification plant—with a regasification capacity much higher than the demand from the Basque market—could access the French market.[4] The initial interconnection capacity of the Euskadour gas pipeline was 0.5 bcm, which rose sharply up to 2 bcm a year after a compression station came into service in Irun at the end of 2015 (involving an investment of €15 million).[5] In 2022, thanks to the increased power of that station, the transport capacity increased up to 3.5 bcm a year.[6]

Both gas pipelines are the sole point of connection to the gas networks of Spain and France, and are a great step forward in the creation of a European single gas market in order to ensure greater diversification of the supply sources, even though its degree of use has been and continues to be very low, and it is more important in terms of gas imports to Spain that for the exports, which were very low until 2020. Due to the consequences of the war in Ukraine, gas exports from Spain and France only exceeded imports in 2022 (see Figure 9.4).

In 2022, natural gas imported through both connections accounted for 5% of all gas entering the Spanish system (natural gas and liquefied natural gas) and 17% of natural gas transported through the international gas pipelines to

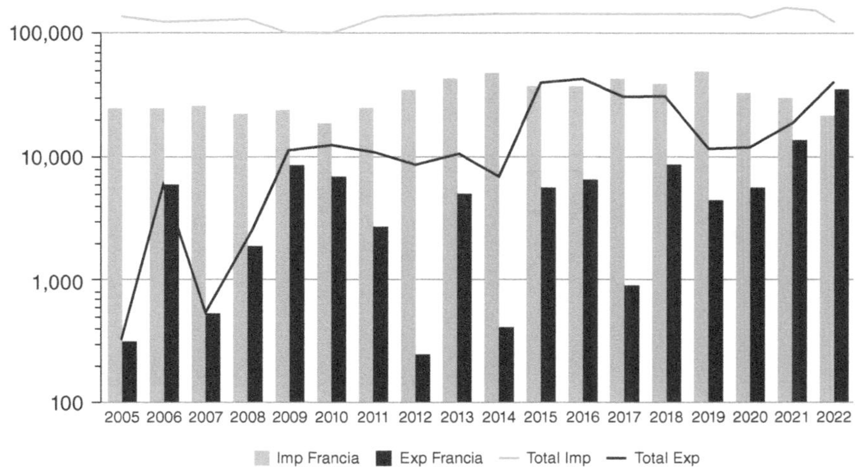

Figure 9.4 Natural gas imports and exports through the Pyrenean interconnection, 2005–2022 (GWh, semi-logarithmic scale).

Source: Enagás, Spanish Gas System Reports, several years.

which Spain is connected.[7] In fact, the existence of this connection and its relatively low use has been one of the reasons wielded by Spanish and French regulators to reject the MidCat project in 2019, which envisaged a gas pipeline between Spain and France through Girona, and which we discuss next.

9.5 The failure of the third connection: The MidCat gas pipeline in the eastern Pyrenees (c. 2007–2022)

The original Midi-Catalunya (MidCat) gas pipeline was proposed in 2007 and aimed to improve the gas connections of the Iberian Peninsula with Europe. It envisaged a route of 235 kilometres that would link the Spanish town of Martorell (where the Spanish–Algerian gas pipeline that entered Spain through Almeria and ran along the whole of the Mediterranean coast where the Cartagena, Sagunto and Barcelona regasification plants were also located) to Barbaira in France over the La Junquera–Le Perthus border, along with a series of works to improve the adjoining Spanish and French networks (see Figure 9.5); and a transport capacity of 7,300 million m^3 (7.3 bcm), approximately the same as the connection already existing through Larrau and Irun (8 bcm); and at an estimated cost of €3,100 million (Pöyry, 2017, pp. 14–15; Heather, 2019, p. 9).

The work got underway in 2010, but the reluctance and lack of interest of the French Government (with an energy mix mainly based on nuclear energy and with a gas network in poor condition that would have to be overhauled for the project to go ahead) meant that it would grind to a halt a year later, at Hostalric (Girona), 100 kilometres from the French border. In 2013 Spanish

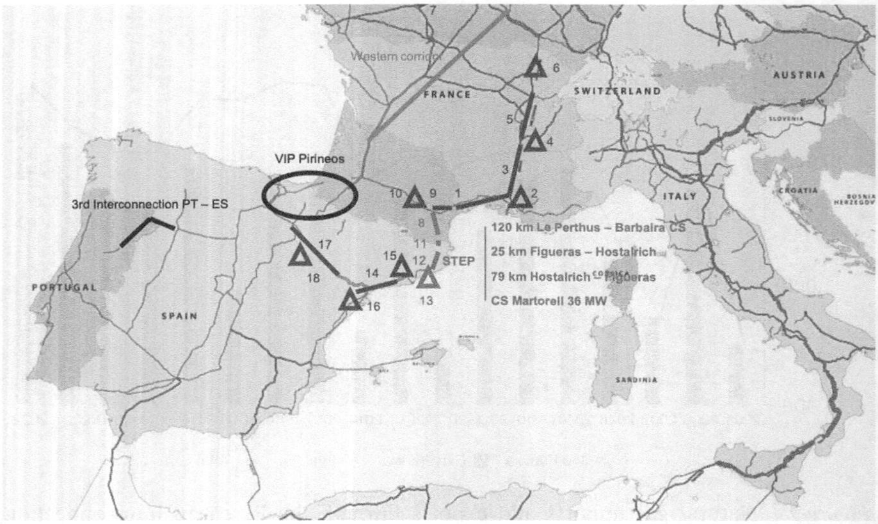

Figure 9.5 The MidCat and STEP projects.

Source: Pöyry (2017), p. 33. The works planned for the MidCat are in green (numbers 1–6, 9–10 and 14–17) and for STEP in orange (numbers 8 and 11–13).

endeavours resulted in a less ambitious version of the project, known as South Transit Eastern Pyrenees (STEP), being included in the list of EU projects of common interest, with an estimated investment of €470 million, two thirds of which would be for investments on the French side and the remainder in Spain (Heather, 2019, pp 9 and 34; Secretaría de Estado de Energía, 2019, p. 51). However, the political support for the project by the three countries involved and by the European Commission itself (Madrid and Lisbon Declarations in 2015 and 2018, respectively) never led to its direct financing (Heather, 2019, p. 10). Furthermore, the cost-benefit analysis commissioned from a specialist consultant concluded that the investment to be made in the new gas pipeline would only be cost-effective in a scenario of reducing the gas supply from Algeria and high LNG prices, and that the benefits of the project would exclusively be obtained on the Iberian Peninsula (Pöyry, 2017; CRE, 2018, p. 80).

Finally, in 2019, the French and Spanish regulators (Commission de Régulation de l'Énergie–CRE and Comisión Nacional del Mercado y la Competencia–CNMC, respectively) rejected the project due to the high cost of the infrastructure and the existence of a cross-Pyrenean connection (Larrau-Irun) with a very low use capacity and used more for gas imports than exports.[8] In 2021, according to the Enagás report on the Spanish gas system, the natural gas imported through those connections, a total of 30,905 GWh, accounted for 7% of all gas entering the Spanish system, while the exports through that same channel were 13,776 GWh, less than half. In addition to those more technical aspects, there was the intense reaction against the project by environmentalists in Catalonia (and also in France, although to a lesser extent) and the lack of enthusiasm of the French and Spanish governments for the project, for different reasons (the greater weight of nuclear energy in the French energy mix, the lack of support by the Spanish government for natural gas and its preference for renewables). After the Russian invasion of Ukraine in 2022, there was a last attempt to revive this project by the Spanish Government, which proved to be unsuccessful, particularly due to French opposition for the reasons already given and, furthermore, citing, to justify its refusal, the low use capacity of the interconnection already existing in the western Pyrenees. Moreover, the EU's commitment to a rapid decarbonisation timeline reduced the service life of the new infrastructure and, therefore, the rate of return on the investment.[9]

Moreover, the closure of one of the gas pipelines between Algeria and Spain, due to the tensions between Algeria and Morocco, shifted the Spain's key role as a preferential entry point for Algerian piped natural gas to Italy, thus reducing, the expectations for using the Morocco gas pipeline. In 2021, 22 bcm of gas reached Europe along the Transmed pipeline between Algeria and Italy, while there were 11 bcm using Medgaz (the only one currently operational between Spain and Algeria). Additionally, the total amount of gas that could be transported to Europe using the two Pyrenean interconnection would be no more than 18 bcm, when the EU demand is around 500 bcm, meaning that the pipeline would not solve the problems of supplying Europe with natural gas. Therefore, some countries of northern Europe, such as Germany, have opted to invest in LNG regasification to achieve greater supply autonomy and not fully depend on transnational gas pipelines (Guasch, 2022; Valdaliso and Lobo, 2022).

9.6 Conclusions

The comparative analysis of the successes and failures of the gas pipelines and interconnections between the French–Spanish gas transport and distribution networks reviewed in this chapter, and of its explanatory factors allows some more general reflections to be made about this type of transnational energy infrastructures and their conditioning factors. They can be divided into three categories: economic, political and geo-strategic (and diplomacy). Even though the role of each group of factors has been analysed separately, a systemic relationship obviously exists between them and, therefore, the final explanation in each case is multi-causal or, if preferred, holistic.

First, the geostrategic factors and, in particular, the existence of good trade and diplomatic relations between the countries through which the gas pipelines run seem to be a type of precondition for their construction and operating. The failure of the transnational gas pipeline projects proposed by Eurafrigas in 1955, Segamo in 1973 and by the Spanish Government in 1983 was due to diplomatic tensions and even military and political conflicts between several of the countries in question (Algeria, France, Morocco and Spain); the halting of the Maghreb gas pipeline in autumn 2021 due to the tension between Algeria and Morocco is another recent example. In the opposite case, the construction of the Larrau–Calahorra and Euskadour gas pipelines, particularly in the latter, should be set in the context of setting up a European single energy market and a strategy to diversify the energy supply in both countries.

Yet apart from that precondition, other factors should come into play for that type of transnational energy infrastructures to be implemented. The energy mix of each country and the relative clout of the stakeholders associated to each of the primary energies, two factors that are closely related, have played a very important role. In Spain, the interests of the Asturian coal mines in the 1950s or of the oil industry in the 1960s and 1970s help to explain the failure of the gas pipeline projects that would connect the Spanish network with the Lacq gas field in south-west France; the Spanish government's commitment to renewables explains its lack of interest (until 2022) in the MidCat project. By contrast, the success of the Larrau-Calahorra and Euskadour gas pipelines has been due to a great extent to the Spanish Government's firm commitment to the gasification of the country and to natural gas to replace coal and oil in the energy mix. As regards France, its interest in Siberian gas explains its lack of commitment to the 1983 North African gas pipeline product; more recently, the relative importance of nuclear energy in its energy mix and the great political weight of that industry, along with the fact that its most important supply sources for natural gas are Russia, the Netherlands and Norway, and not North Africa, are factors that help to understand its lack of interest in the MidCat gas pipeline that, if it came to fruition, would also require large investments to overhaul a very old gas distribution network.

As far as economic factors are concerned, the life cycle of energy and the relative size of the market seem to have played a more important role than the relative cost and the rate of return on the investment or the availability of capital, even though both are strictly related. One of the reasons that explains the failure of the French–Spanish gas pipeline in the 1950s and 1960s was the natural gas industry and market being at such an early stage in Spain and the existence of energy alternatives that were more widespread among consumers, such as first coal and, above all, oil later (and whose interests, as has already been previously said, had greater political influences and power). In contrast, the success of the Calahorra–Larrau and Euskadour gas pipelines can be explained in the context of fast and growing penetration of natural gas in a Spanish energy market on the rise and a strategy of diversifying the supply sources. Financing was only a problem for the 1958–1959 project, in the context of a Spain at risk of defaulting, and even then it did not seem to be the most important reason of the failure. However, in the case of MidCat, the looming decarbonisation timeline set by the European Union, which reduces the relative importance of natural gas in the energy mix, also lowers the rate of return on the investment in the project. The fact that the existing connection between France and Spain has been underused until very recently—and has been used more for importing gas from Europe than for exporting it—has been another significant factor in the failure of the project.

Nearly 30 years after the European Commission committing to a common and integrated energy market, Spain and the Iberian Peninsula in general continue to be an energy island as regards natural gas. Only a small part of the responsibility for this isolation must be attributed to the weak interconnections between the gas networks of Spain and France, which were underused until very recently. Furthermore, it could be said that one of the reasons of the failure of many of the projects considered in this chapter—between two neighbouring countries, and integrated since 1986, in a common supranational space—has been the low amounts of natural gas exchanged between both, which is explained by the different energy mix of each country and their supply sources and strategies. Even though transnational gas pipelines, in the same way as other such energy infrastructures, play a very positive role in the commercial and economic integration of countries and economic areas, their construction, functioning and operability require many geostrategic, political and economic factors to come together between several countries, which is not always simple. The failures examined here, along with the recent problems of other gas pipelines already in service, such as the Maghreb and Nord Stream 1 and 2, are good proof of that.

Acknowledgements

Grant PID2021-122846NB-I00 funded by MCIN/AEI/10.13039/501100011033, ERDF A way of making Europe; and Basque Government, Research Group IT1523-22.

Notes

1 According to Hayes (2004) these latter factors explain the success of the Transmed gas pipeline between Algeria and Italy in the 1980s and the failure of the gas pipeline projects between Algeria and Spain in the 1970s and 1980s. On the origins of the energy security concept and the politics of gas pipelines, see Amirova-Mammadova (2017), chapter 3.

2 The transnational gas pipelines were owned and run by investee companies of the countries in question: Algeria, Spain and Portugal in the Maghreb pipeline, https://www.gem.wiki/Maghreb-Europe_Gas_Pipeline (last accessed 6 September 2023); and Algeria and Spain in the Medgaz (49% Medina Partnership, 50% Naturgy and 50% Black Rock, and 51% Sonatrach), https://www.medgaz.com/medgaz/pages/socios-eng.htm (last accessed 6 September 2023).

3 Ballestero (1989, pp. 227–28), and Ballestero (2017, pp. 130 and 133–134). The estimated cost accounted for 15% of the company's investment in tangible fixed assets between 1990 and 1992, (Vela, 1995, p. 347). Regarding the subsequent expansions, *El Economista*, 7/12/2007, in https://informalia.eleconomista.es/empresas-finanzas/amp/326728/Economia-Empresas-Industria-autoriza-a-Enagas-la-construccion-de-una-estacion-de-comprension-de-gas-natural-en-Navarra, last accessed 27/04/2023, and Enagás, *2010 Spanish Gas System Report*, pp. 90–91.

4 Vela (1995, p. 365); Ballestero (2017, p. 136); Valdaliso et al. (2022, pp. 436–37 and 460); Naturgas Energía, 2006 and 2010 Annual Reports; and *El Correo*, 20/10/2008, p. 42, and 16/10/2010, p. 37.

5 https://www.bbg.es/compartiendo-ideas/noticias/euskadour-ensancha-la-puerta-para-el-gas/, last accessed 10/02/2022.
6 https://www.estrategia.net/noticias/el-gasoducto-euskadour-amplia-su-capacidad-de-interconexion-hasta-los-3-5-bcm, last accessed 27/04/2023.
7 Enagás, 2022 Spanish Gas System Report. Gas imports through the Pyrenean connection were 21,546 GWh, while exports were 35,370 GWh. In 2014, these two physical interconnections were merged into a single virtual interconnection known as Pyrenees VIP (Heather, 2019, p. 8).
8 The regulators likewise highlighted the "probability of interruption" of the new interconnection capacity, therefore not offering "capacity to enter into firm contracts with the retailers", CNMC, Press Release 22/01/2019, in https://www.cnmc.es/2019-01-22-la-cnmc-y-la-cre-acuerdan-rechazar-la-solicitud-de-inversion-de-la-nueva-interconexion, and CRE and CNMC Common Decision regarding the Gas Interconnection between France and Spain, https://www.cnmc.es/sites/default/files/editor_contenidos/Notas%20de%20prensa/2019/20190122_DECISIÓN_COMÚN_SOBRE_EL_PROYECTO_STEP_ESP_VS-NO_OFICIAL.pdf, date last accessed, 11/02/2022.
9 Fernandez (2021, p. 175). Regarding the French gas network, Heather (2015, pp. 50–51) points out that its poor state of repair seriously limited the gas flow between the north and south of Europe. The French position in CRE (2018, pp. 79–80). In a recent interview, the CNMC Chair at that time put the failure of the gas pipeline down to the French demands for exclusive control of the gas pipeline, whose cost had to be met in full by Spain, https://www.elmundo.es/economia/2022/03/24/623b2583e4d4d823738b4577.html (date last accessed, 24/03/2022).

References

Amirova-Mammadova, Sevinj. 2017. *Pipeline Politics and Natural Gas Supply from Azerbaijan to Europe. Challenges and Perspectives*. Wiesbaden: Springer.

Ballestero, Alfonso. 1989. *Buscando petróleo*. Madrid: Espasa Calpe.

Ballestero, Alfonso. 2017. *El gas natural en España*. Madrid: LID.

CRE. 2018. *Les interconnexions électriques et gazières en France*. Rapport. Julie 2018. https://www.cre.fr/documents/Publications/Rapports-thematiques/Rapport-interconnexions-2018

Di Bella, Gabriel et al. 2022. *Natural Gas in Europe: The Potential Impact of Disruptions in Supply*. IMF Working Paper WP/22/145.

Enagás. *El Sistema Gasista Español*, annual reports, several years.

Enagás. *Informes Anuales*, several years.

Fernandez, Alexandre. 2018. Un yacimiento de gas natural en el origen de la formación de una región industrial del suroeste de Francia: Lacq-Mourenx (1957-2013). *Revista de Historia Industrial* 27 (71): 35–54.

Fernandez, Alexandre. 2021. Quelques réflexiones sur les trajectories croisées des politiques du gaz en France et en Espagne depuis la Deuxième Guerre Mondiale. In *Estado, política industrial y energía en Francia y España (siglos XIX y XX)*, edited by Joseba de la Torre, Alexandre Fernandez, Gérard Chastagnaret and Antonio Escudero, 159–179. Alicante: Publicacions Universitat d'Alacant.

Fernández-Paradas, Mercedes, y Sudrià, Carles. 2018. La transición de la industria del gas de carbón al gas natural: dos modelos, España y Cataluña. *Revista de Historia Industrial* 27 (71): 121–149.

García Alonso, José M., and Iranzo, Juan E. 1988. *La energía en la economía mundial y en España*. Madrid: Editorial AC.

Guasch, Alberto. 2022. Spain's Energy Ambitions Are Looking Like a Pipe Dream. *Foreign Policy* April 8, 2022.

Hayes, Mark H. 2004. *Algerian Gas to Europe: The Transmed Pipeline and Early Spanish Gas Import Projects*. CESP Stanford IIS, Working Paper # 27.
Heather, Patrick. 2015. *The evolution of European traded gas hubs*. PAPER NG 104, Oxford Institute for Energy Studies.
Heather, Patrick. 2019. *A Hub for Europe. The Iberian promise?* PAPER NG 143, Oxford Institute for Energy Studies. https://doi.org/10.26889/9781784671327
NATURGAS. *Informes Anuales*, several years.
Pöyry. 2017. *Cost-Benefit Analysis of STEP, as first phase of MIDCAT – Final Report*. Pöyry Management Consulting.
Russell, Martin. 2021. *The Nord Stream 2 pipeline. Economic, environmental and geopolitical issues*. European Parliamentary Research Service. PE 690.705.
Secretaría de Estado de Energía. 2019. Plan de Acción Preventivo del Sistema Gasista español. In https://energia.gob.es/gas/Legislacion/Documents/Legislacion-2020/Preventive-Action-Plan-2019-2023.pdf
SEDIGAS. *Informes Anuales*, several years.
Terzian, Pierre. 1998. *Le gaz natural. Perspectives pour 2010-2020 (disponibilités, contraintes et dépendances)*. Paris: Economica.
Tortella, Gabriel. 2022. Petróleo y política en la España del siglo XX. In *Energía y política. Una historia del petróleo en España*, edited by Gloria Quiroga Valle, 17–39. Madrid: Catarata.
Valdaliso, Jesús M., Alvarado-García, Carlos, and Suárez, Patricia. 2022. *Nortegas (1845-2021): Historia de la industria del gas en el norte de España*. Madrid: Marcial Pons.
Valdaliso, Jesús M., and Lobo, Jacinto. 2022. Gasoductos, suministro energético e interconexión en la frontera entre Francia y España: lecciones de dos fracasos. *The Conversation*, August 30, 2022, https://theconversation.com/gasoductos-suministro-energetico-e-interconexion-en-la-frontera-entre-francia-y-espana-lecciones-de-dos-fracasos-189404
Valdaliso, Jesús M., Suárez, Patricia, and Alvarado-García, Carlos. 2024. ¿Gas natural, carbón o petróleo? Los determinantes del retraso de la transición energética en el norte de España (1958-1974). *Revista de Historia Industrial* 33 (90): 81–104. https://doi.org/10.1344/rhiihr.40496
Vela, Antonio. 1995. *El gas como alternativa energética*. Madrid: Alianza Universidad.

10 Gas supplies to France and Italy from the end of the Second World War to the present day*

Andrea Giuntini and Jean-Pierre Williot

10.1 Introduction

In France, when Gaz de France was created by the 1946 law on the nationalisation of the electricity and gas industries, 600 gas plants were scattered across the country. Over 53% produced less than 500,000 m^3 of gas per year. For a long time, manufactured gas constituted the industrial means of supplying distribution networks. The solutions for the future focused on concentrating production or finding other resources. In the north and east of France, gas producers were considering the development of coking plants. In the southwest, the presence of natural gas was already changing the outlook. The transformation that took place in the following years was a veritable industrial revolution. The exploitation of domestic gas deposits increased following the discovery of Lacq in 1951. A gas transmission network was justified and a cross-border pipeline was constructed to transport Dutch gas imports. LNG technology further expanded the possibilities for bringing gas from Algeria. In the 1970s, France continued to import gas, increasing its number of suppliers and European connections as far afield as Russia. The economic and political trade-off resided in the choice of these contracts to balance the risks. Before the Russian gas import crisis began, Russian gas accounted for no more than a fifth of the gas consumed in France.

Meanwhile, Italy's energy history over the past 80 years clearly shows its weakness in domestic energy resources, a long-term problem that the country has always suffered from since its first industrialisation at the end of the nineteenth century. After an initial phase of excitement regarding its possible autonomy, thanks to the entrepreneur Enrico Mattei (Giuntini and Pozzi,

* This research forms part of the results of the R+D+I Research Project "Gas in Latin Europe: A comparative and global perspective (1818–1945)", PID2020-112844GB-I00, financed by the Ministry of Science and Innovation of the Government of Spain and ERDF Funds.

DOI: 10.4324/9781003428695-10

2003), a public administrator well aware of Italy's strong dependence with respect to energy supplies, which still prevails today, the country became immersed in market conditions that were exposed to political turbulence and which inevitably affected it significantly.

The two trajectories of Italy and France will therefore be compared here, as they are sometimes similar and often different.

10.1.1 From the absence of natural gas to the discovery of gas in the South-West: French hopes

The search for new gas resources began in the 1950s in France as part of the drive to replace coal with other raw materials. Coal represented 80% of supplies to gasworks and coking plants. The decline of coal to produce gas began with the use of petroleum products, which reduced the price per m^3 of gas produced by 75% (Beltran and Williot, 1992, p. 61). Propane distribution was another solution. Natural gas was first used very locally. On the one hand, there were very few known deposits in France. Geologists had identified resources in Juré and especially in the Pyrenees. The Saint Marcet gas field, discovered in 1939, led to the creation of a national south-western gas company after the war. In 1948, this deposit produced 166 million m^3 of natural gas, which was used to supply a number of towns, including Toulouse and Pau. The consumption of natural gas in France was five times lower than in Italy (Beltran and Williot, 1992).

The discovery of the Lacq deposit at the end of 1951 represented a major new opportunity. First, due to the reserves that would be very useful to the economy of the south-west. Second, Lacq reduced France's need to import raw materials to produce gas. And finally because several companies could ensure its growth. Difficulties arose from the complex technical operating conditions and the need to coordinate the operating companies, with Gaz de France claiming responsibility for distribution. There was another problem associated with the Lacq that proved decisive. To make use of this national resource, which was sufficiently abundant to exceed local needs, the construction of a transmission network was the preferred solution. Other regions, and ultimately the Paris region, would be supplied with Lacq gas. The international context of the events in Suez in 1956 and the tension over energy supplies led to the change. In 1960, the Lacq deposit represented almost 20 times the production of south-west France before it was discovered. In just a few years, France had fully entered the era of natural gas which was transported from the south to Paris. Until then, in 1952 for example, the gas consumed was produced mainly by cracking or reforming petroleum products (80.7%), using propane or propane air (0.11%), together with coal gas produced in factories (17.6%). Natural gas accounted for a very small share. In 1960, purchases of natural gas in south-west France accounted for 26.6% of gas emissions.

10.1.2 Natural gas research and production in Italy immediately after the Second World War

In Italy, during the Reconstruction of the country, discoveries of natural gas wells multiplied after the first tentative explorations in the fascist era (Giuntini, 2020). The deposits were found in the north-eastern area of the country, concentrated in the Po Valley; they raised both hopes and perplexities, with some considering it an enormously relevant moment in the history of energy in Italy while others showed distrust from the outset (Samorè, 2010). The role played by Enrico Mattei was decisive in this phase. He was a convinced supporter of national energy autonomy within a context of public monopoly and understood the need to direct the energy sector into the hands of the state with the creation, in 1953, of the Ente Nazionale Idrocarburi (ENI), thus inaugurating a true methane policy in Italy (Pozzi, 2009). In fact, only a public player was able to guarantee sufficient investment in research and production as the hydrocarbons industry is typically capital intensive in which the company has to be very large in order to exploit economies of scale. This was considered by Mattei, who faced opposition from the world's large oil companies because he sourced himself from producing countries without their intermediation, which was cheaper than the fragmented ownership of the methane wealth among small producers, as many liberalists argued at the time. ENI, which is still Italy's largest state-owned company, became the exclusive concessionaire for both the exploration and cultivation of hydrocarbon deposits in the Po Valley and for the construction and operation of pipelines for the transport of hydrocarbon minerals.

Meanwhile, during the same decades, there was a sharp reduction in the production of manufactured gas, which is far less flexible than methane and, as such, is unable to adapt production to both daily and seasonal fluctuations in consumption. It should also be emphasised that the transition from one technology to another represented a major difficulty for those working in the sector, to the point of jeopardising the technological transition. From being a supplementary element, methane gained a space of its own as a gas produced by distillation, and gradually grew to influence the economic destiny of a country historically suffering from energy shortages: In 1955, 3,600 million m^3 were produced and distributed, three years later methane gas provided the largest contribution to the national energy balance, supplying around 12% of the available energy, a percentage certainly lower than the hopes raised in the euphoric climate of the early 1950s. The impact on energy needs still remained modest: compressed gas production represented 19.26% of the national total in 1943, 8.81% in 1944, 11.30% in 1945 and 5.02% in 1946. Oil production accounted for 2.13% of the national total in 1943, 6.97% in 1944, 9.11% in 1945 and 10.91% in 1946.

10.1.3 Gas exploration in Algeria: Another hope for the Sahara

For a long time, France has also sought other energy resources in its imperial territory. The Saharan deposits were mostly discovered by the oil companies.

A succession of borehole drilling exercises led to the identification of In Salah in southern Algeria in 1953, followed by Edjeleh in 1956. The gas deposits were certainly interesting, but too far from the sea to be easily exploited. This was not the case at Hassi R'Mel, where Algeria's national oil exploration company discovered a considerable gas deposit. France could envisage being supplied with gas from the other side of the Mediterranean. The resources estimated in 1956 were more than eight times those known at Lacq. Ten billion m^3 could be produced per year. In a meeting of the Gaz de France Board of Directors on 18 July 1958, the view was expressed that this resource, which was still French, could supply metropolitan France despite the war that had begun.

France was not the only country involved, as the considerable resources at Hassi R'Mel were of commercial interest throughout the Mediterranean basin, particularly in Italy. The trade-off was less about transporting the gas than about how to do it. While the Italian gas companies opted to transfer the gas across the Mediterranean by pipeline, the French implemented another technical solution. This was also being explored by the British with the creation of British Methane by Constock and the Gas Council. In France, it was Gaz de France's research departments, working step by step with various partners such as special steel producers, insulation manufacturers, shipyards and L'Air Liquide, that brought the technology of LNG carriers, gas liquefaction stations and regasification terminals to fruition. L'Air Liquide set up a subsidiary under the name Méthane Liquide in 1957. The Société d'Etudes pour le Gaz Naturel du Sahara set up a research station at the Centre d'essais des propulseurs de Villeras in the Paris region and The New Studies and Techniques Division of Gaz de France created a liquefied methane department in 1959. A year and a half later, an experimental station opened in Nantes. In March 1965, the first deliveries of Algerian gas arrived at the Le Havre terminal (Beltran and Williot, 2016b). In Algeria, the Société nationale de recherche de pétroles en Algérie, founded with French capital, came under the control of the new Algerian Government. From then until 1971, Algerian gas was exploited and delivered by Somalgaz, a company owned 50% by the Algerian company Sonatrach and 50% by the French oil company Compagnie française des Pétroles-ERAP.

10.1.4 From Mattei's dream to the diversification of energy supply from foreign markets

The growth pace of the Italian economy in the 1950s and 1960s soon showed that the gas reserves stored in the Po Valley were not sufficient, despite the undeniable success of numerous drilling operations. From 1946 to 1965, the production of natural gas in northern Italy rose from 62 million m^3 to around 6.8 billion m^3, which confirms that the discovery of sizeable methane reserves in the Po Valley initially represented a providential opportunity to foster national industrial development by expanding the supply of energy. The availability of gas represented an important support for Italy in its expansion phase and an energy supply that allowed imports to be contained. There was undoubtedly a strong imbalance: production and demand were mainly concentrated in the north of the country, where in the period under consideration there was an alternation between the exploitation of the deposits in Lombardy and those in Emilia Romagna, due to the progressive depletion of the former.

But this was still not enough. As the years went by, it became increasingly difficult to discover new deposits and the energy supply did not expand in line with economic development and the requirements of the country's productive fabric. In terms of production, since the possibility of discovering new deposits in the Po Valley had now almost been ruled out, except at great depths, which was interesting from a geological point of view but at the time unfeasible from a technical and economic standpoint, there remained the possibility of exploring the Adriatic coastal strip, where the preliminary surveys carried out up until then had indicated the existence of interesting reserves. Even this second hypothesis, however, would have required a long time and considerable investment, since most of the work would have had to be carried out offshore. The last year of growth was 1962 in terms of physical quantities in industrial thermal consumption until the start of imports and the exploitation of new discoveries in the offshore Adriatic.

The expansion of a number of energy-intensive sectors of the Italian industrial system soon scuppered Mattei's dream of an energy autonomy that the country had never had and would never obtain. Therefore, Italy had no choice but to resort to importing gas, as well as oil, in an attempt to supply its consumption levels, which were increasing dramatically.

10.2 The increase in external supplies

10.2.1 The first cross-border networks and supply from the Netherlands

France's gas supply was slowly coming into line with supplies from outside the country. Algerian gas became the property of the new state and changed its commercial nature for France, which no longer saw it as a national reserve but as an import. Dutch gas already had this status. The discovery of the enormous gas field in the province of Groningen in 1959 had laid the foundations for a European gas market (Kielich, 1988). Exploitation forecasts were based on a considerable amount of data. Reserves were soon estimated at over a thousand billion m^3. In 1963, the French and Dutch expressed their convergent interest; the former to supplement their energy resources, the latter to sell their gas. The first gas purchase contract from Groningen was signed in 1966. It was intended to serve mainly the northern and eastern regions of France, mostly due to technical reasons related to the compatibility of the gas in the network with manufactured gas and gas from Lacq. While until 1965 none of the natural gas supplied by Gaz de France came from abroad, five years later, in 1970, 55.6% of the natural gas purchased by the national company came from the Netherlands. In 1976, when other suppliers were included in the imports,

Dutch gas accounted for 58.4% and Algerian gas for 18.7%, complemented with gas from Lacq and imports of so-called Soviet gas.

10.2.2 The opening of an international perspective

At the same time, and in alignment with the principle of broader diversification, the ENI began to penetrate the international energy market, over time becoming highly specialised in the field of exploration and exploitation of deposits, an activity in which it gained positions of absolute prominence on a global scale, which it still maintains today. At the same time, the political weight of the public decision-maker in the energy field was evidently being strengthened.

Following the line already drawn by Mattei, the prospect of supplementing the national methane gas resources with imports from Libya, the Netherlands and the Soviet Union, and later also Algeria, took shape definitively from the mid-1960s. The discovery of large quantities of natural gas in these countries, together with the progress made in transport techniques by pipeline and by LNG carriers even over long distances, made the Italian turnaround possible. In addition to policies aimed at energy saving combined with a new environmental sensitivity, gas imports were also supported by the need to differentiate the types and origins of energy raw materials as much as possible so as to achieve both greater security in energy supplies and to implement a certain amount of competition between the various energy sources in the domestic market, with favourable effects on prices (De Focatiis and Maestroni, 2013).

Another advantage for the national economic system derived from gas imports resided in the availability of methane. This would have made it possible to reduce the imbalances in the refining yield of petroleum products. Even though the production of fuel oil was pushed to the maximum at that time, it did not fully cover the domestic demand, and the difference had to be imported. The security of being able to dispose of a considerable amount of methane in the future, regardless of the outcome of the search for new deposits in the national territory and in the surrounding seabed, would have made it possible to fully exploit the existing gas pipeline network. In fact, the country, especially in the Po Valley, had an efficient network of methane pipelines, the economic life of which extended beyond the period of presumed availability of national methane reserves. Importing large quantities of gas implemented this network and it was not left unused before its time.

In the five-year period 1965–70, ENI signed four different supply agreements. The first, with a duration of 20 years, was signed in 1965 with the Esso company and provided for the import of 3 billion m^3 per year (which began to arrive in 1971), to be carried out by sea, after the liquefaction of the methane, between the Arzew terminals on the Libyan coast, and the Panigaglia storage and regasification station near La Spezia. A second contract, again for 20 years, but for 6 billion m^3 per year, was signed in 1969, with the Soviet state company Soyutz Neft Export. A third agreement, similar in duration and quantity to the one signed with the Russians, was reached with the Dutch company NAM (formed by Esso and Shell). The latter two agreements provided for supply by pipeline, with two pipelines connecting to the Italian network in the Po Valley. The last contract was signed with Algeria and was based on the construction of a pipeline laid on the seabed between Tunisia, Sicily and Calabria. The imports envisaged by the first three contracts gradually materialised, making it possible to dispose of a foreign supply of almost 12 billion m^3 in the mid-1970s, which added to a domestic production of just under 15 billion m^3.

Italy was one of the western countries that suffered most from the dramatic rise in oil prices following the 1973 oil shock. The consequence of this was also the acceleration of the transition to methane, which had already begun earlier, in order to secure a suitable alternative to crude oil.

All this obviously entailed a technological transformation, which had a major impact. From a technological point of view *stricto sensu*, the switch to natural gas implied, in fact, considerable interventions in the distribution network. It was therefore necessary to adapt the end devices. This intervention that was on the whole extremely demanding, also because it had to be carried out over a period of time that was strictly scheduled to coincide with the replacement of the old gas. This also explains the logic of gradually increasing supplies of methane, rather than immediately introducing full methanisation. Moreover, it was unthinkable to dismantle the existing workshops extremely quickly, an operation that was completely inefficient. Ultimately, a supplementary rather than a replacement role was envisaged for methane. In the final analysis, the personnel problems should not be overlooked either. The loss of the professional identity of the workers, even of the most senior managers, was a constant concern due to the opposition to change that had been created with respect to the fear of wiping out the professional know-how accumulated over the years.

10.2.3 Using LNG technology to complement gas pipelines

By the mid-1980s, France's gas supply situation had changed radically. The first change was in the proportion of imported gas of Gaz de France's supplies. Natural gas purchases had increased 16-fold in 20 years. The proportion of gas purchased in mainland France had fallen to 15%. Three foreign exporters supplied similar levels: Algeria (28%), the Netherlands (24.6%) and USSR (22.9%). This distribution highlights a second essential element in French gas supplies. The balance between supplies by land and through the LNG chain played a strategic role as soon as the supply of natural gas began.

At the same time, heavy technical investments were made in the domestic gas transmission network. The Lacq gas network had expanded to almost cover the country. Later, supplies at border crossings required further investment, both in interconnections and in the transport of different gases. The transmission network increased from 9,000 kilometres in 1960 to 23,000 kilometres in 1985. The arrival of Dutch and Russian gas made a major contribution to this. The national dispatching of gas flows was introduced in 1963.

Interconnections known as "Stars" enabled the different sources of gas to be linked up (Beltran and Williot, 2012, p. 76). Taking advantage of France's coastline was another way of balancing resources. Three LNG terminals were built in Le Havre, Fos-sur-Mer and Montoir-de-Bretagne between 1960 and 1980. Finally, other means of gas production almost completely disappeared for several decades. In 1985, Gaz de France bought less than 120,000 tonnes of liquefied petroleum gas and no more coal or light distillates. Twenty years earlier, the company had sent a level of production to the gas distribution network that still justified the purchase of one million tonnes of coal (compared with four times as much in 1947) and 400,000 tonnes of light distillates. While only a quarter of the French population received natural gas directly and three quarters received manufactured gases in the mid-1960s, ten years later the proportion was 84.7% in favour of natural gas and 98.5% in 1985 (Williot, 2020).

10.2.4 The development of GNL

Liquefied natural gas is the energy source that has grown the most in international energy trade in recent years (Dorigoni, 2009). In addition to the technological and infrastructure investments required to construct regasifiers, it should also be underlined that this resource is extremely important for those countries that still suffer from difficulties in accessing gas pipelines. In Italy there are currently four regasifiers—Panigaglia, Livorno, Piombino, Rovigo—where an increasingly significant amount of LNG arrives by ship. Other regasifiers, identified in the south of the peninsula and on the Adriatic Sea, are currently being studied. However, in addition to the construction data, the frequent opposition of the resident populations must also be taken into account.

Between 2008 and 2020, LNG trade increased by 6.2% per year compared to 2.3% for crude oil and 4.2% for coal. In 2000, LNG's share of global consumption reached 6% and that of pipeline trade 16% of total demand; throughout the decade of 2008–2018, global gas consumption increased by an average of 2.5% per year and most of this growth was met by increased LNG use. Italy imports LNG mainly from Qatar, with which it has secured a long-term contract. However, imports from the United States, which are increasingly decisive due to the growing production of shale gas, and those from North Africa are also essential. Supplies from Tanzania and Mozambique are also beginning to emerge and could enter the market. In short, the system is run by private companies similarly to the United States and is very much linked to the fluctuating prices of the product and the often changing contracts, which affect the quantities traded. In fact, the LNG market increasingly resembles the crude oil market rather than the natural gas market.

10.2.5 Major gas contracts negotiated by Gaz de France under state supervision

There are three main reasons for this decisive switch to imported supplies of natural gas in France. As part of the process of European integration, energy trade was to become increasingly important. This was reflected in the creation of Europe-wide transport infrastructures (Beltran and Williot, 2012, pp. 104–126). Gradually, an extensive network of gas pipelines and links with LNG terminals enabled France to receive gas from distant Russia, the North Sea, the Benelux countries and the Mediterranean. But very little of the gas purchased came from the European Community, with the exception of the Netherlands. The gas only crossed borders. At the beginning of the 1960s, natural gas accounted for just 9.7% of total available gas resources in Europe (Beltran and Williot, 2016b). Only Italy had natural gas production to supply its distribution network.

The situation in Europe then changed slightly. In the North Sea, systematic prospecting by the United Kingdom from 1964 onwards led to the discovery of exploitable deposits off the English and Scottish coasts. The prospect of accession to the European Community by countries with gas reserves, such as Norway and Denmark, and of course the United Kingdom, was an argument that favoured European enlargement in 1972. In the end, Norway preferred to remain outside the Community and the United Kingdom to exploit its gas. The majority of gas in France came from Russia and Algeria. This choice highlights a second essential factor. All the major contracts negotiated to import gas were signed by buyer consortia. But there was no question of France contributing to them without state intervention. Whether with Algeria, where negotiations were often tough and driven by historical ties with a former territory of the French Empire, or with the USSR in the 1970s, where the commercial relationship formed part of a diplomatic effort at the highest level of government, each gas contract had a strong political content (Beltran and Williot, 2016a). The third factor is the position of Gaz de France, which was created following the nationalisation of the electricity and gas industries in 1946. It had a public service mission to fulfil. When they decided to convert their networks to natural gas, the directors of Gaz de France knew perfectly well that they would have to rely on external resources to support an ambitious commercial policy. They constantly argued in favour of expanding supplies. In 1977, Gaz de France Informations proudly ran the headline "Eldfisk, Cod and others, our first offshore gas" (GDFI, 1977, p. 1).

10.3 France and Italy faced with gas energy dependency

10.3.1 Diversified supply of the French gas market from the 1990s

This strategy took full effect in the 1990s. On 12 July 1993, Gaz de France and Gazprom signed a new cooperation agreement to strengthen the tasks of the coordination committee set up between the two companies in 1992. In the same year, Gaz de France opened a representative office in Kiev. International activities were also developed with gas transit countries such as Hungary, the Czech Republic and Slovakia. Partnerships in Central Europe had largely existed since the MEGAL (Mittel-Europäische Gasleitung Gesellschaft) pipeline project, which brought together Austrian (WAG), German (Ruhrgas) and French (GDF) companies in 1975. In the North Sea, Gaz de France signed agreements in 1986 with producers (Statoil, Shell, Norsk Hydro, Saga, Elf, Conoco and Total) to acquire 220 billion m³ of gas over a 30-year period. But above all, at the beginning of the 1990s, Gaz de France looked for new horizons. An LNG project in Nigeria, cooperation with Iran, whose gas reserves appeared to be colossal and interest in Oman were all part of the objective of a gas supply that would become global. In 1993, the situation was only prospective. Algeria still accounted for 27% of natural gas imports, Russia 32%, the North Sea 18% and Groningen 13% (Revue de l'énergie, 1994, p. 202).

The complexity of building new infrastructure and the lengthy time it took to set up long-term gas contracts meant that this pattern evolved very slowly. In the mid-2000s, the same suppliers continued to dominate the market, but the trade-offs between LNG and pipeline supply were more open. The entry of new producers such as Qatar, Nigeria and Egypt and the more frequent use of short-term spot contracts, similar to buying by the load, have slightly altered the geographical structure of France's gas supplies. In the early 2010s, GRT Gaz's transmission system could count on a firm entry capacity of 780 GWh per day at the Montoir de Bretagne and Fos LNG terminals, and more than double that by land (Beltran and Williot, 2012, p. 249). Unlike Spain, which reserved more than 60% of its supplies for LNG, France still only subscribed to 28%. The main sources of supply were, therefore, still those that had been determined by long-term contracts for many years.

10.3.2 The risks of a dependent country

At a time of a real gas war, the crisis due to the Russian–Ukrainian conflict has shown Italy's energy vulnerability even more clearly (Frusciante, 2012; Bellodi, 2022). However, collapse has been avoided thanks to the policy of diversification of sources, which Italy began some time ago, foreseeing that sooner or later such an outcome would occur. It is diversification, in fact, that makes it possible, in the absence of energy self-sufficiency based on abundant domestic reserves as in the Italian case, to protect one's national sovereignty, threatened by excessive dependence on a preponderant supplier (Corazza, 2008). It should also be remembered that Italy decided to renounce nuclear energy production in a referendum held in 1987. A simple figure helps to understand Italy's condition: in 2021 it produced 3.34 billion m³ of natural gas for a consumption of 76.1 billion, that is, 4% of national needs, 38% of which were met by Russian exports.

A crucial alternative source of supply for Italy is North Africa and in particular Algeria, from where more than 20 billion m³ of gas is imported, a figure that has increased further to cope with the interruption of Russian supplies. Tunisia and Libya are the other two countries that enable Italy's energy survival. No less important is the pipeline that brings gas from Azerbaijan to the Salento coast, which covers 9.5% of the country's consumption. Finally, gas also arrives to Italy from the north: Norway and the Netherlands contribute 2.9% of imports.

The Trans Adriatic Pipeline (TAP), the gas pipeline cutting through the Adriatic Sea, is a key resource for Italy. The gas comes from Azerbaijan and passes through Turkey, Greece and Albania before arriving on the coast of Puglia. Besieged by opposition from environmental movements because of the alleged environmental impact, the project has actually proved providential for the country, although doubts about the geopolitical risk of passing through Turkish territory still prevail.

This scenario shows how exposed the country is to geopolitical instabilities that can potentially damage its energy supply, to which Italy is unable to respond with domestic resources (Floros, 2020).

10.3.3 France and European dependence on Russian gas: Between weight and risk

Therefore, questions must be asked about the level of dependency on each supplier. France is a unique case in Europe. It was far less dependent on Russian gas than other countries when recent geopolitical developments condemned supplies. In 2017, Gazprom sold 53 billion m^3 of gas to Germany by pipeline, 29 to Turkey and 24 to Italy. France was only the fourth largest buyer, with 12 billion m^3 imported. This lesser dependence of France is both the result of geography, which encourages it to rely just as much on supplies from other horizons, and the reflection of a certain historical caution. The political and gas conflict between Russia and Ukraine reinforced this position. With the bypass routes envisaged by Gazprom, through the highly controversial Nord Stream 2 (the outcome of which we now know) and through Turkstream, aimed at exporting gas via the Black Sea, France could oppose other solutions. Some of these are commercial choices, such as favouring LNG supplies, which are just another form of dependence on Algeria, Qatar, Nigeria or the United States. But others are linked to France's energy policy, in which electricity plays a much more important role than gas in the energy balance sheet, and no doubt to the pressure of an increasingly important context. Energy sobriety, the phasing out of fossil fuels and the greening of everyday practices will perhaps constitute other factors that limit dependence. Would this benefit new autonomous gas production?

10.4 Conclusions

A brief review of the events in the two countries allows us to highlight similarities and differences. In both cases there have been discoveries—in the Po Valley in Italy, in the south-west in France—that push towards the methane solution, but which in the long run will prove to be insufficient, especially in the Italian case. Both France and Italy, thus, find themselves obliged to resort to certain producer countries, both European and non-European, to which they will remain linked in terms of imports. The advent of LNG makes imports easier and less costly, but still necessary to meet energy needs. The Italian case stands out for the creation of ENI in 1951, thanks to a long-term strategic vision, which proved decisive for a country historically lacking in energy.

The history of Gaz de France took another turn when it was absorbed by Suez to create Engie. In France, gas remains an energy source that is not a leader due to a political choice made in the 1970s to favour nuclear-generated electricity. This is no doubt partly due to the country's dependence on external gas supplies. However, today, France suffers less from a dependence on Russian gas due to a wide differentiation of sources. In addition to these differences, which stem from the resources or political choices of each country, there are forms of gas cooperation that unite the two countries. The creation of an interconnected European network has made gas trading possible on both sides.

References

Bellodi, Leonardo. 2022. *Gas e potere. Geopolitica dell'energia dalla Guerra fredda a oggi*. Roma: LUISS University Press.
Beltran, Alain, and Williot, Jean-Pierre. 1992. *Le Noir et le Bleu. Quarante ans d'histoire du Gaz de France*. Paris: Belfond.
Beltran, Alain, and Williot, Jean-Pierre. 2012. *Les routes du gaz*. Paris: Cherche Midi.
Beltran, Alain, and Williot, Jean-Pierre. 2016a. Gaz de France and Soviet Natural Gas: Balancing Technological Constraints with Political Considerations, 1950s to 1980s. In *Cold War Energy: Oil and Gas between Western and Eastern Europe*, edited by Jeronim Perovic, 231–252. London: Palgrave Macmillan.
Beltran, Alain, and Williot, Jean-Pierre. 2016b. Le gaz alternatif: les méthaniers et les routes maritimes du GNL des années 1950 aux années 2010. In *Les routes du pétrole. Oil Routes*, edited by Alain Beltran, 33–49. Bruxelles: Peter Lang.
Corazza, Cristina. 2008. *La guerra del gas. I nuovi padroni dell'energia, i rischi per l'Italia e l'Europa*. Milano: Il sole-24 ore.
De Focatiis, Marinella, and Maestroni, Angelo. eds. 2013. *Il mercato del gas tra scenari normativi e interventi di regolazione*. Milano: Giuffrè editore.
Dorigoni, Susanna. 2009. *Il gas naturale liquefatto per l'Europa. Le ragioni, l'impatto sul mercato e le prospettive*. Milano: Franco Angeli.
Floros, Demostenes. 2020. *Guerra e pace dell'energia. La strategia per il gas naturale dell'Italia tra Federazione russa e NATO*. Santarcangelo di Romagna: Diarkos.
Frusciante, Alessandra. 2012. *Le vie del gas. L'Italia e le politiche energetiche dell'Ue, storia e problemi*. Roma: Edizioni Nuova Cultura.
Gaz de France Informations (GDFI) n°344, novembre 1977, p. 1.
Giuntini, Andrea. 2020. La vicenda del gas naturale in Italia dai primi ritrovamenti dopo la seconda Guerra mondiale al boom economico. In *Cercanas pero distintas. La desigual trayectoria de la industria del gas en las regiones del sur de Europa (siglos XIX-XX)*, edited by Isabel Bartolomé Rodríguez, Mercedes Fernández-Paradas, and Jesús Mirás Araujo, 43–60. Madrid: Marcial Pons.
Giuntini, Andrea, and Pozzi, Daniele. eds. 2003. *Energia per il territorio. Enrico Mattei e l'industria del metano in Italia*. Lodi: Giona.
Kielich, Wolf. 1988. *Subterranean commonwealth. 25 years Gasunie and Natural Gas*. Amsterdam: Uniepers.
Pozzi, Daniele. 2009. *Dai gatti selvaggi al cane a sei zampe. Tecnologia, conoscenza e organizzazione nell'AGIP e nell'ENI di Enrico Mattei*. Venezia: Marsilio.
Revue de l'énergie, n°457, mars–avril 1994, p. 202.

Samorè, Francesco. 2010. *La piramide del gas. Distribuire energia al territorio (1945–2009)*. Milano: Bruno Mondadori.

Williot, Jean-Pierre. 2020. La conception régionale des réseaux gaziers en France: intérêts économiques, structuration du territoire, opportunités techniques. In *Cercanas pero distintas. La desigual trayectoria de la industria del gas en las regiones del sur de Europa (siglos XIX-XX)*, edited by Isabel Bartolomé Rodríguez, Mercedes Fernández-Paradas, and Jesús Mirás Araujo, 23–42. Madrid: Marcial Pons.

11 The redevelopment and repurposing of historic gas sites

Russell Thomas

11.1 Introduction

The manufacture of gas was one of the key developments during the industrial revolution, bringing the first effective form of lighting. Originating as a commercial offering in 1806, gas was manufactured on sites referred to as gasworks, which eventually became present in most towns and cities across Europe. The technology was initially spread by British companies such as the Imperial Continental Gas Association and British engineers seeking new opportunities abroad (Thomas, 2020a, Moyano and Thomas, 2016).

The technology constantly evolved and with new processes developed across the world and the technology transferred between countries. This enabled the gas industry to increase production, flexibility and utilisation, whilst entering the cooking and heating markets when competing with the emergence of electricity (Thomas, 2018).

Gasworks had a profound impact on the landscape in which they were situated. In many small towns they were the only significant industrial activity. The most notable feature visually, the gasholders were in many cases the largest industrial structures in the area, dominating the skyline along with cathedrals and church spires. The gasworks were important culturally and socially, through its architecture, people it employed and societal changes it introduced (Thomas, 2020a).

The design of the gasworks could be ornate, such as the restored gasholders at Kings Cross, London, the architecture of Gaswerks Augsburg in Bavaria (Figure 11.1), or the ornate private gasworks built to supply Sudbury Hall in England. As the industry moved into the early decades of the twentieth century, gasworks became more utilitarian. Steel framed structures dominating, some enclosed by bricks or as became common with some German designs, the plant inside the frame, received little protection from the elements (Thomas, 2020a; Thomas, 2020b).

Within Europe the manufactured gas era ended between the 1960s and 1980s. They left a legacy of by-products and wastes which found their way into the ground. The survival of structures from the gas industry is limited and varies between countries. The redevelopment of gasworks provides an

DOI: 10.4324/9781003428695-11

Figure 11.1 The restored Ofenhaus at Gaswerks Augsburg.
Source: Russell Thomas.

interesting challenge, made all the greater if historic structures survive and are incorporated in the redevelopment.

11.2 The evolution of coal gas manufacture

The first commercial gas plants were erected by 1806 by William Murdoch and Samuel Clegg (Murdoch's former apprentice). These gasworks were constructed to light the mills of Philips and Lee (Salford) and Henry Lodge (Sowerby Bridge) respectively. In the years following many gasworks were built to light other mills and factories across the United Kingdom. In 1812 the world's first company was established in London to provide a public gas supply, the Gas Light and Coke Company (GLCC). Constructing three initial gasworks, they produced gas which was supplied by underground pipes connected to street lights, lighting in public buildings and those wealthy enough to be able to light their homes. This model formed the structure of future energy utilities, being replicated first in London, then across the UK and Europe. The evolution of the gas industry has been described in more detail by the author previously (Thomas, 2018; Thomas, 2020a).

The process of manufacturing gas from coal consisted of heating coal in a sealed long tubular vessel called a "retort", in an oxygen-free environment, the heat caused the coal to decompose, releasing gas and other by-products. The gas industry first used small benches of horizontal cast iron retorts which were loaded by hand. These were heated from a furnace beneath the retorts to a temperature of ≈600°C. As retort design evolved using fireclay and silica, higher temperatures could be withstood. The introduction of the regenerative heating of incoming air; and the use of producers, allowing gas to be burnt adjacent to the outside of the retorts, allowed temperatures within the retorts to eventually reach ≈1200°C (Thomas, 2020b).

Retort design evolved across Europe (see Figure 11.2). In Rheims, France, Emile Coze developed the inclined retort from the horizontal retort; it was later improved upon by Frank Morris at Brentford gasworks in London. It saved labour, utilising gravity to aid loading and unloading down the incline (Thomas, 2020b).

To maximise on the benefits of gravity, many engineers had attempted the use of vertical retorts. It was not until Dr Julius Bueb of the German Continental Gas Company in Dessau, who developed an *intermittent vertical retort* in 1902, that any success was achieved. A few were built in Britain, the first being Ayres Quay in Sunderland (Thomas, 2020a).

This design was improved by British engineers Woodall-Duckham and Glover-West, who developed a system which could be operated continuously with certain British coals. Referred to as *continuous vertical retorts*, they were widely adopted across the UK and on some gasworks across continental Europe (Meade, 1921; Thomas, 2020b).

Another development in Europe was that of the "by-product coke oven". This was an adaptation of traditional coke ovens, which thermally decomposed coal to make coke for metal production. The development by-product coke oven dates to the 1850s, where Antoine Pauwels and Vincent Dubochet (cofounders of the Parisian Gas Lighting Company) patented a by-product coke oven, used in Saarbrucken by 1854. Two years later another French engineer Carl Knab constructed by-product coke ovens in Commentry, France. Further developments were made by Haupart and Carvès, Simon, Coppee, Hilgenstock and Koppers to give the design still used today (Thomas, 2020b).

Despite the efforts of industrialist Henry Simon, Britain was late adopting their use, due to the concern the process would reduce coke quality. However, by 1920 the process started to predominate. The surplus gas produced by the coke ovens, became an additional source of coal gas, similar in composition to that produced at gasworks. In areas of coke manufacture, the gas started to be used to supplement or replace gas manufacture at gasworks, with only storage and distribution activities maintained, the production buildings demolished. The West Yorkshire Gas Distribution Company was established to distribute surplus coke oven gas in West Yorkshire (UK) to gas undertakings (Thomas, 2023). Whilst they were a useful additional source of gas, only 5 by-product coke ovens were built on British gasworks (Thomas, 2020b).

Within mainland Europe similar situations arose where coke oven gas became important. In Belgium for example, following the destruction of the gasworks along the Western Front in the First World War, it was decided not

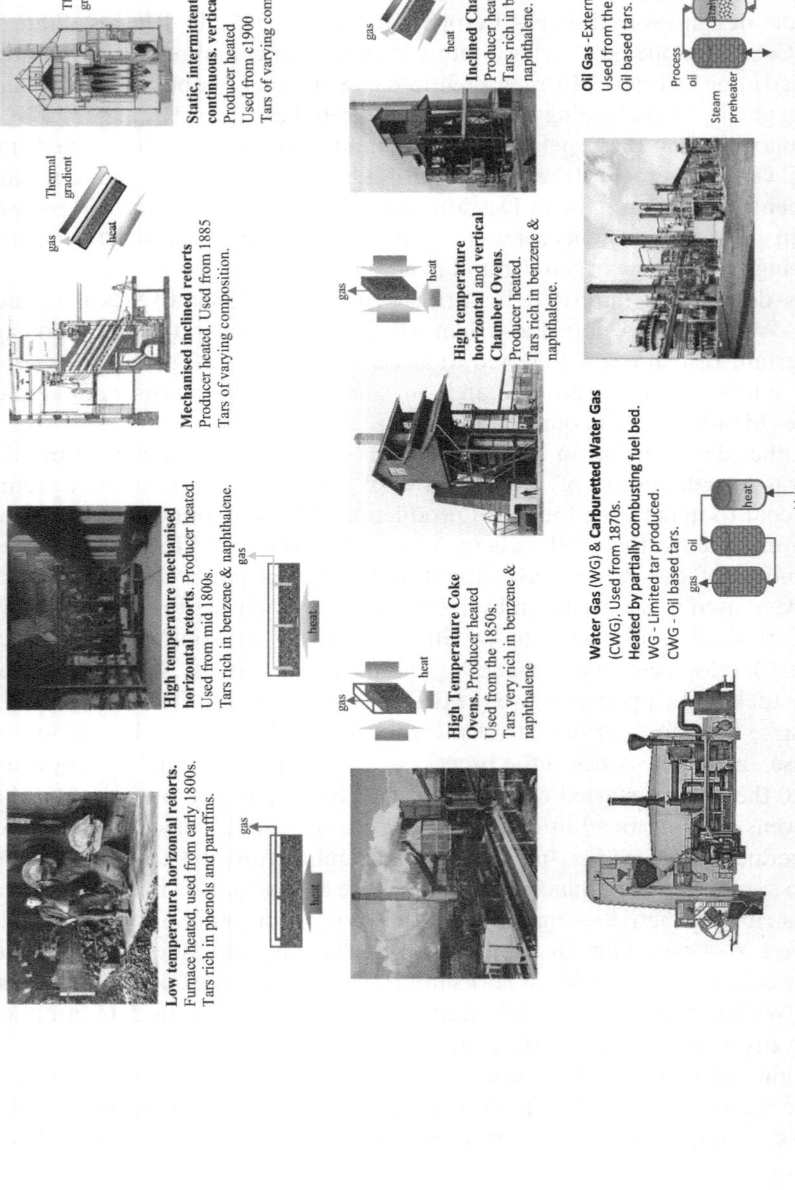

Figure 11.2 The evolution of gas making processes.

Source: Russell Thomas.

Figure 11.3 A chamber oven plant built at the Lund gasworks in Sweden.
Source: IGEM Archive.

rebuild the gasworks, but provide a supply of surplus gas from surviving coke ovens distributed by a new gas transmission system. This approach led to most the gasworks in Belgium being replaced by supplies of coke oven gas. Gas transmission pipelines were also built for supplying coke oven gas in parts of Germany, France and the Netherlands, leading to the predominance of coke oven gas and the closure of many gasworks in those areas (Thomas, 2018).

This development of by-product coke ovens was mirrored by the gas industry in the form of chamber ovens (Figure 11.3). These designs included horizontal, inclined and vertical chamber ovens; they were largely developed by German companies such as Klönne and Stettiner Chamotte Fabrik. They became popular across continental Europe, as they could use a wider range of coals than retorts, including poor-quality coals. As British gas coals started to decline, a few chamber ovens were built in Britain, including the last traditional coal gasworks, the White Lund gasworks in Morecambe (Thomas, 2020b).

11.2.1 Gas processing and its environmental legacy

The raw coal gas produced was not suitable for distribution to customers as it had many noxious impurities which required removal. These processes are described in brief here and in detail by the author elsewhere (Thomas, 2014a, b, c; Thomas, 2020b).

11.2.2 Tar removal

Once the gas left the retorts by means of the ascension pipe, it travelled through the hydraulic main and then the foul main. The hydraulic main, a water sealed trap above the retort, prevented the backflow of gas, but along with the foul

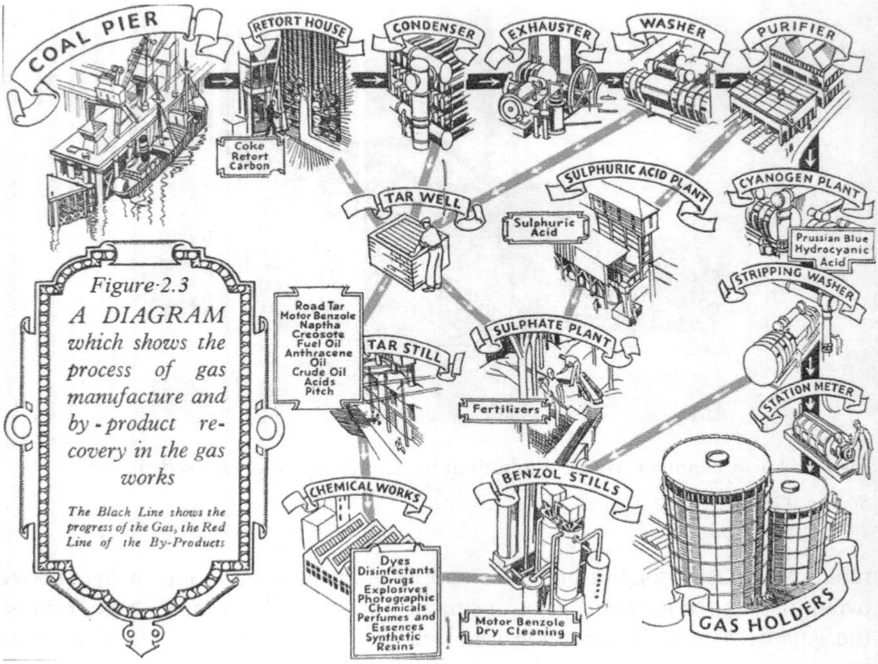

Figure 11.4 A diagram showing the gas manufacturing process and recovery of by-products.

Source: Gas Council 1950.

main also cooled the gas. The coal tar and liquor drained into the tar and liquor tank. The gas would then travel through a condenser, these came in many forms, and used the difference in the temperature of the gas and the coolant (ambient air or water, or a combination of the two) to cool the gas (Thomas, 2014a, b, c).

To keep the gas flowing from the retorts through the processing plant into the gasholder, a pump called an exhauster was used (see Figure 11.4). After the exhauster another set of "secondary" condenser were sometimes used on larger gasworks. These were replaced by a new innovation that was introduced in the 1930s, the electrostatic detarrers which used high-voltage positive charge to attract negatively charged tar droplets from the gas.

11.2.3 Washing and scrubbing

Washers and scrubber were employed for the removal of any entrained droplets of tar using a tar washer and the removal of soluble components such as phenols and ammonium. They would expose the gas to as much moisture as possible, passing the gas through seals or weirs of liquor (washer) or the exposure of the gas to wetted surfaces (scrubber).

Within the tar washer, the gas passed through tiny holes in a wire gauze, on which the tar was deposited. The Pelouze and Audouin tar extractor developed in France performed a similar function for removing residual tar (Thomas, 2020b).

The most common form of scrubbers took the form of tall circular towers, which were filled with material to provide a large surface area such as wooden boards or bricks. The liquor was sprayed down the tower and the gas passed upward (Thomas, 2014a, b, c).

The scrubber evolved into a mechanical washer/scrubber device, which consisted of a cylindrical vessel containing a series of rotating discs with a high surface area. The discs were wetted by liquor within the vessel and then exposed to the passing gas. Multiple units could be used, with the strength of the liquor in the secondary unit weaker to maximise the removal of impurities (Thomas, 2014a, b, c).

The liquor (once concentrated enough) and coal tar collected drained via pipes to the tar and liquor tank.

11.2.4 Purification

Two further noxious substances had to be removed: hydrogen sulphide and hydrogen cyanide. Hydrogen sulphide was present at a much higher concentration than cyanide, and formed noxious fumes of sulphur dioxide when burnt, leading to the deterioration of property within houses. Hydrogen cyanide was toxic in raw gas, although was destroyed when burnt. These substances were removed by passing them through iron boxes filled with hydrated lime or granular iron ore, or a combination of the two. Both the lime and iron oxide could be regenerated up to three times by exposure to air within the yard, before becoming either "foul" or "spent", respectively, containing high concentrations of cyanide (>6%) and sulphur (50–60%). Foul lime could be used as a fertiliser; spent oxide was used as a feedstock for sulphuric acid production. There were times when no market existed for either by-product and they were dumped as waste either on site or off.

There were also a range of processes which removed cyanide directly from the gas by passing the gas through a solution of iron carbonate or an iron salt. The cyanide being removed as soluble ferrocyanide. The cyanide was used in the metal industries or as the dye Prussian Blue. The cyanide was collected in large vats, often below ground which could potentially leak.

11.2.5 Benzol and naphthalene removal

Two organic substances could be removed from the gas directly, these were benzol and naphthalene. Benzol, which was a mixture of benzene, toluene, ethyl benzene and xylene, could be used as a replacement for motor fuel.

Naphthalene was troublesome for the gas engineer, its deposits blocking the gas mains, due to its bulky crystalline form. Both could be removed by circulating the gas through a static or rotary washer through which gas oil was circulated. The gas oil was then distilled to remove the substance.

11.2.6 Other gas making processes

A problem with coal gas manufacture was the time taken to get the gas plant producing gas, a couple of days. This required reliance on storage in gasholders; otherwise, retort would have to be kept hot to enable them to be brought into use at short notice, both inefficient and uneconomic.

An alternative gas making process called *Water Gas* had been perfected in 1873 by the American Thaddeus Lowe. It worked by injecting steam into a chamber (called a *generator*) filled with hot coke, to produce a gas consisting primarily of hydrogen and carbon monoxide. It required a continuous cycling between blowing air into the generator to increase the heat in the fuel bed and then injecting steam into the generator which produced the water gas but cooled the fuel bed. This gas lacked illuminating power, but could be enriched by the injection of oil, a process called Carburetted Water Gas (CWG). The first major installation of a CWG plant in Europe was at the Beckton gasworks near London, but the technology spread across Europe (Thomas, 2020b).

In the twentieth century other gas making processes evolved from thermally decomposing oil into gas, these evolved in Britain (SEGAS process), France (Microsimplex) and the United States (Hall process). The gas from the CWG and oil gas plants was processed in a similar way to that described for coal gas; however, as the tar produced originated from an oil-based feedstock, it had different properties (Thomas, 2014a, b, c).

In the 1960s the gas industry started to produce gas from refinery by-products such as naphtha using gas reforming technology. This plant soon became redundant, as natural gas became available across Europe and gas networks converted (Thomas, 2018).

11.2.7 Gas storage

With the by-products removed, the gas was stored in a gasholder (see Figure 11.5). The gasholder consisted of a cylindrical vessel which was closed at the top but open at the base, it was placed in a cylindrical water-filled tank. As gas entered the gasholder vessel, it would rise in the water tank, the water acting as a seal to prevent the gas from escaping. The gasholder evolved from small iron vessels of $14m^3$ ($500ft^3$) to huge structures holding $283{,}000m^3$ ($10{,}000{,}000ft^3$). Gasholders were one of the last features to be removed from gasworks, as they were often retained for natural gas storage after gas manufactured ceased. Gasholders are described in brief detail in this chapter and in more detail in Tucker (2014), Berger (2019), and Thomas (2020b).

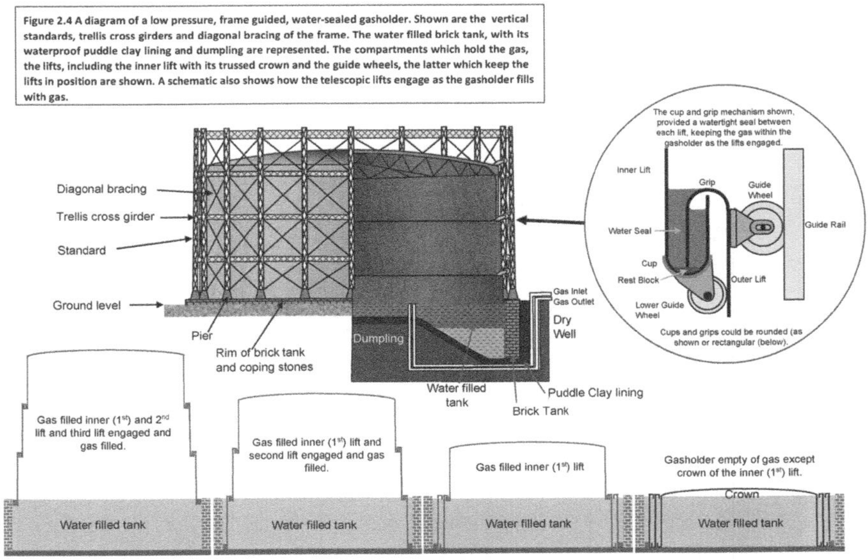

Figure 11.5 Diagram showing the operation of a gasholder.

Source: Russell Thomas.

The design of gasholders evolved over time. The earliest surviving example is the No.2 gasholder at Fulham which dates to 1830; this used a single vessel (lift) guided by individual cast iron tripods (Figure 11.6a). As this design grew larger, the tripods were connected together at the top by horizontal girders. These tripods were then replaced by cast iron columns, again joined by horizontal girders. To increase the volume of gas stored, addition lifts were added to the gasholder, these connected to each other interlocking by cups and grips, which were sealed by water. Up to six lifts were used in the largest gasholders (Thomas, 2020b).

As gasholders grew larger multiple tiers of horizontal girder were used to connect the cast iron columns together. These became limited in size by the weight of the columns. These columns were often highly ornamented and form a majority of the listed gasholder in England. The next development was the construction of frame guiding for gasholders, cast iron columns were replaced by wrought iron and later steel standards connected by horizontal girders. This design further improved by George Livesey using geodesic framing on the listed No.13 gasholder at Old Kent Road (Figure 11.6b); the lighter frames allowed larger water-sealed gasholders to be built (Thomas, 2020b).

The final iteration of the water sealed gasholder dispensed with framing altogether, using spiral guiding combined with more rigid lifts. These highly utilitarian structures were extensively built in the UK, with much fewer built abroad. Their limited visibility when down has led to only one listed example.

(a)

(b)

Figure 11.6 Examples of listed gasholders in England whilst operational – (a) No.2 Gasholder Fulham the world's oldest gasholder in 1950 and (b) No.13 Gasholder Old Kent Road in 1960.

Source: IGEM Archive (a) and National Gas Archive (b).

The gasholder tanks which held water were constructed below ground from brick or stone, waterproofed on the outside by puddle clay. Later concrete tanks were rendered on the inside to make them waterproof. Where ground conditions were unsuitable for below-ground tanks, above-ground tanks were used. These were built from cast iron sections bolted together. The gasholder at Fakenham in England is typical of this type of tank. These were superseded by steel tanks, built from steel sections, initially riveted and later welded together. The gasholder tanks often contained sludge in the base of the tank, containing residues from gas manufacture, oil and lead from the gasholder paint (Thomas, 2020b).

Dry gasholders were developed in the early twentieth century; they used a fixed Polygonal (MAN) or circular (Klönne) tank, with an internal piston, which used a tar or oil/grease seal respectively. The tar, oil and grease can be problematic when dealing with the remediation of these structures. A later American design (Wiggins) used a piston sealed with a rubber membrane. High-pressure gasholders were also used from the 1930; these spherical or torpedo-shaped vessels were specially reinforced to store gas at high pressure in a compressed form. These designs were typically free of contamination apart from condensate which may be deposited within them (Thomas, 2020b).

11.2.8 Tar and liquor tanks

The tar and ammoniacal liquor from the plant described were drained by gravity to underground tar and liquor tanks. These tanks could be constructed from cast iron, steel, brick or concrete and often reused the tanks of former gasholder, which had become too small. They incorporated a weir system which separated the tar from the liquor. The liquor which was rich in ammonium was processed to produce ammonium sulphate fertiliser and the coal tar distilled into different fractions at a tar distillery. Both of these processes were operated on larger gasworks, or the by-products transported to a chemical works for processing. They had many uses from wood preserving to medicines and plastics (Thomas, 2020b).

11.3 Contaminants associated with gasworks

The many thousands of gasworks built across Europe left a considerable environmental legacy in the waste and by-products which occasionally leaked from plant or had to be dumped as waste (see Table 11.1).

Tars are the primary concern on gasworks. Tars are produced from the thermal decomposition of coal and oil and are complex mixtures of organic compounds, which reflect the temperature, the feedstock and the type of process used to produce them. They contain polycyclic aromatic hydrocarbons (PAH) and their heterocyclic derivatives The PAH contain carcinogenic compounds such as Benzo(a)Pyrene, and others, for example, naphthalene are toxic. Tar also contains other harmful substances such as benzene, phenol and petroleum hydrocarbons, is flammable and does not readily biodegrade, all factors which

Table 11.1 Contaminants of concern typically found on a gasworks

Contaminant	*Associated waste or by-product*
Heavy metals, in particular arsenic and lead	Ash
Polycyclic aromatic hydrocarbon (PAH)	Ash, coal, tars (coal tar, water gas tar, oil gas tar) and ammoniacal liquor
Phenols	Tars and ammoniacal liquor
Benzene, toluene, ethyl benzene, xylenes	Tars and benzol
Petroleum hydrocarbons	Tars and benzol
Ammonium, sulphur and sulphate, cyanides (complex and free cyanides), thiocyanate	Spent oxide, foul lime, ammoniacal liquor, sulphate plant and acid plant residues
Asbestos-containing materials (ACM)	Lagging on pipes, boilers and ACM tiles, gaskets and panels

Source: Russell Thomas.

make coal tar a hazardous and difficult substance to remediate of gasworks (Thomas, 2014a, b, c).

Coal tars were typically denser than water and would sink in the water table below the site until they reached an impermeable stratum. Oil-based tars from CWG or oil gas processes reflect the parent oil used to produce them and can produce tars of a similar or lighter density than water, making them more mobile and more likely to migrate off site in groundwater. The composition of these tars is described in greater detail in McGregor et al. (2012) and Gallacher et al. (2017).

Ammoniacal liquor is rich in ammonium and phenol; it is a particular problem if entering ground or surface water, where it may be toxic to aquatic life and cause eutrophication, due to the high nitrogen content (Thomas et al., 2022).

The tar and liquor tanks and the pipework connecting it to other plant tend to be the most significant source of coal tar or ammoniacal liquor on a gasworks sites (see Figure 11.7); other sources include tar distilleries, concentrated ammoniacal liquor plants and sulphate of ammonia plants (Thomas et al., 2022).

Toxic heavy metals, lead and arsenic in particular, are typically found in elevated concentrations in ash. The ash, a waste from burning coke, was used for ground raising activities and can be found in across former gasworks sites.

Due to the high-temperature processes operated on gasworks, asbestos-containing materials (ACM) were used for insulation purposes. ACM were also used in the construction of buildings and are typically of concern when investigating the sites, due to their known carcinogenic properties.

Each country follows its own policy governing how land contamination is dealt with. For example in England the Environment Agency provides the *Guidance: Land Contamination Risk Management*, published online.[1] Approaches vary between countries, but most typically follow a risk-based approach, which is briefly described herein.

Figure 11.7 A former tar and liquor tank exposed during remediation works.
Source: Russell Thomas.

Where a former gasworks site is being redeveloped, a desk-based preliminary risk assessment will be undertaken to develop a Conceptual Site Model (CSM) to establish whether there are potentially any unacceptable risks. A Source-Pathway-Receptor approach is used to assess whether there is a potential for an unacceptable risk, where a *source* (contaminant with the potential to cause harm) requires a *pathway* (a route between the *receptor* and *source*) to adversely affect a *receptor* (e.g., person, important water body, organism).

The desk study will collate desk-based information, such as geology, historical maps and information about the processes operated on the site. It may include previous investigations of the site and any work undertaken to remove contamination previously (remediation). A site workover is typically undertaken to enable a better understanding of the site.

Following the desk study, where there are concerns that the site could pose a potential risk of harm to receptors, an intrusive investigation will be undertaken. This includes the excavation of trial holes in the ground, to identify below-ground structures, to take soil samples and install boreholes to sample groundwater, collect ground gases or vapours. This information is used to inform the CSM. The results of soil, water, gas and vapour analysis will then be screened against assessment criteria to assess the level of risk. If the investigation demonstrates a significant risk of harm to receptors such as a leaking tar tank over an important aquifer, then remediation would be required. This can take many forms and CL:AIRE (2015) provides a useful overview of gasworks remediation technologies.

The presence of protected historic structures on a gasworks may limit the investigation due to the risk of damaging the historic structure. In England, guidance for dealing with Land Contamination and Archaeology is provided by Historic England (Anon, 2017).

11.4 The challenges of a sustainable gasworks redevelopment

Given the challenges posed by gasworks sites, why preserve and redevelop former gasworks? The reasons are largely based on their social context within the societies they served.

11.4.1 The challenges of a sustainable gasworks redevelopment

Gasworks were one of the few industrial features in some towns and villages; they can therefore be unique industrial features in otherwise rural settings. The gas industry also employed large numbers of people in the manufacture and distribution of gas, creating strong links with modern society through the discovery of ancestors who worked in the industry. It was typical for multiple generations of the same family to work within the gas industry, so the links with some families are very strong and, in some case, still present today (Thomas, 2020a).

The societal improvements of gas were significant, being the first effective form of lighting in the home with later developments included cooking and heating by gas. It greatly improved hygiene and living standards across society, well demonstrated in Kensal House, a GLCC housing development designed by Modernist Maxwell Fry and social reformer Elizabeth Denby. It showed how a modern building could run cheaply and safely on gas (Jackson and Holland, 2016; Thomas, 2020a).

Although gas had originally only been available to the wealthy, the development of the prepayment gas metre in 1870 allowed the poorer members of society access to gas and the ability to hire gas appliances (Thomas, 2020a).

The position of the gas industry in society has been reflected in culture and art. Gasworks have frequently appeared in artwork (see Figure 11.8). The French artist Gustav Dore produced prints of London's gasworks, a notable British artist Norman Wilkinson painted many scenes of London's Gasworks, and Vincent van Gogh used the gasworks in The Hague as a subject for his art. The industry produced some iconic advertising artwork including "Mr Therm" created by Eric Frazer and Cyril Farey's views of Beckton gasworks, both produced for the GLCC (see Figure 11.9).

Gasworks also featured in the literature of the day including the famous authors Robert Louis Stevenson and Charles Dickens. Stevenson penned the Poem "The Lamplighter" and Dickens wrote in his essay "The Genii of the Lamps" about the wonders of gaslighting and the not so wonderful conditions in which the gas was made (Thomas, 2020a).

Figure 11.8 Norman Wilkinson's painting of the coke breeze plant at Fulham gasworks.

Source: National Gas Archive.

Gasworks in Great Britain, especially around London, became important backdrops for film and television. The most notable site was London's former Beckton gasworks, once the largest in the world. After closure, they became the backdrop for Stanley Kubrick's "Full Metal Jacket", the opening sequence for the James Bond film "For Your Eyes Only", John Wayne's Thriller "Brannigan" and the Pet Shop Boys music video "It couldn't happen here". The Munich gasworks were used as the chocolate factory in the original film version of *Willy Wonka and the Chocolate factory*. The former gasholder at the redeveloped Westergasfabriek in Amsterdam has become a location for the reality television music programmes the Voice of Holland and ARIA. Many other examples exist.

11.4.2 The extent of the gas industry

The extent of the gas industry varied significantly across Europe. The main determinant being the access to gas making coals, which were available from British coalfields by ship, but also became available from coalfields in continental Europe. Coal was not the only feedstock that could be used. In the early years of the gas industry, whale and vegetable oils were used for gas manufacture, their high cost made them less economical, gradually failed. In some parts of Europe wood was used as a feedstock for gas manufacture but degraded the gas making plant faster. New gas making technologies enabled gas to be made

Figure 11.9 Cyril Farey's depiction of the Beckton gasworks.

Source: IGEM archive.

from a wider variety of coals available from across continental Europe, spurring the growth of the industry (Thomas, 2018).

Annual Year Books listing public gas undertakings were published by British journals from 1880s to the 1960s, which give insight into the extent of the gas industry across Europe. The countries included changed, as the national boundaries changed during this period because of the two world wars. Data compiled from four yearbooks (1889, 1898, 1937 and 1940) are shown in Table 11.2.

Table 11.2 Selected countries in northern Europe and the number of gas undertaking providing a public supply recorded in gas industry year books between 1889 and 1940

Country	*Number of public gasworks*
Great Britain	2,160
France	1,087
Germany	991
Netherlands	279
Poland	154
Belgium	112
Denmark	112
Sweden	40
Norway	18
Finland	3

Source: Anon (1889), Anon (1898), Anon (1937), Anon (1940).

Where coal was available within country, as it was in Great Britain, France, Germany, Belgium, the Netherlands, and Poland, then an extensive network of gasworks developed across the country. The figures for Great Britain are skewed by the more detailed information available to the British publication. Denmark, which had no native coal, did have access to coal through neighbouring countries and, by sea, had a much larger gas industry than other Nordic countries which imported coal by sea alone. The gas industry only developed in those locations with ports to import coal.

The only comprehensive published study of gasworks undertaken in a single European country is the *Manufactured Gas Industry – Gazetteer* produced by Historic England (Thomas, 2020c). This accompanied an historic assessment of the importance of the industry. The *Gazetteer* lists over 3,600 former public and private gas sites, detailing their location, brief history and current state. It provides insight as to the extent of surviving structures at the time of the review in 2020 (Thomas, 2020c).

The report showed few public gasworks' buildings survive in England. The one exception was South West England, where the South Western Gas Board had a policy of selling the surplus gasworks land and buildings once the plant had been removed. Examples of significant surviving gasworks in the region include the Hele Gasworks at Ilfracombe, Devon and the Ilminster gasworks in Somerset. In other parts of the country very few buildings survive; for example, only one site in the county of Surrey, at Horley, has any significant surviving buildings (Thomas, 2020c).

Where buildings do survive on gasworks, they tend to be individual buildings, or small groups, and typically not associated with gas production. The most common surviving features tend to be the gas manager's house. These survived as they were tenanted and had an ongoing use. Some examples of such buildings which have protection (Grade II listed) include the entrance

Figure 11.10 The Fakenham gasworks Norfolk, England.
Source: Russell Thomas.

buildings to the former Sleaford Gasworks (Lincolnshire) and the former manager's house and offices of the Bath Gasworks in Somerset (Thomas, 2020c).

The most complete gasworks in England is at Fakenham in Norfolk; it is protected as a scheduled monument (Figure 11.10). It contains the original plant and is typical of the type of small country town gasworks which operated across England and today serve as a gas museum (Thomas, 2020c).

There are no complete large gasworks which survive in England; the two best examples are Louth in Lincolnshire and Farnworth in Lancashire. They contain the only surviving large steel framed horizontal retort houses. Both had been operated by the United Kingdom Gas Corporation prior to the nationalisation in 1949, the initials of which feature in the wall of the retort house in Louth. Bost sites are now industrial estates, their history largely forgotten with the exceptions of the Gas Lamp pub located in the former Louth Gasworks offices and features gaslighting. These sites are not protected by listing but the Louth site is part of a conservation area (Thomas, 2020c).

Private gasworks associated with country houses have tended to survive in greater numbers and relatively more have statutory protection from listing such as Sudbury Hall gasworks and Cliveden House gasworks (Both Grade II). These structures have tended to survive because they have found new uses, such as housing or workshops (Thomas, 2020c).

The survival of buildings from former gasworks varies from country to country. For example, Finland had three public gasworks and significant buildings survive at two sites: Turku and Helsinki. Both sites include preserved and redeveloped former gasholder houses. The later site contains many interesting buildings from the original gasworks designed by the local architect Selim Lindquist. Poland has many wonderful examples of former gasworks buildings. The best examples are the gasworks museums at Górowo Iławieckie, Paczków and Warsaw. Germany has many former gasworks with surviving structures across the country; the most notable of these is Gaswerks Augsburg in Bavaria, designed by architects Gebrüder Rank. Greece is another example where there were only known to be nine public gasworks, but the largest of these in Athens has been restored with many or the original surviving features.

11.5 Effective gasworks redevelopments

To make a gasworks redevelopment meaningful to its past but also of value to the future is a significant challenge. The redevelopment should be considerate of its heritage, address environmental legacy issues and provide financially viable and sustainable end use. Such a positive redevelopment should allow the site to tell its story, conveying a sense of the site's industrial history through to the present day. Such examples that achieve this are Technopolis in Athens, Gaswerks Augsburg in Bavaria, Warsaw Gas Museum, the Danish Gas Museum in Hobro and the Sudbury gasworks restoration in Derbyshire. Each tells the story of the site and the industry within the redevelopment.

Other interesting examples include the King Cross Gasholder redevelopment in London, which include four restored and relocated gasholder frames (Figure 11.11). Three of these contain apartment blocks with a further single frame containing a small park open to the public. Such a development was made feasible by the high value of the apartment blocks constructed, which was not an option in many locations. London developments at Bethnal Green and the Oval gas sites look the replicate this residential reuse of gasholder frames approach, funded entirely from the private sector.

Other reuses include theatres; the surviving gasholder house at the Østre Gasværk in Copenhagen found a new life as a theatre in 1979, being fully renovated in 2018 and regular staging plays and musical theatre. The former gasholder at Westergasfabriek has also become a venue for the Dutch National Opera, and Gaswerks Augsburg hosts the state theatre onsite reusing the former Ofenhaus. These reuses provide a sustainable long-term income to maintain the sites. The Technopolis site in Athens former gasworks hosts workspace, cultural events, educational facilities, all which help fund the gas museum (Figure 11.12). These great examples show what can be achieved, usually with significant public funding.

Another approach was used with the small gasholder in the village of Lavenham in Suffolk, which dated back to 1868 (Figure 11.13). A scheduled monument, it was restored by its owners National Grid Property and the site

Figure 11.11 The restored Kings Cross gasholders, London.

Source: Russell Thomas.

Figure 11.12 A repurposed gasholder at Technopolis, the former Athens Gasworks, Greece.

Source: Russell Thomas.

Figure 11.13 The restored gasholder at Lavenham, Suffolk.

Source: Russell Thomas.

Figure 11.13 (Continued)

with the gasholder transferred to the local council, who have now redeveloped the remainder of the site as much needed car parking with electric car charging points.

Where unprotected structures survive on former gasworks, there is no requirement for the structure to be retained in the development. Heritage structures and gasholders can be very expensive to refurbish and maintain, this includes gasholder frames, which are typically the protected element. A developer, however, may choose to incorporate unprotected structures to enhance the redevelopment. The Bethnal Green development in London is such an example where two gasholder frames are to be refurbished and reused.

Reusing former industrial structures is more sustainable, than starting afresh as promoted by the Royal Institute of British Architects (RIBA), who have done much to promote the creative transformation of an existing building through their *Built for the Environment* report, their *Sustainable Past and Future Guide* and the *RIBA Reinvention Award*. These focus heavily on reusing existing structures with the aim of environmental, social or economic sustainability (RIBA, 2021; Smith et al., 2023).

Sadly, in the case of most former gasworks, as was shown from the review of former gasworks in England, little or no surviving above-ground structures survive. Despite this there are often many below-ground features which may be present. These can impede development, but in some cases beneficial reuse can be made. Such features may include tanks and voids (infilled or not) such as flues, basements or subways and foundations. In the proposed redevelopment of the Wandsworth gasworks in London, the concrete gasholder tank is intended to be reused as a foundation for a new development. Firebricks from a below-ground flue structure on the former Milburngate gasworks in Durham were reused in the redevelopment of the Sudbury gasworks. Parts of structures from the gasworks can be incorporated in redeveloped gasworks, as was done at the former Stepney and Battersea gas sites in London.

It also may be possible to gift artefacts from the former gasworks sites to museums, as was done with the Windsor Street Gasholders in Birmingham, where part of the gasholder frame was gifted to the local science museum along with a written history of the site.

It requires a team with a shared vision, imagination and sufficient finance to deliver the project. It requires the planners behind the project to work closely with the local authorities and regulators. It requires that the engineers undertaking the project understand the complexity of the environmental and structural challenges that may be involved especially if historic structures are to be incorporated into the final design. For a project to be successful, it needs to be financially viable, if heritage structures are to be retained then a long-term plan to ensure funding for maintenance is required. This is particularly important where the site may contain a museum element, which may itself not be self-funding. In this case use of the wider site for other events such as concerts, letting parts of the site to tenants or obtaining long-term funds from an industry body, company or charitable foundation may be important.

11.6 Conclusions

The gas industry has had a significant impact on European society, providing the first effective form of lighting and significant improvements in cooking and heating. The by-products brought smokeless fuels, new medicines and plastics. The gasworks became significant features on the landscape, often being the largest industrial feature in the town.

The few remnants of Europe's once extensive manufactured gas industry are to be found across the continent, often in unexpected places such as country estate and more likely locations such as the industrial areas of cities. The structures that survive do so because they found a new use or gained some form of protection.

To enable long-term survival former gasworks structures need to find sustainable uses such as museums, cultural destinations or residential redevelopments which can provide the long-term revenue to maintain the structures and mitigate the environmental risks associated with their past use. Gasworks structures offer an opportunity to enhance developments. By incorporating and enhancing through interpretation these culturally significant structures, it can help strengthen the longstanding links they have to surrounding local communities. Without a long-term use, however, these structures can become a blight and hazard, so it is important that any heritage protection enables a sustainable long-term future, which balances the complex issue of heritage protection and financial viability.

Note

1 https://www.gov.uk/government/publications/land-contamination-risk-management-lcrm

References

Anon. 1889. *The Gas Engineer's Text Book and Companies Directory*. J.G. Hammond Co. Ltd, Paternoster Square.

Anon. 1898. *The Gas Engineer's Text Book and Companies Directory*. J.G. Hammond Co. Ltd, Paternoster Square.

Anon. 1937. *The Register of the Gas Industry 1937*. The Gas Times, Victoria Street.

Anon. 1940. *Gasworld Yearbook 1940*. Gas World, Benn Brothers, Bouverie House.

Anon. 2017. *Land Contamination and Archaeology – Good Practice Guidance*. Historic England.

Berger, Barbara. 2019. *Der Gasbehälter als Bautypus*. TUM University Press.

CL:AIRE. 2015. *Soil and Groundwater Remediation Technologies for Former Gasworks and Gasholder Sites*. CL:AIRE.

Gallacher, Christopher, Taylor, Chris, Lord, Richard, Thomas, Russell, and Kalin, Robert. 2017. Comprehensive database of manufactured gas plant tars. *Rapid Communications in Mass Spectrometry* Aug 15; 31(15): 1231–1260.

Jackson, Iain, and Holland, Jessica. 2016. *The Architecture of Edwin Maxwell Fry and Jane Drew: Twentieth Century Architecture, Pioneer Modernism and the Tropics*. Routledge.

McGregor, Laura A., Gauchotte-Lindsay, Caroline, Daéid, Niamh Nic, Thomas, Russell, and Kalin, Robert M. 2012. Multivariate statistical methods for the environmental forensic classification of coal tars from former manufactured gas plants. *Environmental Science and Technology* 46 (7): 3744–3752.

Meade, Alwyne. 1921. *Modern Gas Works Practice*. Benn Brothers, 2nd ed.

Moyano Jiménez, Florentino, and Thomas, Russell. 2016. William Richards and the unrecorded success abroad: A British engineer in the Spanish gas industry in the nineteenth century. *The International Journal for the History of Engineering & Technology* 86 (2): 124–146.

RIBA. 2021. *Sustainable Past and Future Guide*. RIBA, London.

Smith, Maria, Apperley, Joshua, Couling, Alex, Dillon, Martha, Forth, Andrew, and MacDonald, Phoebe. 2023. *London: Built for the Environment*. RIBA.

Thomas, Russell A. P. 2014a. *Gasworks Profile A: The History and Operation of Gasworks*. CL:AIRE 2014.

Thomas, Russell A. P. 2014b. *Gasworks Profile B: Gasholders and their Tanks*. CL:AIRE.

Thomas, Russell A. P. 2014c. *Gasworks Profile C: Water Gas Plants*. CL:AIRE.

Thomas, Russell A. P. 2018. The development of the manufactured gas industry in Europe. *Geological Society, London, Special Publications* 465: 137–164, 14 May.

Thomas, Russell A. P. 2020a. The Manufactured Gas Industry, Volume 1 - History, Research Report Series no. 182-2020, Historic England.

Thomas, Russell A. P. 2020b. The Manufactured Gas Industry, Volume 2 – Gasworks, Research Report Series no. 182-2020, Historic England.

Thomas, Russell A. P. 2020c. The Manufactured Gas Industry, Volume 3 – Gazetteer, Research Report Series no. 182-2020, Historic England.

Thomas, Russell A. P. 2023. Lessons Learned from Past Energy Transitions in the Gas Industry. NIA Project Report (In Press).

Thomas, Russell A. P., Riding, Matthew J., Robinson, Jamie D. F., Brown, Stuart J. A., and Taylor, Chris. 2022. Distinguishing sources of ammonium in groundwater at former gasworks sites using nitrogen isotopes. *Quarterly Journal of Engineering Geology and Hydrogeology*, 55. https://doi.org/10.1144/qjegh2021-13

Tucker, Malcolm. 2014. London Gasholders Survey. The Development of the Gasholder in London in the Late Nineteenth Century, Part A, A general Report for English Heritage.

12 Epilogue

EU, war and energy: Geostrategy and gas pipelines

Pere-A. Fàbregas

12.1 Introduction

During the last decades, the European Union (EU) has developed an important strategy to become the world leader in the fight against climate change, although it is not the area with the highest greenhouse gas emissions in the world, a position reserved for China and the United States.

With this orientation, it had begun to reduce, in recent years, its consumption of coal, largely from its own internal production, replacing it with natural gas, energy with a much smaller environmental impact. The closure of nuclear power plants had also begun, due to the problem of nuclear risk at the facilities, and the difficulties in managing radioactive waste. As is known, nuclear power plants do not generate greenhouse gases.

All of these lines of action were called into question when, on 24 February 2022, Russia invaded Ukraine, starting a long-term war with uncertain consequences. Suddenly, Europe realised that it had reduced its own energy production, and that imports from other countries had increased, and that the main supplier of natural gas was Russia, a country with which a serious, difficult and probably long-haul confrontation was beginning.

12.2 Energy in the European Union

In the year 2020, despite the efforts made, the European Union still depended on fossil energy at 69.9% and nuclear energy at 12.7%, with renewable energy contributing only 17.4% (Eurostat, 2022a). The process of substitution of fossil energies is slow; it has taken 30 years (1990–2020) to reduce dependence on fossil energies from the 82.6% recorded in 1990 to current values. In the same period, renewable energies have tripled their share in the European energy market.

Oil continues to be the leader of the European energy market, with a share of 34.5%, that has been gradually reducing over the years. Coal has been displaced from second place in 1990 to fifth today, with lower importance than renewables. Natural gas rose to second place in 2000, thanks to its lower ecological impact and its increasing availability. Nuclear energy peaked in 2000, very slowly reducing its share since then.

DOI: 10.4324/9781003428695-12

Table 12.1 Gross available energy by fuel, EU, share in %

Energy	*1990 (%)*	*2000 (%)*	*2010 (%)*	*2020 (%)*
Solid fossil fuels	25.7	18.1	15.3	10.2
Natural gas	16.8	20.1	22.6	23.7
Oil and petroleum products	39.0	40.3	36.5	34.5
Renewables and biofuels	4.8	6.3	10.8	17.4
Nuclear heat	12.7	14.4	13.7	12.7
All other fuels	1.1	0.8	1.2	1.5

Source: Eurostat (2022a).

The situation for the EU as a whole is what has been presented, but there are great differences between the 27 member states, depending on their history, their resources and the energy policies applied. For example, Italy depends 40% on imported natural gas, due to its decision not to allow nuclear power plants to be installed on its territory, taken in 1987, after the Chernobyl nuclear accident, which occurred on April 26, 1986.

Sweden is an example of a country with an option for renewable energy, which already represents 48%, almost three times more than the European average, and also for nuclear energy with 25%, double the EU average. France is the leader in nuclear energy in Europe with 41% of its needs covered by its nuclear power plants, thus promoting its important advances in nuclear technology. Denmark has very quickly reduced its dependence on fossil fuels, basically Danish coal itself, replacing it with significant growth in renewable energy, which now represents 38% of the supply.

Member states with significant coal reserves continue to maintain significant proportions of this energy in their energy mix, such as Poland or the Czech Republic, with 40% and 30% respectively. In the case of Spain, energy demand has less coal than the EU average, but it compensates for this with a higher than average share of oil.

The growth models of energy demand are also very different, if we compare the evolution of the EU 27, for example, with Spain, over the last 30 years.

EU energy demand grew softly until the international financial crisis of 2008. Subsequently, it was reduced until 2015 when it began to rise, falling again due to the impact of COVID-19, declared a pandemic by the WHO (World Health Organization) on 11 March 2020. Finally, EU energy demand in 2020 was 7% lower than in 1990.

The Spanish case has similar tendencies, but with much more abrupt movements, and spectacular increases in energy demand. Until 2005, the EU demanded 11% more energy than in 1990; in the Spanish case, the increase was 65%. Afterwards, the EU and Spain follow similar patterns, reduction starting with the 2008 crisis, return to growth starting in 2015, and drastic reduction due to COVID-19 in 2020, but maintaining, in that year, a demand that is not lower than in 1990 like Europe, but almost 30% higher.

Table 12.2 Gross available energy, EU and Spain, Index 1990 = 100 %

Country	*1990*	*1995*	*2000*	*2005*	*2010*	*2015*	*2020*
EU	100	100	103	111	108	100	93
Spain	100	115	141	165	150	142	128

Source: Eurostat (2022a).

Domestic energy production in the EU during the years 1990 to 2020 was characterised by a massive reduction in coal production, going from about 13,000 Petajoules (PJ) in 1990 to less than 4,000, combined with unstoppable growth of energy renewables, which grew from 3,000 PJ to more than 10,000 in 2020.

The low oil production, about 2,000 PJ in 1990, has been reduced to practically zero in 2020. Natural gas production, basically due to the depletion of the Groningen gas field, has also been reduced from about 5,000 PJ to less than 2,000 PJ in 2020. It should be noted that the countries with hydrocarbon reserves in the North Sea, the United Kingdom and Norway, are not EU member states at this time.

EU nuclear production has basically remained around 8,000 PJ, with slight growth until 2005, and a slight reduction since that year.

The maintenance of the EU's energy demand and the reduction of its own energy production have resulted in an increasingly high dependence on energy imports from non-member third countries, in order to continue to operate normally the economies of the EU different member states.

The main change has occurred in natural gas imports, which have gone from around 7,000 PJ in 1990 to around 13,000 PJ in 2020, practically double. Oil imports have remained at the level of 20,000 PJ, while coal imports have been reduced by approximately half from 5,000 PJ.

In summary, the energy situation of the EU in the period 1990–2020 presented a certain stability of demand, with a reduction in the internal production of coal and natural gas, combined with a rapid introduction of renewables, and a clear increase in natural gas imports.

Another element of the analysis is the efficiency with which energy is used, which can be measured by the primary energy demand per capita, and also by the energy intensity of the economy. The first indicator measures how much energy a citizen needs on average, allowing us to compare countries with very different population levels, and the second allows us to observe how much energy is necessary to develop a specific economic activity or the entire GDP of a country. The two indicators present very different results in the different member states.

The primary energy demand per capita of the EU in 2020 is 129 TJ pc (Terajoules per capita), the most extreme values are Finland with 240 TJ pc, and Romania with 70 TJ pc, while Spain with 100 TJ pc is in an intermediate situation, but with 30% per capita energy demand lower than the European average. The differences between countries are mainly explained by the climate, the type of industry, the level of per capita income and other cultural, historical or sociological circumstances.

It is important to analyse the evolution of primary energy demand per capita over the last 30 years, as these are years in which pressure for energy savings, financial crises, policies to adapt to climate change, and the introduction of new technologies have conditioned its evolution. In the period 1990–2020, primary energy demand per capita has been reduced in the EU by 13.5%, a reduction led by Germany with 40%, Estonia (48%) and Romania (39%). In the German case, progress is due to an important energy transition program, the Energiewende of 2011, with special emphasis on the introduction of clean energies and the improvement of energy efficiency. In the case of Estonia and Romania, the reductions come mainly from the reconversion of their heavy industry to lighter and more efficient models. Other countries have had different evolutions, in Spain the indicator has increased slightly, while in Portugal it has risen by 20% and in Austria by 9%.

We will calculate the energy intensity of the economy as the energy demand necessary to increase GDP by €1,000. In the last ten years, all the countries analysed have improved their indicators, but with clear differences. The countries with the greatest energy consumption to be able to increase their GDP are those that had belonged to the former USSR, due to their heavier industry, a certain technological delay and the historical lack of incentives to improve productivity. However, also in recent years there are differences between these countries due to the policies applied and the efforts made, such as Estonia, which has improved by 43%, while Bulgaria only improved by 14%.

Spain is among the countries that require less energy to advance its economy, although its improvement is not among the most relevant. In the industrialised economies of the EU, the greatest effort has been made by Germany, which requires less than 100 kilos of energy to generate €1,000 of GDP. The case of Ireland is absolutely singular, a country that is not very industrial, having managed to attract many headquarters of multinational companies to

Table 12.3 Energy intensity of the economy, kilogram of oil equivalent per € thousand GDP

Country	*2010*	*2015*	*2020*	*% 2020/2010*
Bulgaria	470.48	458.89	403.34	−14%
Estonia	416.51	295.61	236.00	−43%
Poland	283.57	229.44	210.18	−26%
Finland	196,68	174,52	161,92	−18%
Portugal	138.31	140.71	125.43	−9%
Spain	129.15	121.66	112.33	−13%
France	136.32	124.65	108.02	−21%
Germany	132.98	114.95	99.50	−25%
Ireland	90.81	62.45	44.63	−51%

Source: Eurostat (2022a).

its territory due to its attractive tax system, achieving a great economic movement with few energy needs.

If the data is corrected to present them after equalising the purchasing powers in the different countries, known as PPS (Prices Purchasing Standard), Finland and Bulgaria stand out (with more than 6,000 GJ per thousand EUR PPS) as the largest energy demanders to obtain economic growth, followed by France, Holland, Spain and Poland (between 4,000 and 5,000 GJ). Next, Italy, Portugal, Romania and Germany (between 3,000 and 4,000 GJ). And two unique cases, Denmark with less than 3,000 GJ, and Ireland, with less than 2,000 GJ. Over the last 30 years, all EU countries have clearly improved their records in this basic efficiency indicator.

To go from primary energy demand to final energy consumption, the different energies must go through a transformation process, basically to convert primary energies into electricity; this process is a main energy consumer in the EU, absorbing 24% of the available energy. The final energy in Europe, in 2020, is consumed by transport (28%), homes (28%), industry (26%) and services (14%).

In the period 2007–2020, the final energy consumption was reduced in all sectors: in industry (16%), in transport (14%), in services (4%), and in homes by only 0.4%. The behaviour of citizens is where it is most difficult to improve consumption patterns.

12.3 Energy dependence

In the EU, the reduction in fossil energy production and the decisions on nuclear energy have produced an increase in imports from other countries, clearly enlarging energy dependence and, therefore, the Union's supply risk.

In 1990, the EU's energy supply was 50% dependent on external sources, an indicator that had worsened to 58% in 2020 (Eurostat, 2022b). In 2020, the EU imported 97% of its oil consumption, 84% of natural gas and 36% of coal, very important proportions of its supply, with a clear strategic risk.

The analysis of the data allows us to indicate that it is not only that the EU was increasingly dependent on foreign countries to guarantee its energy supply,

Table 12.4 Energy imports by supplier, EU, 2020, share in %

Supplier	*Oil*	*Natural Gas*	*Solid fuels*
Russia	29%	43%	54%
USA	9%		16%
Norway	8%	21%	
Algeria		8%	
Qatar		5%	
Australia			14%
Other	54%	23%	16%

Source: Eurostat (2022b).

but that it was increasingly dependent on Russia. And not only for natural gas imports, as was emphatically commented by the media. In 2020, Russia was the EU's leading supplier of natural gas (43%), and also the leading supplier of oil (29%), and coal (54%). In short, when the war in Ukraine began, the EU's strategic dependence on energy supplied by Russia was very relevant, with a high geopolitical risk.

The analysis of natural gas imports indicates that in 2020, Russia was the leading supplier to Germany and Italy, representing 66% and 43% of their imports respectively. On the other hand, in the French case the main supplier was Norway (36%), and in the Spanish case, Algeria (29%). In 2022, in Spain the situation had already changed, with the United States being the main supplier of gas from fracking processes.

12.4 Natural gas transportation

The extreme dependence of the United States, and mainly Germany, on Russian gas forces us to delve deeper into this energy, its transportation systems, its reserves and its alternatives.

Transporting natural gas is not easy, but there are two great alternatives: transport by gas pipeline or transport by ship. Both systems require significant investments and sophisticated technologies. Gas pipeline transport requires steel pipes capable of working at high pressures, for example, 60 bar. Gas pipelines require the installation of compression stations depending on the route design, which allow the pressure that is reduced over the distance to be overcome. Europe has gas pipelines that connect it with Russian fields in Siberia, those in North Africa, mainly in Algeria, and with other areas, for example Azerbaijan.

Transport by ship is carried out with LNG carriers specialised in this transport, which take advantage of the characteristics of natural gas, which at 160° below zero is transformed into a cryogenic liquid that reduces its volume about 600 times. Transporting an LNG tanker in these conditions is equivalent to transporting 600 ships of natural gas in the gas phase. Obviously, special materials and technologies are required to operate at such low temperatures, known as cryogenic technologies. The energy that moves the methane tanker is natural gas itself. The system operates in the producing country with a gas pipeline that transports gas from the field to the coast, and a liquefaction terminal on the coast that transforms the gas into liquid and loads ships. In the receiving country, a regasification terminal must be built on the coast, which allows gas to be stored at 160° below zero and regasified at ambient temperature in accordance with the demand curve.

In 2018, the EU had 18 regasification plants in operation, installed in 9 member states. Additionally, there were two FSRU plants (Floating Storage and Regasification Unit) located in Italy and Turkey, and one FSU (Floating Storage Unit) plant in Malta. In Spain, the "El Musel" plant was hibernated awaiting authorisation. Outside the EU there were three plants in United

Table 12.5 EU Large-scale LNG import terminals, 2018

Country	*Terminal*	*Installation Year*	*Ships (10^3 m^3)*	*Storage (10^3 m^3)*	*Production capacity (bcm/year)*
Spain	Barcelona	1969	266	840	17,1
Italy	La Spezia	1971	70	100	3.5
France	Fos Tonkin	1972	75	155	3.4
France	Montoir	1980	267	360	10.0
Belgium	Zeebrugge	1987	266	380	9.0
Spain	Huelva	1988	173	620	11.8
Spain	Cartagena	1989	266	620	11.8
Greece	Revithoussa	2000	135	130	5.2
Portugal	Sines	2003	216	390	7.6
Spain	Bilbao	2003	270	450	8.8
Spain	Sagunto	2006	267	600	8.8
Spain	Mugardos	2007	266	300	3.6
Italy	Rovigo	2009	152	250	8.0
France	Fos Cavaou	2010	267	330	8.3
Netherlands	Gate	2011	266	540	12.0
Lithuania	Klaipėda	2014	160	170	4.0
France	Dunkerque	2016	267	600	13.0
Poland	Świnoujście	2016	216	320	5.0

Source: King and Spalding (2018).

Kingdom and three more in Turkey (King and Spalding LLP, 2018; Howell and Quigley, 2022).

The first LNG plant in the EU was the one in Barcelona, installed by Catalana de Gas y Electricidad and Exxon, with successive posterior expansions. It is currently the largest plant in Europe, in terms of both storage capacity and production capacity. Plants from the same era such as La Spezia have not had similar growth.

Spain is the country with the most facilities; it had six plants in operation in 2018, with the largest storage and production capacity in the EU, followed by France with four plants. In the case of Europe's leading industrialising country, Germany, in 2018 there was, strangely, no LNG plant, depending solely on Russian gas pipelines for its supply.

12.5 Case study: Germany and Spain

The comparison of the cases of Germany and Spain on the issue of natural gas is interesting, as they are the two extreme cases in the presence of LNG plants, six plants or none. Also, from the perspective of dependence on Russian gas, absolutely basic in Germany and very residual in Spain.

12.5.1 Germany. Russian gas pipelines

Germany's relations with Russia began in 1970 when the two Germanys created after the end of the Second World War in 1945 still existed: on the one hand, the Federal Republic of Germany (FRG), and on the other, the German Democratic Republic (GDR). It was the world before the fall of the Berlin Wall, in which the old USSR existed.

The USSR had discovered important oil fields of natural gas and was searching for customers for its gas, while the German steel and industrial machinery industry of the FRG was also looking for customers for its companies. They reached an agreement to build a gas pipeline called Transgas, which would link Russian territory with Germany, via Ukraine, Czechoslovakia and Bavaria. The steel and compressors would be German, and the Russians would pay with natural gas supplies, a clear example of barter trade. The United States lobbied hard against the deal, offering American coal at a good price, but was unsuccessful. The pipeline was finally inaugurated in 1973, in a clear sign of collaboration between a clearly communist country and a clearly capitalist country (Fàbregas, 1975).

Subsequently, the world experienced great changes: the first two oil crises (1973 and 1979) (Fàbregas, 1981), the fall of the Berlin Wall (1989), the reunification of the two Germanys (1990) and finally the dissolution of the USSR (1991).

The increase in the gas relationship between Germany and Russia was again imposed in 1997, with the inauguration of the Yamal gas pipeline, which from Siberia was supposed to reach Germany via Belarus and Poland. The Yamal reached its maximum capacity in 2006.

The next step would be the Nord Stream 1 underwater gas pipeline, designed to supply natural gas from Russia to Germany by crossing the Baltic Sea with an underwater tube. The agreement was signed by German Chancellor Gerard Schröder and Russian President Vladimir Putin on 8 October 2005. The signing took place, coincidentally or not, just ten days before the German elections won by Angela Merkel. The gas pipeline came into operation in 2012.

Shortly thereafter, in 2006, the project to double the Baltic gas pipeline, known as the Nord Stream 2 project, began to be developed, with former German Chancellor Schröder being appointed president of the Russian company, who was also appointed president of the Russian oil company Rosneft in 2017, all of this consistent with the German policy of reducing the presence of coal in its energy mix, although with some strange personal protagonisms. In 2021, the construction of Nord Stream 2 was completed, but it had not yet entered into operation.

The Fukushima nuclear accident in 2011 caused, at the proposal of Chancellor Merkel, Germany to decide on a plan to close its nuclear plants with a horizon of 2021–2022, and launching, in the same year 2011, the ambitious energetic transition program called Energiewende. Strategy that made Germany more dependent on Russian gas in the short term.

With all this background, natural gas imports into Germany, from Russia, went from 37% (2011) of the total to a significant 66% of said imports in a very few years (2020). In this context, on 24 February 2022, Russia invaded Ukraine, and Germany discovered its great dependence on Russian gas and also discovered that it did not have a single LNG plant that would make its supply more flexible, that its former chancellor Schröder had positions in Russian energy companies from which he had to resign, and that Nord Stream 2 had not worked. Finally, on 26 September 2022, a sabotage action disabled Nord Stream 1 and 2 with explosions, with the perpetrators still unknown. A very relevant change of scenery in a very short time.

12.6 Spain: Plants and gas pipelines

The introduction of natural gas in Spain has followed very different patterns from those in the German case, basically due to the availability of natural gas in North Africa, first in Libya and later in Algeria, the lack of technology for the construction of deep-sea submarine gas pipelines in the 1960s, and the availability of cryogenic technologies for ship transportation (Fàbregas, 2018).

The beginning was the discovery of natural gas deposits in Libya by Exxon, which developed a project to bring the gas to the Libyan coast (Marsa el Brega), build a liquefaction plant and transport the gas in cryogenic methane tankers to Barcelona (Spain) and La Spezia (Italy), where the corresponding regasification plants would be built.

In the case of Barcelona, an agreement was signed between Exxon and Catalana de Gas y Electricidad (1965) for the development of the project in Spain, with the corresponding regasification plant inaugurated in Barcelona in 1969, a plant that is currently the largest in Europe. In those years Catalana de Gas was the main manufactured gas company in Spain.

All this happened during the years of General Franco's dictatorship. The most reactionary forces of the regime thought that natural gas should be a product of the State, as was oil in Spain at the time, and for this purpose they established a State company in 1972, Empresa Nacional del Gas, S.A. (ENAGAS), which acquired by political imposition the Barcelona plant from Catalana de Gas in 1975. Meanwhile, supplies from Algeria had already begun, also in methane tankers.

The political discussions and the difficulties of managing a public company in Franco's Spain caused the country to accumulate a significant delay in the introduction of natural gas in relation to Europe, not recovering the historical lack of infrastructure, and with a strange situation in the market with a massive presence of bottled gas unique in Europe. The situation continued until 1985, when an aggressive plan for the introduction of natural gas was launched, known as the Gas Protocol, a public–private collaboration plan in a democratic environment that managed, with great effort and professionalism, to normalise the demand in European terms in a few decades.

In this context, ENAGAS built the LNG plants in Huelva (1988) and Cartagena (1989). The first distributor in Spain, Catalana de Gas, absorbed Gas Madrid, which was in second place, in 1992, creating Gas Natural SDG, a company that bought ENAGAS from the State in 1994. Finally, in 1996, Gas Natural SDG inaugurated the Maghreb-Europa Gas pipeline, which connected the gas fields of Algeria with Spain and Portugal, crossing Morocco and the Strait of Gibraltar.

The liberalisation of the European gas market forced Gas Natural SDG to divest from ENAGAS, which began trading on the stock markets (2002). But the system continued to grow, and new regasification plants became necessary: Bilbao (2003), Sagunto (2006), and Mugardos (2007), and also a new gas pipeline, the MEDGAZ, which directly connected Algeria with the southeast of Spain (2011). Finally, in 2011 the first shipments of fracking gas arrived from the United States.

Additionally, the MIDCAT project was studied to connect Spanish gas pipelines with France through Catalonia, but the project was abandoned in 2019. Finally, in October 2021, Algeria cut off the supply through Maghreb-Europe due to its political disagreements with Morocco as a country of passage.

Therefore, this is a very different model from that of Germany, with gas pipeline connections with Algeria, but also with the capacity to receive natural gas from anywhere in the world through the LNG plant system. In short, a greater operational flexibility, mainly in times of crisis, although relations with Algeria have hardened since the change in position of the Government of Spain on the issue of the former Western Sahara.

12.7 Natural gas reserves

Despite how important the logistics of natural gas supply is, as well as the infrastructure available in EU countries, a relevant point to consider is where the reserves of this energy are geographically located worldwide, and their quantification. This information is basic to guide the future strategic framework for the positioning of natural gas in Europe.

Russia is not only a country close to Northern Europe and has gas pipelines and also LNG tankers in operation, but it is also the country with the most natural gas reserves in the world, with 37 tcm (trillion cubic metres), practically 20% of the world total.

Algeria, despite its importance as a supplier to Southern Europe, with gas pipelines to Spain and Italy, and with liquefaction plants and methane tankers, only has 1% of the world's natural gas reserves. A clearly distinct and weaker long-term position than that of the Russian Federation.

Europe's great alternatives to supplies from Russia and Algeria are Qatar and the United States, which together have reserves like those of Russia, although geographically they are further away, a situation that has been

Table 12.6 Natural gas reserves by country, 2020, tcm (trillion cubic metres)

Country	*Reserves (tcm)*	*Share total reserves (%)*
Russian Federation	37.4	19.9
Iran	32.1	17.1
Qatar	24.7	13.1
Turkmenistan	13.6	7.2
US	12.6	6.7
China	8.4	4.5
Venezuela	6.3	3.3
Saudi Arabia	6.0	3.2
United Arab Emirates	5.9	3.1
Nigeria	5.5	2.9
Iraq	3.5	1.9
Azerbaijan	2.5	1.3
Australia	2.4	1.3
Canada	2.4	1.3
Algeria	2.3	1.2
Kazakhstan	2.3	1.2
Other	20.2	10.7

Source: British Petroleum (2022, p. 34).

resolved for years with transportation via methane tanker, which is easy in Spain due to its large number of terminals and difficult in Germany, which began to consider the construction of terminals only after the start of the Ukrainian war.

Other countries with reserves, and relatively close to Europe, are Azerbaijan, on the west coast of the Caspian Sea, close to Armenia and Turkey. Also, Turkmenistan, on the east coast of the Caspian Sea, which has large reserves, and beyond, already in Central Asia, Kazakhstan. Gas is currently arriving in Italy by gas pipeline from Azerbaijan.

12.8 Strategic visions

The EU has been working very seriously and for many years to become the world's leader in the fight against climate change, setting the ambitious goal of zero emissions by 2050 and developing very ambitious energy transition programs in areas such as:

- The introduction of renewable energies
- Policies to improve energy efficiency
- Carbon removal
- Oil reduction
- Closure of nuclear power plants
- And natural gas, as transition energy

But the war in Ukraine has changed all frames of reference. Suddenly, the EU has discovered that it depends a lot on energy imports, that Europe's main energy supplier is Russia and that Russia has started the war in Ukraine, practically on the borders of the EU.

If the EU continues to import energy from Russia on a large scale, what it is doing is financing the country that has invaded Ukraine, which would like to become a member of the EU. And if it returns to less clean energy than natural gas, it clearly puts its position in the fight against climate change and greenhouse gas emissions at risk.

The questions that the EU had to ask itself in the first months of 2022 were transcendent:

- How had this situation come about? What could be done?
- And while it was being discussed whether to help Ukraine more or less: How and where could the natural gas that Europe needed be obtained?
- Many problems, all new, but the basic question was: could this whole situation have a solution? How to achieve a new balance?

12.9 The EU plan: REPowerEU

Finally, on 18 May 2022, the EU published its first plan of action in the energy field, consequence of the change in circumstances produced by the Russia–Ukraine conflict, calling it REPowerEU (European Commission, 2022a).

The plan had a budget of 210,000 million euros of investment in the period 2022–2027, with the objective of reducing import expenses by 94,000 million euros, mainly for natural gas, including measures of:

- Energy saving, with a 13% increase of the objective of the Energy Efficiency Directive.
- Diversification of imports, with a common natural gas purchasing platform, synchronisation of the electricity networks of Ukraine and Moldova to the EU, and replacement of dependence on Russian uranium in five EU countries.
- Substitution of fossil fuels, with a significant increase in the speed of the deployment of renewable energies, introduction of green hydrogen infrastructure and biomethane expansion.

12.10 Conclusions

The EU must manage to reduce its greenhouse gas emissions, even though the goal of zero emissions in 2050 is, in technical terms, very difficult with the technologies currently available. Furthermore, the way of life of the European population should not be significantly affected. Citizens think that climate change should be fought, but not with their own sacrifices, for example, by voluntarily agreeing to pay more taxes or giving up traveling by plane (León et al., 2022).

An important part of what can be done is based on the energy transition from fossil energies to renewable energies, with the consequent technological advances, which additionally allow improving the efficiency of the system.

To optimise the EU's future energy supply, it is important to obtain sufficiently distributed suppliers that do not generate political risks. The EU has a great purchasing capacity and therefore influence in international markets. The future may be conditioned, more than by energy, by new materials, for example, the necessary components of electric batteries, a market where there is great positioning and dependence on China.

But the capacity for action of a truly united EU and with all countries working in the same direction is very great, and the case of the reaction to dependence on Russian gas is a good example.

During the months of war, the situation has changed drastically, due to the decisive reaction of the EU by implementing measures to reduce energy dependence on Russia. In the second trimester of 2023, imports from Russia only represented 14% of imported gas (43% in 2020), 4% of imported oil (29% in 2020), and in the case of solid fuels imports from Russia had already disappeared (54% in 2020) (European Commission, 2022b; Eurostat, 2023). For the future, the EU must build a solid strategy that does not facilitate a return to situations of exaggerated energy dependence on other countries.

References

British Petroleum. 2022. *Statistical review of world energy 2021*. London: BP.

European Commission. 2022a. *Communication from the Commission to The European Parliament, The European Council, The Council, The European Economic and Social Committee and The Committee of the Regions: REPowerEU Plan*. Brussels, COM (2022) 230 final.

European Commission. 2022b. *REPowerEU. Affordable, secure and sustainable energy for Europe*. https://commission.europa.eu/strategy-and-policy/priorities-2019-2024/european-green-deal/repowereu-affordable-secure-and-sustainable-energy-europe_en (accessed June 18, 2023).

Eurostat. 2022a. *Energy statistics – an overview. European Union*. https://ec.europa.eu/eurostat/statistics-explained/index.php?title=Energy_statistics_-_an_overview (accessed May 4, 2022).

Eurostat. 2022b. *From where do we import energy?* https://ec.europa.eu/eurostat/cache/infographs/energy/bloc-2c.html?lang=en (accessed May 4, 2022)

Eurostat. 2023. *EU imports of energy products continued to drop in Q2 2023* https://ec.europa.eu/eurostat/web/products-eurostat-news/w/ddn-20230925-1 (accessed October 8, 2023).

Fàbregas, Pere-A. 1975. Problemática energética. Semana de Estudios sobre Política Energética. Málaga: Colegio Mayor Javier, Universidad de Málaga.

Fàbregas, Pere-A. 1981. *Un ensayo de estructura energética comparada: España y la C.E.E.* VII Asamblea Técnica de Gas. Tarragona: SEDIGAS.

Fàbregas, Pere-A. 2018. *Naturgy. 175 years of commitment to energy and society (1843–2018)*. Barcelona: Naturgy Energy Group.

Howell, Nina, and Quigley, Adam. 2022. LNG in Europe 2021: Current trends, The European LNG landscape and country focus. *The National Law Review* 144. https://www.natlawreview.com/article/lng-europe-2021-current-trends-european-lng-landscape-and-country-focus (accessed May 24, 2022).

King and Spalding LLP. 2018. *LNG in Europe 2018. An overview of LNG import terminals in Europe*. Atlanta, GA: King & Spalding LLP.

León, Sandra et al. 2022. Radiografía de las divisiones y consensos de la sociedad española en torno al cambio climático. EsadeEcPol-Center for Economic Policy. https://www.esade.edu/ecpol/ca/publicacions/radiografia-de-las-divisiones-y-consensos-de-la-sociedad-espanola-en-torno-al-cambio-climatico/ (accessed June 30, 2022).

Index

Pages in *italics* refer to figures, pages in **bold** refer to tables, and pages followed by n refer to notes.